KATHY MEXTED is a writer, photographer and editor. Inspired by her father, she learnt to fly in 1991, before she became a writer. Now she writes more than she flies, though her eyes and mind are usually turned skywards. She grew up in Finley, New South Wales. She married into, and then created, a flying family. She currently lives with her husband Denis on 40 hectares in Central Victoria, and they fly a Cessna 180. She is the author of *Australian Women Pilots*.

'Beautifully written, these captivating stories about women in flight will make you wish you had even half their bravery and passion.'
LISA MILLAR, TV presenter

'Who doesn't need a little inspo in their lives? When women who choose to fly have their remarkable stories collated, prepare to have your own heart and mind soar!'
CATRIONA ROWNTREE, TV presenter

'Amazing flyers, amazing women, amazing lives. From flying with swans in the freezing skies over Europe to piloting choppers in the outback to – of all things – BASE jumping in the Himalayas, and many more. Kathy Mexted writes brilliantly, vividly, sometimes even breathlessly, bringing us this remarkable collection of stories of women who have chased down their lighter-than-air dreams. The word 'inspiring' doesn't even come close.'
MICHAEL VEITCH, author

'Kathy Mexted captures beautiful insights into these normal yet audacious and courageous women and their breathtaking aviation adventures. I'm inspired.'
LINDA BEILHARZ, Polar explorer and pilot

'The writing and the stories are so good that the book itself deserves to take flight off the shelves.'
MICHAEL DILLON, filmmaker

'Wonderful and diverse! Kathy Mexted's passion, inquiry and talent has created a book that inspires flight, energy and the desire to turn the page.'
AMANDA-LYN PEARSON, pilot, circus aerialist, creator and director of *The Crackup Sisters*

'From free falling to paramotor and adrenaline-pumping aerobatics – a masterful recount of those who take flight.'
RYAN CAMPBELL, pilot

INCREDIBLE STORIES OF AUSTRALIAN WOMEN WHO REACH FOR THE SKY

KATHY MEXTED

NEWSOUTH

UNSW Press acknowledges the Bedegal people, the Traditional Owners of the unceded territory on which the Randwick and Kensington campuses of UNSW are situated, and recognises the continuing connection to Country and culture. We pay our respects to Bedegal Elders past and present.

A NewSouth book

Published by
NewSouth Publishing
University of New South Wales Press Ltd
University of New South Wales
Sydney NSW 2052
AUSTRALIA
https://unsw.press/

© Kathy Mexted 2024
First published 2024

10 9 8 7 6 5 4 3 2 1

This book is copyright. Apart from any fair dealing for the purpose of private study, research, criticism or review, as permitted under the *Copyright Act*, no part of this book may be reproduced by any process without written permission. Inquiries should be addressed to the publisher.

A catalogue record for this book is available from the National Library of Australia

ISBN   9781742237619 (paperback)
        9781742239088 (ebook)
        9781761178054 (ePDF)

Internal design and illustrations Josephine Pajor-Markus
Cover design Luke Causby
Cover images Alida Soemawinata flying an AS350 Squirrel over Kata Tjuṯa by Natalie Luescher (front, upper); Heather Swan wearing her wingsuit by Graeme Murray (front, lower); Emma McDonald debuting her solo aerobatic display on the Gold Coast by Matt Hall Racing (back, left); Speed skydiver Jessica Johnston flying head down by Debbie Murphy (back, right)
Printer Griffin Press

All reasonable efforts were taken to obtain permission to use copyright material reproduced in this book, but in some cases copyright could not be traced. The author welcomes information in this regard.

To Denis, Harrison and Beth, Amelia and Kate.

CONTENTS

Introduction: A flying start ... ix

1 **The human swan:** *Sacha Dench, paramotor pilot* ... 1
2 **From tourism to aeromedical rescue:** *Alida Soemawinata, helicopter pilot* ... 26
3 **From the tallest mountain:** *Heather Swan, wingsuit BASE jumper* ... 50
4 **Soaring to great heights:** *Catherine Conway, glider pilot* ... 85
5 **Two crazy ideas:** *Stef Walter, wing walker and Moomba bird(wo)man* ... 110
6 **On eagles' wings:** *Kirsten Seeto, paraglider pilot* ... 130
7 **On a roll:** *Emma McDonald, aerobatic pilot* ... 155
8 **Head down, fast as you can:** *Jessica Johnston, speed skydiver* ... 177
9 **It started with the stars:** *Krystal De Napoli, Gomeroi astrophysicist* ... 195
10 **The earliest aviators:** *Donna Tasker, balloon pilot* ... 212

Glossary ... 230
Sources ... 236
Acknowledgments ... 241

INTRODUCTION: A FLYING START

There's a broad cross-section of aviators – some powered by fuel, and some by their own gumption – who have shared their stories in this book. There are common intersections in the flying, and – from studying the stars, to high-speed aerobatics – some wide diversions. After the release of *Australian Women Pilots*, I was often asked why I only wrote about fixed-wing flying. It's because that was a dominant and logical place to start. For this book I have explored some 'other' types of flight, and the adventures and careers that accompany them.

Aside from their courageous undertakings, I was astonished at some of the personal stories these women told me – stories so surprising that I had to take my hands off the keyboard and wonder, 'Do we stick to the flying, or do we explore these parts that make up their whole? The stories they share to make sense of their experiences. Can I do them justice?' Despite their different pursuits, there are some close crossovers in their flying. Catherine the glider pilot, Kirsten the paraglider pilot, Stef the birdwoman/wing walker, and Donna the balloonist all do or did fly fixed-wing aircraft. Sacha the paramotorist started off in gliders and paragliders. Heather the BASE jumper had to learn skydiving, and Jess the skydiver wants to BASE jump. Emma the aerobatic pilot also flies some aeromedical work in NSW, as does Alida the helicopter pilot in Borneo. Krystal the Gomeroi astrophysicist, with her feet planted on the earth, is looking beyond them all at a universe so vast and colourful that her work is cut out for her just describing it.

My connection to these stories of the sky, and the desire to fly, starts on the back lawn of my childhood home in Finley on the NSW–Victorian border, where summers can be so hot that the dark

TAKE FLIGHT

is barely cooler than the daylight. On one such stifling hot night while I was still in primary school, nobody could sleep. We were leaving for the beach the next day – no matter which way you drove out of Finley, it seemed like a long way to the beach for our annual holiday. On this long hot sleepless night, Dad rallied some of us to go outside and look at the stars. We lay our towels on the buffalo grass under a sky so brilliantly lit that it looked like a sequinned blanket. It was adventurous to be slipping out the back door at this strange hour. I was awestruck by the incredible display above us as, lying in the dark, Dad quietly pointed out the Pot and the Southern Cross. 'See those four stars with a little one just to the side?' For such a bustling household (eight kids plus cousins and interested others), the night was memorable for the silence, which was broken only by our father initiating this moment of connection.

We slept fitfully because the mosquitoes kept eating us, until finally Dad said, 'Bugger it. Let's go now'. At a time that belongs to the wise old owl and the insomniac, Mum, Dad and whichever kids were still living at home, piled into the car with the already packed trailer. The car was facing the exit and we drove off, leaving our hot and dusty small town for two precious weeks at the hot and sandy beach. Forever since, the starry sky has been ours. At a school reunion yesterday a group of friends reminisced about the Riverina skies and the different places they sat or lay to observe them.

In my twenties I returned to Finley after some years overseas and again was stopped in my tracks one night and craned my neck in wonder at the unpolluted sky, spread wide with our endless stars. I felt like I was seeing it for the first time. Had it been so familiar that I never knew I'd missed it? For this reason, I was compelled to include the starry night in the book as it is connected to our fascination with the sky. Gomeroi astrophysicist Krystal De Napoli started her story an hour away at Benalla. On a hot summer's night, her mother lay with a couple of her children on the trampoline, pointing out the same patterns in the sky. That simple moment of connection inadvertently set the pattern for Krystal's future, during which she learned to understand the skies in a way that was beyond the reach of most of us.

In 1969, television brought the moon landing into our school library. I sat in my scratchy box-pleat grey winter tunic, squashed into the tiny room with the whole class and more, supervised by nuns, and surrounded by books and the distinct smell of methylated spirits and purple ink on the Gestetner. I remember so clearly watching the grainy black and white footage of Neil Armstrong stepping onto the moon, saying those immortal words, 'One small step for man …'

Reaching the stars was clearly off limits to me, but the desire to try flying was irresistible and a few years later we four younger siblings started on the roof of our back verandah. My brother Brendan jumped off it without fear and assured me I'd be fine. 'Come on', he encouraged, laughing the way kids do when even they don't believe what they're saying. Soon there was a steady stream of us and the neighbourhood kids shrieking, 'I can fly!' for the couple of seconds that we were airborne. Eventually Mum came out to see what the din was, just as we were attaching a cape to the youngest. She told us to get down, so we went back to kicking the footy until she went back to peeling the potatoes, and then we got back on the roof.

Brendan recently reminded me that our intention was to make the cape stream out behind us like Superman. I loved it then, when I saw a clip of Heather Swan learning to BASE jump. She ran off the edge of a clifftop and shrieked, 'I can flyyy!' before throwing her chute.

Eventually we kids graduated to the roof of the shearing shed on our farm at Blighty. The freefall from that roof was about as high as we were brave enough to jump. It was BASE jumping without the parachute! Dad soon put a stop to our shenanigans with the old adage, 'you'll break your leg'.

'Maybe', I thought, 'but what if we don't?'

I think the desire to fly is as primal as the first person who saw the first bird and thought, *hmmm* ... In a more sophisticated Superman-like moment a couple of years ago, I jumped off a mountain to fly like a bird. Fortunately, I was attached to Kirsten Seeto and we flew from 'Mystic', the paragliders' launch place outside of Bright, Victoria. Once rigged up and attached to Kirsten, the instructions were simple. I had to run as fast as I could towards the edge of the 2200-foot mountain. At some point there would be a jolt as the wing lifted, and I just had to keep running. So I ran, the wing jolted, I jolted, she shouted, 'Keep running!'; 'I'm running, I'm running', I called back, and as the hill sloped away and the pine forest came into view, the wing gently lifted us aloft and we spent the most beautiful nine minutes hovering above the blue hills, doing a slow turn back to look where we'd just been, and then silently floating over a ridge line down to the landing zone. I could see how it is addictive, and so much better than jumping off the shearing shed roof.

I hope you enjoy meeting these women of the skies and take inspiration from them. I've told the stories as best I can, and generally as they were presented to me. Thanks for reading.

1

THE HUMAN SWAN

SACHA DENCH, PARAMOTOR PILOT

'A remarkable and original way of telling the story of the journey of the birds, of learning more about them and passing that knowledge on. This is an enormously brave and exciting undertaking.'

Kate Humble, BBC television presenter

TAKE FLIGHT

Across western Russia, thousands of kilometres from home, Sacha Dench guided her fragile paramotor away from the icy polar north on a broad track south-west. As she flew, in company with two cameramen in trikes, the swirling tundra landscape bubbled and boiled beneath her. Before it stopped thawing, the permafrost continued burping in defiance at the approaching winter. Soon, it would re-freeze into silence.

Over the next few months Sacha would fly from the Russian Arctic through Estonia, Latvia, Lithuania, Poland, Germany, the Netherlands, Denmark, Belgium and France, terminating in the UK.

On a similar path were the beautiful Bewick's swans, who departed with their young. They'd been trained by their parents for the journey. On arctic winds, the swan families made for the central parts of Europe, and largely spread to the southern parts of the United Kingdom. The Bewick's swans' graceful two-metre wings beat slightly faster than those of their larger cousins, the mute and the whooper swans, as they hauled their 6-kilogram summer weight back to more temperate winter areas. They would be back in the north the following summer to breed and feed on summer grasses and shoots.

It was so cold up in the air that Sacha could only fly for a couple of hours at a time. Her face stung and her legs dangled redundantly as she powered along under the paramotor's reassuring hum. The propeller, which is usually driven by a two-stroke engine, was strapped to her back, and they were suspended under a 10-metre fabric wing connected to her backpack by fine coloured ropes. Its versatility is its strong point as the pilot can depart on their feet, usually with a running start from a paddock free of obstructions. As the paramotor industry is self-regulated, participants can land wherever the ground is suitable.

Up in the air, Sacha could feel every change in the sensitive wing, constantly checking her reserve chute and scanning for birds and landing options. The Arctic seemed a little desperate and deserted as the winter triggered its various occupants to either hibernate or head off. The migrating swans would fly for up to 48 hours at a time, while Sacha scouted for remote villages and communities to stop and speak to; to have first-hand conversations and seek insight into why the swan numbers were declining so rapidly. On their long flights, Sacha is flying with, but not beside, the migrating swans to understand their journey and most importantly their challenges.

IN A CAREER THAT BEGAN WITH SHARKS AND TURTLES, THE birds were a natural progression when Sacha worked as Head of Media at the UK's Wildfowl and Wetlands Trust (WWT), a British conservation charity that restores, creates, and protects wetlands. The trust was established by Sir Peter Scott, the son of English Antarctic explorer, Captain Robert Scott, who died when Peter was only two years old. After the Second World War, Peter, a veteran, founded the Severn Wildfowl Trust, now WWT, at Slimbridge in Gloucestershire. From his house by the lake, Scott would paint the Bewick's swans gliding by the large picture window of his study, which is now the WWT head office.

In an accent that is Australian to the English ear, and vice versa, Sacha reflects on her own childhood, which began a long way from Slimbridge, on Sydney's northern beaches where she ran between a small unlocked house and the sandy shores of the coast. Both her parents were interested in nature and encouraged their free-spirited daughter's innate curiosity. Her telling of it is like a postcard from Australia, splashing around in the rock pools, snorkelling, and watching her parents spearfish, dive and surf. There, she learned to understand the moods and motions of the oceans, beaches, and reefs – to love and respect the water and all that it held.

Then the family moved, and her mother went to the extreme south of New South Wales. Six hours' drive from Sydney, Eden is now a bustling tourist destination, but back in the 1970s it was a sleepy fishing town with a busy port and a wealth of fish that were caught and shipped to Sydney and beyond. Alongside the fish were many whales, which are abundant now they were no longer being hunted for their oil, bones and meat.

The family were self-sufficient in a bush house that was 45 minutes (two buses and a hike) from Sacha's nearest school. Woodchipping was big business and the pristine ancient forest behind Eden was being savagely logged and sent to Japan as mulch. 'The Forest Wars' ensued and at school Sacha straddled the middle ground between the families of the loggers and the conservationists. It was an early lesson in diplomacy.

Her mother's 16-hectare bush block was a kid's dream. The house was an unpowered one-room dwelling on stilts and had an air of earthy freedom. Young Sacha would take herself down the hill to a riverside camp or trek a couple of hours beyond it to see her best friend. With the isolation came the chance for the kids to explore and to learn to trust their instincts, navigate the landscape, and enjoy camping for a couple of days within striking distance of a responsible adult. She remembers endless hours to herself and an affinity with nature; a tomboyish existence that fuelled her enquiring mind and love of wildlife.

Meanwhile, her father Steve had moved onto a rural property in the north of the state where – though still a 45-minute trip to school – Sacha experienced remoteness in a different way. The 600-acre cattle property had a pool, which she got to know well, and laid the foundations for future achievements. Her strong body – perfect for endurance – excelled underwater as she held her breath longer and longer. Like a mermaid, she swam the length of the pool underwater, while Steve egged her on. Fifty cents to swim two laps underwater. Fifty more if you can do it backstroke. He wondered what else she could be capable of.

By the time she turned 15, the swimming pool was in a different setting altogether. At her grandparents' manor house in Suffolk in the UK, the pool was flanked by manicured rose gardens, evergreen lawn mown into exacting stripes, clipped hedges and a river that tootled past the lot. There was not a snake or a bindi-eye in sight. This was Enid Blyton country in real life. Sacha also spent time with her maternal side of the family in French and Swiss villages. Here, she saw how the different landscapes and circumstances formed human characters, largely based on the chance of birthplace.

After school Sacha studied marine science and biology at University College London and began work as a marine turtle and shark geneticist. During her master's degree studies in the UK, she had a go at freediving, which is the act of underwater diving without breathing apparatus. She was exceptionally good at it, holding her breath for more than six minutes. Within a few weeks she was competing for the UK and in 2001 she won the British National Depth Record at the world championships in Ibiza. She later led and won for the Australian freediving team.

BACK IN SYDNEY'S OCEANS, SACHA WOULD SWIM OUT TO THE protective shark nets installed to keep dangerous sharks away from the beaches and their bathers. There were no sharks, but the nets were full of dolphins, whales and fish. An awareness-raising article inspired by her team about one of their projects, with photographer Alejandro Rolandi, advises that there are only three types of potentially dangerous sharks in NSW: Bull, Tiger, and Great White. The article continues, 'You are more likely to be killed by a falling coconut, or by lightning, than by a shark'.

The poor sharks. Without the cuddle factor of a koala, it was difficult to get people to care about them, and just as difficult to sort the net problem. By telling their story, and gently approaching those who mattered, Sacha realised she could gain more traction than if she were to ram it down people's throats. Her real storytelling break came, though, when she was acknowledged as a freediving champion. She found that she got more airtime as an athlete than as a scientist. It didn't matter; they were listening, but progress is slow as even today shark nets remain in place along the eastern coasts of Australia, while other surveillance technologies are being developed. Her media production and photography skills developed to the point that back in the UK, wildlife charities sought her out. It was a shift in focus, but still a long step to flying across remote Russia.

PARAMOTORING HAS BEEN A USEFUL HOBBY AND WORK TOOL for Sacha, and it came about after a succession of flying experiences. Years before she began piloting the paramotor, she had developed a fear of flying, stemming from a horror trip in the back of a light aircraft in the Caribbean. Some of those islands are so tiny that the airstrips run from one side to the other, and even then, they can jut out into the sea. In a stormy sky over such territory, a terrified pilot frantically searched for a pinpoint island, while his white-knuckled passengers were suggesting that he return to their departure point. It affected Sacha deeply for years afterwards.

'He couldn't find [the island], and it went on for about half an hour. The pilot was obviously petrified because he went pale, and we couldn't get any information. One of the two locals in the back with us got out her prayer book and started praying and crying. It was horrible. It was half an hour of extreme fear.' Down in the airport terminal, the pilot lay on the floor and stayed there. The fallout was a lasting fear of turbulent air. 'It left me scared. Bear in mind I do cave diving and I'm generally not a scaredy-cat, but if we hit any turbulence, I would almost uncontrollably grab hold of the person next to me and I'd turn into a bit of a gibbering wreck.'

Fear of flying can be debilitating for anyone cursed by it. To take control of the fear, Sacha had a go at gliding, to learn about air and turbulence. She didn't love gliding so much, and so turned her interest towards paragliding. She went to northern Victoria, where she watched brightly coloured silky paraglider wings grace the skies at Bright. She carefully followed their launches from a mountaintop, observing their flights and landings. She credits her scientific brain with rationalising her fear of turbulence and reckoned that if she could understand air, then she could conquer it. 'The best way to do that is in a paraglider. Its little strings connect the wing to your body. I learnt to read the air in a new way.'

It took a couple of years to become comfortable with paragliding, and when it clicked, Sacha really enjoyed it; however, the drawback was that so much of the flying relied on finding the right lift from the rising air. Eight years later she discovered paramotoring, where the versatility of having a motor was a game changer. Paramotors have a similar harness and principles as a paraglider, but the paramotor pilot is propelled by a two-stroke engine attached on a backpack. The pilot starts the motor and then runs across a field, hauling the wing above them. Once the wing is up, the pilot advances the throttle. With the right amount of speed beneath it, the wing lifts off and the throttle allows the pilot to control the altitude and direction; it uses similar principles to the unpowered paraglider; however, there is no need to hang around ridgelines looking for thermals [rising masses of warmer air] to provide lift. This new vehicle enabled low and slow flight, keeping pace with the birds. It meant Sacha could easily and affordably take aerial photos and carry out much of her conservation work this way. And that's how she got her brilliant idea.

IN 2014 SACHA WAS WORKING FOR THE WILDFOWL AND Wetlands Trust (WWT). A regular sight on the water at their

Slimbridge headquarters, near the Welsh border, is the Bewick's swan. It rests there from September to March, before returning to northern Russia. In the 1960s a frustrated Peter Scott caught some and dyed their rear ends yellow. He correctly assumed that people up the flyway would be enraged at this disfiguration of the white birds. The complaint letters duly arrived from various parts of Europe, and Scott was able to piece together a migration map.

Fifty years later at WWT headquarters Sacha joined a group of swan researchers. The countries along the Bewick's swans' flyway had agreed on an international action plan to halt the decline in their numbers, but the large maps and depressing spreadsheets told an alarming tale of continuing decline. Her colleagues turned to her, as their media engagement specialist, imploring her to help find some fast solutions. How could they engage with the various stakeholders along the swans' flyway? Why did today's arrivals only number half of those 20 years ago? Why did a third of them have shotgun pellets in their bodies? And how could they deal with poisoning in swans and other waterbirds that ingested spent lead shot when feeding?

While Sacha considered the glacial pace of correspondence exchanges she'd have to embark on with the agencies of 11 different governments, 'Hope' literally flashed before her eyes. On a mounted digital map, she watched as a small blinking dot over Arctic Russia made its way towards Slimbridge at about 20 metres per second. It was from a GPS tracker on the slender neck of a female Bewick's, which researchers had named Hope. As the swan's 4000-kilometre journey began, Sacha wondered about Hope's flight plan and the dramatically changing countryside that it covered. Who and what does she see and how are her lifelong partner and their young cygnets handling it? Even though migration is instinctive for many birds, the Bewick's swans are traditionalists who, while instinct plays a role, must also be taught the way, each time negotiating a landscape shaped by urbanisation, agriculture, and climate change. Is the wetland now a golf course? With a reducing wetland offering fewer green shoots to feast on, can they find sustenance in a nearby crop? Will they be shot? Will they hit a powerline or (less likely) a wind turbine? Sacha had to bring this story to life and inspire those involved to want to be part of the solution. It was an easier sell than the sharks: elegant, fluffy, non-threatening swans are easily tracked and counted, and never going to frighten you. She tossed the idea around for a couple of months and decided that she needed to take the problem to the people. Perhaps by flying her paramotor along the swans' migration route, she could understand more about their journey and stir the communities along the way into caring. Because paramotorists are so versatile, she could land virtually anywhere that she could stand up. That would need to be at least every couple or few hours to refuel and to thaw out.

Many people deemed the plan 'ridiculous, bonkers and mad'. WWT's response came with an unexpected addendum, though: 'but it just might work'. With that encouragement Sacha spent the better part of two years planning the expedition. The most pressing part was how to convince the Russian authorities to allow her and her photographic team aerial access across five of Russia's heavily guarded border regions. Maybe it was her infectious enthusiasm that helped Sacha and her project manager Pete Cranswick bring together a band of volunteers who were equally caught up in this incredible scientific endeavour. The physical training alone was rigorous. She trained for months in arctic conditions of minus 25 degrees. She had to prove herself capable of emergency procedures in the air, specifically to recover the wing if it collapsed from an errant change in airflow, or worse, collided with an object. Her all-important underwater escape training wasn't much warmer – it was done in a cold swimming pool.

By August, having only just secured a sponsor to provide her with a wing, some of the team was in Russia for final preparations. During their six-week transit into Estonia, when they did get going, they would gain crucial support from the communities along the way. They would also work with the Nenetski National Nature Reserve, the Russian Academy of Sciences, and the Baltic Fund for Nature in Russia. First, they would cross the boundless Russian tundra and then the dense taiga forest. When things were almost set to fly, the devil reared its head in the detail. Two weeks before departure, the swans were about to leave, and the expedition still didn't have Russian government approval. Endorsements from Sir David Attenborough, perhaps the world's most widely regarded naturalist, and Sir Ranulph Fiennes, credited in 1984 by the Guinness Book of World Records as the world's greatest living explorer, held no sway. No permits – no dice.

The desperate but invaluable Russian fixer, Vlad, turned to Sacha and asked if she had any more influential friends. Anyone? What a perplexing question. Sorry, no – her relevant friends were all on the table. He enquired about her surname. Was she related to Dame Judi Dench, one of Britain's best actresses, loved worldwide? And if so, could she write a letter of endorsement to the Russians as a matter of urgency? Judi Dench had too many acting awards to name, but some pivotal roles that you could name in a hurry were as M, the lead character in seven James Bond spy films. The Russians love James Bond and Vlad clutched at this straw.

After a hurtle through the internet, Sacha asked a relative to do the research, which returned some astonishing family news. Judi Dench's great-grandfather is Sacha's great-great-grandfather; however, Sacha is descended from his secret second partner, Bessie from Battersea. She earnestly tracked down Judi's agent, explained the situation, then explained it all again to Judi, who dispatched a letter. 'Flight of the Swans is fascinating, full of adventure and passion. I'm proud to support it. We need to work together if we're to help these beautiful birds, and I am looking forward to following the expedition.'

Russian approval, when it came, was ambiguous. They wouldn't allow her to fly through the country, but they wouldn't try to stop her either, so long as she didn't fly over 'here'. They wished her and the swans the best of luck. Avoiding 'here', when plotted on the map, meant a 400-kilometre diversion.

ON 19 SEPTEMBER 2016 TEMPERATURES DIPPED TOWARDS ZERO, and after the swans' last supper on the tundra's rich aquatic plants, England beckoned.

Extending their wings to a two-metre span, the birds push them down quickly, then retract and repeat. The first beat or two raises them onto their feet, and they pump against the drag to gain momentum. Whoosh-retract-whoosh and their belly is light on the water. Another few cycles and they are running across the water, each step timed to the beat of the wing. With half a dozen steps to go they run lightly, like a cartoon of somebody not wanting to get their feet wet, and then they are airborne. Half a dozen of them (tagged) would be tracked by WWT headquarters. While Sacha would take weeks to get to the Estonian border, many of these birds would fly the 1200 kilometres non-stop and be there in 48 hours for a few days' stopover before the second push home.

Spreading her lightweight wing on the ground behind her, Sacha gathered up the cords at her side and shook the wing into the gentle breeze. Hauling the full weight of her kit, she started its two-stroke motor, took a few steps forward and then jolted as the wing caught and lifted on the icy breeze. She ran a bit further, another few dozen steps, straining against the resistance of the wing and the weight of the motor until at last she was lifted from the ground and the motor took over the work. Settling into her seat, she turned with the breeze and followed a 1000-kilometre pencil line on her map that would take her to Arkhangelsk and her waiting support team.

She was departing from the research station on the Pechora Delta with a sleeping bag, a tent, two GPS units, a phone and two radios.

TAKE FLIGHT

Each expeditioner needed to be self-sufficient in case of emergency, particularly if they were separated from the group. And while the swans were kept warm by the constant flapping of their powerful wings and their 25 000 feathers, Sacha wrapped four layers of clothing around her legs and more than that around her upper body.

The paramotor's fine coloured lines held taut. They reacted to every thermal glitch by tugging on the fine wing above. Sacha sat back in her seat while her legs dangled above the gloriously coloured treeless tundra slowly passing below. The first of the tracked swans streamed ahead, and some families lingered. They would fly a few long hops to Sacha's many short ones. It is important to note that the team was not trying to parallel or interfere with the swans, which form V-shaped groups of up to 100. They were merely trying to follow their flyway and see what they see. Beneath Sacha's feet, the swirling colours of the Arctic slid by, a leadlight pattern of earthy ochres and lime greens that coloured the huge undisturbed network of pools and lakes. Gaseous bubbling water betrayed the shifting landscape, which Sacha continually scanned for landing options and for wildlife. To help her relax, she crossed her feet. It didn't do anything practical, but was somehow calming.

The flight team headed for a fuel drop at their first location after covering 60 kilometres. They landed on a wide sandy beach where the river joined the Averent Strait. There was not a soul in sight; oh, hang on. There was one guy, celebrating his birthday, who eyed the visitors with amazement. What on earth ... He watched curiously. Out of the sky with a strange buzz, a bulky pilot disengaged from her apparatus. Tumbling from beneath the helmet was a mass of wavy blonde hair that fell unrestrained almost to her waist. The face of this fugacious traveller told a less glamorous story; she was frozen!

Vlad, who had helped arrange the fuel drops, arrived bearing a generous picnic for the ravenous crew. The village of Tobseda's only visible resident cycled up to the group and asked the obvious: 'What are you doing?' He was an old fisherman, alone and immersed in nature. He reckoned he knew about swans and pointed to a nearby family with three young. He insisted he could talk to them. He turned and started flapping and calling out. 'There was a call-back!' says Sacha. 'We were completely humbled by this guy.'

The group continued to their next stop, a research station, for a fruitful discussion about the tundra's nomadic hunters, who, in an area without agriculture, live on reindeer, birds, and foraged foods. They also legally hunt geese. To a distant eye, the Bewick's swans, with their short necks and loud calls, are strikingly similar. And if it talks like a goose and flies like a goose, the chances are it will be hunted as a goose. Some interesting exchanges took place, with lessons learnt on both sides. As they said farewell, the hunters good-naturedly promised not to shoot the swans anymore, claiming, 'they don't taste very good, anyway'.

Suited up for the last leg of their first day, Sacha hit the start switch. Silence. The paramotor wouldn't start. It was so disheartening to have a breakdown on the first day of the expedition, and the team wondered how it could get this bad this early. Thankfully, Vlad had the right contacts and sent the engine off in a helicopter to be repaired.

A Nenets family had watched from a distance, uneasy about engaging with the visitors, and offered the minimal: wood and water. But they realised the next morning that the adventurers could really use a hand obtaining food. With warming relations, they took them foraging for mushrooms and berries. They offered some of their own food – two-week-old reindeer meat, warm cranberry juice, and a bright pink metallic salty reindeer blood pancake. They wrapped Sacha's shivering body in a toasty reindeer skin and queried, 'You've really come all this way in that thing to talk to us about swans?' Throughout the trip, people wanted to know why Sacha cared so much, and were then motivated to ask how they could help.

TAKE FLIGHT

The engine was returned to a broad sandy beach in a bright orange and white Cessna. As Sacha prepared herself for a boggy 5-kilometre walk to retrieve her new motor, she was confronted with a sled hitched to five energetic reindeer. The grinning reindeer breeders urged her to jump aboard. Slightly dehydrated and puffy-eyed from cold and lack of sleep, she gladly joined the group on a wild ride across unmade fields. This hospitality was repeated right across the country. That afternoon they were on their way again and spent five days flying across the remote grassy tundra, stopping to speak with nomadic groups where they could, landing every couple or few hours to warm up, rehydrate and eat. 'I can't eat when I'm flying', says Sacha. 'If I so much as let go of a peanut it can fly back into my motor, or into the propeller, and cause a slight unbalance. Over time that unbalance becomes exaggerated and then I have a real problem, so it's safer to eat on the ground.'

The tundra flights finished under a blanket of cloud, over a fir forest. In the distance, great shafts of light shone through tiny breaks in the cloud, creating the Fingers of God (crepuscular rays – light scattered by dry particles in the atmosphere at dawn or dusk) that reach down to the ground. Beneath it, at the mouth of the Mezen river, is the remote town of the same name. For the few tourists who are interested, Tripadvisor calls it a place of powerful pure energy – a point on the map that calls for you to return. The swans return here every year because the nearby White Sea is one of their regular wetlands stops. Afterwards, Sacha would describe the scale and glory of the tundra. 'It looked like it could be from Mars!' she said. 'The tundra ended up being really kind to us. We had some funny crosswinds, but no headwinds. It had more thermals than I expected. When bits of sunshine came through, we had cold air that then heated up in parts, and different colours of the ground produced different thermals. I'd be flying along perfectly normally and then suddenly a section of the wing would collapse. That was quite shocking because we assumed it would all be reasonably stable. Sometimes we had very low cloud cover and sometimes we'd pick between rain clouds, which is not what we would do normally. As the trip went on, our tolerance for rough weather got better as we learnt what the kit was capable of.'

The team had worked hard in northern Russia to bring together the authorities and hunters to learn from them, and discuss ideas and strategies to reduce the problem of inadvertently shooting swans. The ground crew were churning out footage and images that were used then and since for education. A trike was used to fly important people over the wetlands for a different point of view, to show how they were connected to the wildlife. Local and international media became interested, and the expedition gained traction. By this time, Hope and her cohort, Maisie, Daisy Clarke, Leho, Eileen and Charlotte, were making great progress. At this point also, Sacha sadly farewelled her pilot Vlad (Vladislav Vyucheiskiy), who had been instrumental in gaining support for the expedition and was unwavering in his belief in Sacha's ability.

Sacha's next leg was over the taiga forest. Right across the cold subarctic regions of the Northern Hemisphere, taiga forests lie between the tundra to the north and the more temperate forests to the south. The swans tackled the taiga in one mammoth direct flight. Sacha had to make her 400-kilometre diversion. This was an enormous challenge, because not only did it add extra flying time, but the countryside was so densely forested that it precluded many landings. The paramotor whirred on at 80 kilometres per hour as a thick evergreen blanket of spruce, pine and fir trees, coloured by autumnal birch and poplar, passed below. Its floor, carpeted with moss, lichen and mushrooms, was cut by lush bogs, streams and lakes. Winter in the taiga is so cold that even its own birds take off, leaving the littlest animals to hunker down under its spongy floor. Cutting through parts of this forest are narrow winding roads and the ground crew, sometimes having to block roads to make runways, were constantly renegotiating meeting points for pilots who were largely dictated to by the weather. Sacha's flight log shows that she could be as low as 100 feet checking ground conditions and as high as 2500 feet trying to outclimb cloud, where fine icicles would form on the paramotor's flying lines. Ducks, geese and swans shared the same airspace and were forced to make the same inflight decisions. All the while maintaining visual contact – sometimes intermittent glimpses – with the ground, Sacha would always try to fly high enough in her vulnerable and fragile craft to glide to safety in case that little engine failed.

As she obligingly flew the wide arc out to the east, Sacha noticed a huge formation of swans off to her right. They were in company with some noisy geese. It's no surprise, then, that an errant shot can bring down a protected swan. The 41-year-old's concentration was broken by the arrival of a pair of Bewick's swans. She was now three weeks into the trip, and on this unexpected long diversion, the most memorable event happened. Two swans broke from their group's V-shaped formation and edged towards her. They were curious, cheeky, vigilant. Why did they do it? She watched them, closely monitoring their movements, for a collision could be fatal for her. The swans slowly inched closer, eyeing the foreigner in their midst. They were so close that Sacha could see their black beaks rimmed with a thin orange line and the distinctive individual yellow markings where it connected with their heads. Each yellow and black pattern splayed beneath the eyes like a painter's accident tells a different story.

She could see their brown eyes, the slender necks, and the plump bellies. Sacha was mesmerised by the rogue pair; they came so close that she prepared to pull a sharp left hand down to avoid them colliding with the lines of her equipment, presumably invisible to the swans. The birds edged even closer and tucked in behind the right tip, in the vortex, of her colourful canopy. This was no accident. They were flying in formation.

With excitement running high, the Human Swan – a name she reluctantly conceded to adopt as a publicity strategy – truly felt like she was the lead bird in the flock of Bewick's swans making their long journey to their winter home. For the briefest and most beautiful of moments, Sacha was at one with the pair. As slowly and gently as they arrived, they returned to their place in the long V formation making their way to the next wetland. What story would they tell?

The conservation team had been working with authorities to figure out ways to increase surveillance on the migrating birds, then look at designating sites to protect them. Some of the Russian schoolchildren Sacha met were riveted by how conservation and research works. They had no idea where the swans went. Some, as young as nine years old, had been sent to shoot the migrating birds for food. Research shows that each shotgun cartridge releases up to 300 tiny lead pieces, which equates to around 20 000 tonnes of lead each year being left across the ground, mostly where the birds are feeding (because that's where they're being shot). The birds accidentally eat the shot, mistaking it for grain or grit they intentionally seek out to help with digestion. Sacha pales as she recalls the sight of a bird that had choked on its food because the lead poisoning had paralysed its gut and its legs. The swans that don't die from lead poisoning can pass lead poisoning on to any humans who eat them. The poisoning can affect kidneys, heart and thinking. It compromises the swans' immune systems, making them more susceptible to diseases like avian influenza/cancer. According to an article in *Science Direct*, at least 40 bird species are at risk of lead poisoning in European wetlands from gunshot, and a million in the whole of Europe die from the effects of lead poisoning every year.

After two and a half weeks of flying without ground crew, the pilots were pleased to meet their team again at a welcoming camp with a boiling cup of tea. Sacha looked the part as she smilingly unclipped her gear, but she was completely shattered. Her body had shut down. The flying had been mentally and physically exhausting and it was time for a rest.

The trip was going well. The tundra was fast, the taiga was slow, but overall, they were just ten days behind schedule. Sacha's enthusiasm for the project was obvious and her beautiful broad smile reflected that. She'd been so sunny that the camera crew suggested to her that the continual smiling could get a bit dull after a couple of months and could she inject some drama into her reporting? Sacha smiled, of course, and dismissed it as theatre, but the following day she was making one of her last Russian launches from a field east of St Petersburg, planning to catch some of the flocks at the wetlands near the city. She sharply pulled the wing up into the air and stabilised it, then confidently turned to run but twisted and fell in excruciating pain. As the pain dulled, she tried again the next day, but the same thing happened. Her media crew got their drama, complete with screaming so loud it drew an elderly couple out of the forest. Out of great sympathy they bestowed freshly picked cranberries upon her as they are 'good for health and healing'. The MRI team at the local hospital diagnosed a snapped right knee ligament.

As she was now unable to run, or even bear weight, Brian Middleton, the expedition mechanic, modified a buggy from stuff he could find. The buggy was bolted onto the motor at one point, and the wing at another point. Sacha had to learn how to drive it straight long enough for the wing to take hold and lift. It took a dozen attempts to master and reconfigure the gear, and the result was a beautifully tied-together vehicle using ingenuity and paraglider string. She flew the more lightweight contraption for the rest of the journey.

Though the contrast in cultures was stark, Sacha left Russia with an enormous fondness for its people and its huge and remote landscape. The Flight of the Swans team had been well received, both as expeditioners and conservationists. They'd found new stopover sites and picked the brains of researchers, hunters and government officials.

While her knee was being sorted, the team had gone ahead to deliver workshops in Estonia. This country is serious about their responsibility for the Bewick's swans' safe passage by protecting its wetlands under their National Action Plan. They are the only country on the flyway to have an action plan, and their Minister of Environment, Marko Pomerants, drove home the message. 'We are worried about the decline of the swans and encourage our neighbours along the flyway to analyse the reasons for it, and if necessary to create a plan of action the way Estonia has done.' As Estonia is about the halfway mark between the Arctic and the UK, it is a most important rest stop.

The weather was deteriorating by the time Sacha got to Estonia. Beneath her layers of clothing, she was still freezing and becoming run-down, which resulted in a severe head cold. Prolonged time in the open air can potentially result in frostbite of the throat and a chest infection. She was so cold that when she landed, one of her crew raced over and embraced her on landing, then called for somebody to turn on the car heater so she could get her circulation back.

While visiting the Estonian towns of Haapsalu and Tartu, Sacha spoke to local schools and met with swan researcher Leho Luigujõe, after whom one of the tagged swans was named. He too identified hunting, mostly people hunting mallard duck, as the number one threat. The other challenge is the kilometres of above-ground power-lines that crisscross the country at the height that many swans travel. In low cloud, the swans cannot see the powerlines. The third threat is the loss of wetland habitat.

Charlotte the swan was passing through Southern Estonia and the team rushed to get a glimpse of her. To achieve this, they hopped on a ferry, slept under starry forest skies, and did a dawn dash to intersect with her flight path. The weather continued to deteriorate and the staff at Latvia's Lake Lubans expected to run their morning meet and greet without seeing the WWT team; however, to their utter surprise, Sacha made it through to present at the morning for kids and visitors. The Latvian Museum of Natural History ran a wetland-themed national art competition that boasted more than 200 pieces of work.

By late October the team arrived in Lithuania, where a famous photographer generously loaned his long 600-millimetre lens so they could take their own photos. He also found a photo of the swan Daisy Clarke in his recent files and then helped to locate her.

By the first week of November Sacha had arrived in Poland. Travelling across the country would take her more than nine days as she stopped to attend events. The national television station aired a story that prompted 100 emails to its journalist before his head had hit the pillow that night. A few days later the national hunting lobby made themselves known, to argue the case for continuing to use lead shot. That conversation was redirected to the Danes, who countered with a video, made by hunters for hunters, that has been shared across the flyway.

Onwards she flew, through horrid weather into Germany where snow and ice forced her down. The swans also don't fly in foul weather, but by the time Sacha got to the Netherlands, Croupier, one of the oldest Bewick's swans on the WWT records, had arrived home. The 25-year-old and his partner Dealer were already at Slimbridge. Sacha flew along the string of islands that connect Denmark, Germany, and the Netherlands, and was inspired by their beauty. Seeing what the swans see, she got perspective on how important these islands are as both a marker and a haven in transit.

In Belgium they encountered resistance to paramotorists, who are seen as interrupting the passing and breeding birds. In consultation with the local paramotor pilots, an agreement was reached that winter-time nature reserves were a no-fly zone, leaving the birds to breed peacefully.

Sacha Dench, paramotor pilot

By early December, Sacha flew into Wissant on the French coast and spotted the White Cliffs of Dover. For someone so stoic, she suddenly realised how keen she was to get home. She and her team had worked every day and on most days the plans had changed somehow. They had to sit out the weather for a few days on the French side, while the remainder of the tracked swans brought up the rear. She was still being trailed by Leho, who was in the Netherlands; Eileen was in Denmark and Hope was crossing Germany. Sacha's challenge in the 90-minute Channel crossing was to stay warm. In this fine-weather window, the swans departed from frozen lakes and Sacha took off with them. Up at 3500 feet it was colder than when they had flown across the Russian Arctic. As she climbed through 2500 feet the famous white cliffs slowly emerged, creating a fine white line between blue sky and blue water. It was a bigger moment than she'd allowed herself to believe. She was almost home.

The photographer who was filming her Channel crossing had to contend with a frozen hand in minus 25 degrees when he dropped a glove mid-flight, and Sacha had to contend with his swearing through her Bluetooth headset. Supported by a nice tailwind to push her along, she confidently flew the 90 minutes towards Dover and was grinning widely when she passed the halfway mark. In her bright yellow flight suit, she landed smoothly and was greeted by media asking how it felt to be the first woman to cross the English Channel by paramotor. Without missing a beat, she answered with her characteristic smile. She wanted to say, 'I've just flown from the Arctic! The Channel was a mere hop!' but she went on to say how great it was to be the first woman to do anything and presumed it's because not many women fly paramotors that she had the chance for that honour. 'I feel now I have crossed so many countries and communities, that I want to do anything I can to encourage or champion women doing adventures.'

TAKE FLIGHT

The trip ended a few days later when Sacha arrived at Slimbridge to join the swans. 'It was so lovely to come back to Slimbridge, it's amazing to know you'll see the swans there. It's one of the few bodies of water large enough to accommodate large flocks like that.' On the way, though, she delivered a 20 000-signature petition to No. 10 Downing Street.

It asked:

- for wetlands to be protected
- for the creation of another 100 000 acres of wetland
- for the government to ban the use of lead shot in shooting
- to tackle illegal hunting.

Maisie had flown in hops of six to twelve hours and had arrived in the UK after flying throughout the night from the Netherlands. She'd crossed the North Sea and landed at Norfolk after just one rest stop. Her next leg was three-and-a-half hours' flying and she arrived at Slimbridge tired from her long migration. Standing in the shallows, she shook herself down, preened her feathers, then dived into the water for a good stretch. Likewise, that night Sacha dived into a glass of cider, stretched, and finally slept soundly in her own bed.

WWT FORMALLY ACKNOWLEDGED THAT THE TEAM HAD MANaged a complicated expedition that succeeded by drawing together experts, resources, and money. Sacha smiled graciously as they were congratulated on their ambitious, unrealistic, and unrivalled plan.

By paramotoring along the flyway, viewing the journey as the birds do, scientists can now see the challenges and opportunities of the migrating swans. One outstanding legacy is the invaluable visual resources, footage and stills that are used for education. The story captured a wide audience – 1500 media articles, played on every major

TV and news outlet in each country they visited. That brought to the fore the important message of the swans' incredible journey and called for real solutions to protect them. Then came many awards; the one that left her speechless was the UK's Royal Aero Club 2017 Britannia Trophy – the first for a woman in 50 years. Dave Phipps, the aero club's General Secretary, spoke of the size of the challenge and the inspiration it has provided, listing the project as one of the great aviation achievements.

The following year Sacha received the British Women Pilots' Association senior award for female pilots who consistently achieve goals. They acknowledged her diligence, citing her 'amazing feat of planning, logistics, aviation, navigation and endurance'.

The Taiwanese Chou Ta-kuan Foundation invested Sacha as a Laureate of the 'Fervent Global Love of Lives Award', recognising people globally who have overcome great personal adversity, helped others or helped the planet. The project also received Campaign of the Year 2017 by the Environmental Impact Awards for the scale of its ambition, huge profile, and international reach. The *Guardian* named her in their Top Ten Adventurers.

On her bookshelf is a postcard from some Russian hunters inscribed, 'your memories inspire us' and signed with a love heart. There is also a sweet family of three dolls from the Nenets people. The dolls' heads are traditionally made from the beak of a migratory bird.

The swan named Daisy Clarke was a revelation during the expedition, covering 3600 kilometres in just seven weeks. The entire trip was the springboard for further conservation exploration and in 2019 Sacha sublet her home and used the funds to form Conservation Without Borders (CWB), together with Emma White. Their mission is to bring together networks of vital resources to work together for a united push towards fighting climate change and the collapse of biodiversity. The expeditions they undertake follow the path of migratory species across multiple political and geographic regions.

TAKE FLIGHT

With the Flight of the Swans as its model, CWB's expeditions aim to show the real effects of climate change and biodiversity collapse and how that affects the animals within it. In the first five-yearly count of the swans, their number levelled off. It was exciting. In the years since, the impacts of the climate are more extreme and starting to take their toll again. Sacha hopes that every little bit of education might inspire people to enact change.

In early 2020, howling winds whipped up under an apocalyptic sky and her mother's home at Bega was among 400 lost in the devastating Black Summer fires. South-east Australia was in chaos, and alight for months. On New Year's Day, the South Island of Aotearoa/New Zealand awoke to a thick blanket of smoke that had drifted across the Tasman. Ten million hectares of mostly forest was burned and precious natural resources were affected. Speaking to Australia's Channel 7 news, Sacha said, 'Losing our home was devastating yet it's a drop in the ocean compared to the impacts of man-made climate change and habitat destruction on migratory wildlife across the planet as we decimate their global flyways and swimways'. For those living through the bushfires, it felt like the end of the world.

Reignited to raise awareness, Sacha took on an almighty workload to get CWB off the ground. Its first expedition was the Round Britain Climate Challenge. In an electric-powered paramotor, the team circumnavigated Britain and spoke to the people who 'showed us exactly how climate change is changing our country, but also what we can do about it'.

Sadly, the trip ended just short on its last leg after a tragic accident. Sacha was seriously injured, and her great friend and photographer, Dan Burton, was killed. It was devastating. Unbelievably, after months in hospital learning to walk again, she recovered as best she could in time for the 2022 Flight of the Osprey, which followed the migration of the large raptors through ten countries from Scotland to West Africa. Though she was land-based and debilitated for this trip, it did not dampen her dedication to the cause. The next expedition, at the end of 2024, will be the Flight of the Vulture.

For the many people who ask her how they can help, she recommends finding your strength. 'I was really passionate about doing something for the Bewick's swans. So basically, find that area, find a project where you can combine what you're good at with what you're passionate about, and that's probably the best thing you can do.'

Sacha did meet Dame Judi Dench, and also gained support from British actress and animal welfare supporter Joanna Lumley. From her English home, Sacha is physically a long way from Australia and the plants and animals that initially inspired her; however, they are never far from her heart. Her continued love of nature and commitment to conservation has brought her to an international stage, driven by a fragile paramotor, and fuelled by insatiable energy to raise awareness and provide practical solutions for our planetary crisis. As we finish this story, Sacha and CWB are fundraising for state-of-the-art prosthetic legs to enable her to walk efficiently again, to continue her important work. The outstanding film, Flight of the Swans, is winning awards in film festivals around the world.

NOTE: This chapter was mostly sourced from the public record, based on the many hours of media, podcasts and television appearances that Sacha has done. I had a conversation with Sacha afterwards, as time and recovery permitted, and I edited the details with Dr Julia Newth, one of the key WWT scientists involved in the project.

2

FROM TOURISM TO AEROMEDICAL RESCUE

ALIDA SOEMAWINATA, HELICOPTER PILOT

'The desert surrounding Uluṟu is so quiet, open, and flat. It is the true taste of freedom.'

Alida Soemawinata

It's been said that the three best sounds in aviation are the growling Merlin engine on a World War Two Spitfire fighter, the brrrrr of a radial engine on its American cousin, the Harvard, and the wok-wok-wok of a Huey coming at you – the rhythmic slap of its blades mimicking the backbeat to every rock song. You'll know the Huey as a Bell UH-1 Iroquois helicopter from any Vietnam War movie.

Helicopters are not an easy aircraft to master; anyone who's tried will attest to the skill required to simply hover. It is a finely tuned exercise in the coordination of hands and feet, perception and reaction.

When you fire up a chopper, the flying starts immediately. It's a magic carpet ride, albeit a noisy one, that rises from where you're starting and lands right where you're going. They can hover and turn on a point and take you in any direction.

Choppers are excellent for plucking hapless victims from a cliffside, out of the ocean, or off a roadside, and speeding them straight to safety. They are the cool vehicle with the excellent view that you fly in over Victoria Falls, the Twelve Apostles, or the Statue of Liberty. And they're the ultimate getaway vehicle favoured by Hollywood, rescuing an oil-stained hero as the city below burns. Have you ever seen a Cessna fly in and save the day?

For VIPs, they offer immediate access to a departure and arrival point.

When Michael Gudinski ran a series of rock concerts at the Hanging Rock Reserve in the Macedon Ranges of Victoria, he brought out big acts – Springsteen, The Eagles, Rod Stewart, and Elton John. It turns out our front paddock makes a perfect helipad, as we planted the trees around the edge, leaving the paddock flat and clear. It's a short 1 kilometre to the back entrance of Hanging Rock; Elton John flew in for his performance and out again in the depths of the night, the crowd still swaying and singing to 'Goodbye Yellow Brick Road'. He was almost in bed by the time they realised he wasn't coming back. For these pilots there is an intimacy with the clients and the flying experience. It's so hard not to love helicopters, except for the operating costs, but cost is the last thing on your mind when your wide eyes are pinging with the stars of excitement. And that's how 13-year-old Alida Soemawinata felt in 2001 when she returned from a doors-open over-water flight with the military: extremely excited.

It was an A-grade aerial baptism for the young member of the Australian Air Force Cadets (AAFC), a youth development program that enabled her to meet others from all over Australia and (eventually) overseas. The two-week General Service Training camp at RAAF Base East Sale, Victoria, included a week's work experience, and the helicopters were there. With her tiny body strapped into the seat, Alida looked around in adrenaline-fuelled wonder and determined, 'I'm going to do this'. That's the moment she made the decision. It would be expensive, and she knew that it was up to her to make it work. Alida is the fourth of five kids and money was tight; all five had joined Cadets, some Army and Navy, but Alida followed her eldest sister into the AAFC and attended the weekly Cadets meetings at 401 Squadron in Melbourne's Surrey Hills.

The family's story doesn't start in the suburbs of Melbourne, though. Both Alida's looks and surname come from her father Eddy, a Sundanese man from Bandung, West Java's second largest city. It is 140 kilometres south-east of Jakarta and if you keep driving through Bandung, it's another 1000 kilometres to Bali. The fourth most populated city in the country, the volcanic area is elevated and cooler than much of its surrounds. The Soemawinata family have lived in this area since at least the 17th century, when the Dutch East India Company were building roads to link their new tea plantations. Her grandfather brought the family to Australia in his role as an Indonesian emissary. When Eddy's father's four-year diplomatic posting ended, he stayed behind to study electrical engineering. Although he was studying at Footscray, a migrant suburb in Melbourne's west, he lived in share housing in the popular student enclave of Parkville, a leafy suburb on the city's edge. Through this extended group he met his future wife, Margaret, who was studying nearby at the prestigious Melbourne University. One thing the pair shared was a transient childhood, as Margaret had lived in Holland for a large part of her life. They embraced both their Indonesian and Dutch cultures but were keen to stay planted in Melbourne. Alida, their fourth-born child, was named after her Dutch great-grandmother and she uses the shortened version, Li, as her great-grandmother had. Their name means 'small winged one', which was fortuitous as the younger Li never grew past about 163 cm and has spent most of her life thinking about or being in the air.

The close and happy family observed Ramadan and Eid and enjoyed traditional foods such as opor ayam, beef rendang, sate and gado-gado. She'd savour the familiarity of these foods later, when she moved to Borneo. At Christmas time it was a traditional European-Australian roast alongside Aussie prawns and seafood. The Soemawinata family placed importance on being a good person and allowing freedom of cultural or religious belief. The kids followed each other off to Cadets and put their hands up for holiday camps. They learned about aircraft, bushcraft, communication, and some important personal development skills in team building and leadership, with a bent towards officer roles. Alida sought opportunities and was awarded a Boeing-sponsored, four-week International Air Cadet Exchange to the UK in 2003. The Cadet group were flown around to RAF Bases and had a trip on the Queen's flight, where the young Australian recalls the novelty of watching sugar cubes dissolve in the bottom of a fine china teacup. They were hosted at No. 10 Downing Street and visited museums, a firing range for rifle training, Tower of London, and other cultural highlights. They practised scenario team events and formation marching and made lifelong friends.

TAKE FLIGHT

In 2005, Alida had the honour of being chosen Cadet of the Year. It was a huge deal and meant that she could join a group of cadets in Papua New Guinea. They walked part of the Kokoda Track, which she admits was hard enough, never mind doing the whole thing! Then back in Port Moresby, Anzac Day dawned with a still and eerie silence. And though they'd only seen very few expats around town, suddenly there were hundreds of them at the Dawn Service. The uniformed young group took their place among current and retired service personnel for the moving ceremony. 'It was so emotional. In the silence of the dawn, I realised what the meaning was behind Cadets. Even though I wasn't actually in the military, it gave me an understanding of "service". And it gave me access to the old diggers and nurses who had such national pride and sense of community service.'

That service background influences her current work, helping villagers on the island of Borneo, flying medical retrievals and transfers. She bounced home from PNG, full of stories and enthusiasm and even more motivated to learn and to get around in the big world. She mostly sought to be airborne: glider, aeroplane, helicopter. She couldn't raise the funds to go parachuting but did finish high school contemplating a helicopter licence. Should she join the military? The Return of Service (the time required to stay in the military to repay the time it took them to train you) for pilots meant a commitment to them until she was 31.

She wasn't too excited about the locations of the army bases and so looked to the Navy. Nowra! What a beautiful place on the NSW coast, a couple of hours south of Sydney. Ships ... oh, that meant months at sea. None of it felt quite right and so she thought long and hard. *OK. How do I really do this?*

Alida began her first career as a barista at just 15 years old, working at a busy city Starbucks. Hospitality allowed her to work on weekends and after school, with her parents supportively driving her when she needed, sometimes collecting her after midnight. She learned very quickly how to manage money, building her savings in preparation for flight school and of course to fund her travel adventures. Leaving school and Cadets behind, she continued work as a barista, taking on multiple jobs while she completed a science degree at Monash University, majoring in biology and ecology. From uni she went backpacking to Europe for a year, which was a nice way to clear her mind. In 2010, now 22 years old and back home in Melbourne, she went for a Trial Introductory Flight (TIF). The relieving instructor, standing in for the permanent instructor that day, had been a helicopter pilot with the Police Air Wing. His 6 foot 2 inches frame filled the little chopper, a Schweizer 300, and they lifted off from Moorabbin, heading towards the Bay for a one-hour taster. It tasted like fun, and she enquired about flight training.

The helicopter school doesn't have 'intakes' as such. Students start and finish lessons as and when they can. Alida attended ground school classes at night; these were a highlight because she could mix with other students, which helped her to stay motivated. Today she credits her teacher Rob Salvagno and his stories for many of her flight decisions. At around $550 per flight hour, there were a lot of coffees to be made, and a couple of years later, the barista funds stretched to a flying lesson every couple of weeks. Career progression with the company she chose, Professional Helicopter Services (PHS), meant a newbie could see a clear path from first flight to first pay cheque at either their Gold Coast or Uluṟu/Kings Canyon bases. PHS operates charters and joy flights at many major events including the Formula 1 and the MotoGP, and volunteering as ground crew demonstrated her commitment to flying and to the company. Alida was ecstatic at being rewarded with hours of ferry time in the AS350 Squirrel, her dream machine. Ferry flights are done without passengers, and usually to reposition an aircraft for operational purposes. It allows students to log valuable flying hours for free. The course took her six years, and the more cashed-up students overtook her in that time, finishing in less than two; however, a week after her 30th birthday she got her licence. By that time, she was working reception at the PHS headquarters and as a hangar assistant, driving the ground support fuel truck. By the end of 2017 she was ready to go and when she got passed over for a line pilot position at the Uluru Kings Canyon base, she asked why. She had expected to follow the standard career path, starting out in the Red Centre, and then transferring to either the Gold Coast base or returning to the Melbourne base and completing her instructor's rating. Building time as an instructor usually leads to aerial photography work, charter flights, powerline surveys, and aerial fire operations. Exciting work and decent pay.

The reply was that because she had a boyfriend, they thought she didn't want to go.

'I'm already packed', she shot back.

With all there was to look forward to, she was raring to go. First stop, Kings Canyon.

THE FIRST THING TO HIT YOU AFTER A THREE-HOUR SUMMER flight to Ayers Rock Airport is the heat. While the name Ayers Rock has been reverted to the Indigenous name Uluru, the resort and the airport are still officially referred to as Ayers Rock. As the jet's engines spool down and the tingle of air-conditioning recedes from your skin, the dry heat slips on like a winter coat on a summer's day. Sweat forms on your forehead and armpits, and in the small of your back, and by the time you've crossed to your vehicle, you've collected a fine layer of bright red dust. When you plonk yourself onto the seat, a healthy puff of the stuff rises like a cloud, and you wear it until you leave.

Alida was here for a stint as ground crew and to be familiarised with PHS operations. She spent the first night in comfort at the Ayers Rock Resort, Yulara, then with a bunch of downloaded music and podcasts, drove the company car out the front gate and turned right, heading north-east on the Lasseter Highway towards Alice Springs, before turning left onto Luritja Road to Kings Canyon. The phone's reception died ten minutes into the three-hour drive, but her curiosity and enthusiasm were very much alive.

'I saw more animals on that trip than I did in the next four years: brumbies, camels, cows, and lizards. As soon as I turned onto the main road the first dingo I'd ever seen crossed directly in front of me, walked along the road and disappeared into the bushes. I thought, *oh, this really is the outback!*'

At the Kings Canyon resort her old friend from training, Dean Neal, greeted her with a huge grin that matched her own. He had overtaken her by 12 months during their flight training in Melbourne and she was pleased to see his smiling face. The resort has accommodation, a fuel station, a store, and a large dining and bar area. Sitting with the pilots at the end of each day, she was rapt to be there and quietly wondered how soon her turn to fly out here could come. She didn't have to wait long because by Christmas a few weeks later, home was a donga in the desert. The small transportable building was next to the helipad on the edge of Kings Canyon resort. The team ate at the resort and there was plenty of downtime for reading and completing other work. It was a stepping stone to the busier Ayers Rock base and the crew rosters cycled between the two. Ten minutes' drive from the door of her new home was the start of the 6-kilometre trail that follows the Canyon Rim, and she got to know it well. The few hours' walk is regarded as medium difficulty, starting with 500 stairs. In this isolated place, life for the resort workers, and flying for the pilots, was mostly straightforward and predictable. For Alida, also a fitness enthusiast, it was a dream come true because she had plenty of opportunities to hike as well as fly. Even though summer is the quieter time, it is still busy, and her vital skills were consolidated quickly as she punched out so many

TAKE FLIGHT

landings. Most joy flights were either the 'eight-minute dash' or a longer 15-minute circuit. On a busy day she could do up to 30 flights unless the extreme heat or a passing storm grounded them, as it did late on New Year's Day 2018.

The storm from hell was fast and vindictive. Rob Mengler was enjoying his day off at the ranger complex 4 kilometres from the resort. Then in his mid-50s, Rob was the senior District Ranger and Incident Controller for the Parks and Wildlife Commission Northern Territory. Late in the afternoon he watched the full kahuna unleash when massive cells from ex-tropical Cyclone Hilda united into a spectacular rolling dark front with lightning and thunder. His work was centred around biodiversity and conservation and as both the highway and the canyon's main walking trail were flooding, he knew that soon spectacular waterfalls would be in full flow. Rob and the other Kings Canyon rangers must also train as first responders, generally responding to slips, falls, dehydration, and incidents caused by lack of fitness up on the Canyon Rim. By the time he was notified of an emergency, health clinic staff were already on their way. He contacted the PHS staff to put the pilots on standby; however, the pilots knew there was no way they could fly in that weather.

Rob recalls the 'unusual freak storm that went along the full length of the George Gill Range, and that it had lightning in it'. The fierce lightning had struck and killed a hiker, Antony Van Der Meer, and a pair of park rangers scrambled to get to the accident site. Knowing they couldn't fly, Alida and Dean motored off in the PHS van to the canyon car park. She braced herself. Rain was pouring down from further up the range and the creek at the bottom of Kings Canyon was already uncrossable. Dean turned to her: 'We'll do The Rim and see if we can get around to them that way'.

They arrived in the dark 90 minutes later to a confronting scene, with the distraught Van Der Meer family being helped by a couple of other hikers, the park rangers and two health clinic staff. Alida took her place with the group and, through now-drizzling rain over rough terrain, helped carry the heavy stretcher down to the waiting ambulance. Relaying how Alida described the incident to me, Rob's quick to point out that it was a really physical trek with lots of stops. 'Over a hill, down a goat track, along the side of the sandstone ridge, and across boulders and loose footings.' Antony's wife Jessica remembers it as feeling like a cliff face.

Down at the creek, Alida sat for hours, bravely and compassionately, with the stretcher while the rangers set up a water crossing and assisted the distressed family, on the worst day of their lives, across to the emergency vehicles. The 4WD troop carriers, equipped for extreme weather, were able to depart. Meanwhile, the rest of the stranded hikers waited until the wee hours when the water receded enough for them to be ferried out in 4WDs, returning in the morning to pick up their cars and campers.

It is natural for people to help in remote communities; there's nobody else to call on. But despite all of Alida's leadership training and life experiences, nothing could prepare her, even as an outsider, for the toll that witnessing death for the first time, so close and dramatic, would take. She lay awake in her isolated donga trying to process it. A couple of weeks later a friend at the Rock was seriously injured in a helicopter accident and for the first time, 31-year-old Alida, the 'sunshine' in her family, struggled to process her emotions. Her parents were naturally concerned for her, and curious to see where she was living. They came to visit after the helicopter accident, while flying operations were temporarily halted. It was an important visit for the family and Alida appreciated their support. Sensibly, she also sought formal counselling soon afterwards and is grateful that was available.

Margaret and Eddy were as enamoured with the outback as their daughter was. 'It's a really lovely place to be; a beautiful environment', says Margaret. 'Alida has always been tuned into nature and that was part of what she really loved out there. We did all the tourist activities including a helicopter flight over the top of Kings Canyon. We could see the beautiful cycads and palms deep inside it. Over the top of the range is a sheer drop off the edge. She asked us later if we'd noticed how hard the pilot was working his hands and feet at that point, to fly into the updraft over the ledge without the passengers noticing any change in level. That was the first notion I had of the level of skill required to do what she was doing.'

The magic slowly returned after such a turbulent start and Austin McNallen, the base manager, was impressed with how his new charge took to her role. 'Her greatest asset was her interaction with the customers. We all get given a 200-word brief to say in-flight and once we have the basics down, we can give a broader commentary to the passengers. The conversations flow from there. We'd often end up doing our own research on things that interest us and hers was very involved because she had a real interest in the area. The customers really engaged with that.'

When the next round of pilots arrived in the winter, Alida relocated from Kings Canyon to Ayers Rock Airport. The flying is a bit more complex because pilots must contend with a control tower advising of local conditions, more passengers and a busier airspace shared with another helicopter company, fixed-wing aircraft, airliners, and General Aviation activity. With back-to-back Uluru and Kata Tjuta flights of around 25 minutes, each pilot follows a well-worn, legally defined route; a series of purple dots laid out on the aviation maps that keep aircraft to the north and west of Uluru, away from culturally sensitive areas. But Uluru is still close enough to fill the window. 'How did the proposal go?' she remembered to ask one joy-flighter as they disembarked. 'She said yes!' he replied and shared a once-in-a-lifetime photo of himself with his surprised fiancée seated facing him. Uluru loomed large out of the window as a silent witness. It also loomed large from her home at the resort, which was a giant step up from the donga. With perfect timing she got to move into a freshly renovated house with two other junior pilots.

The soft, rounded top of Uluṟu rises 348 metres from the earth, dwarfing the quarter of a million visitors who stand before it each year. They have bike tours, picnics, walks, cultural talks, and many other activities to entertain and inform them. And to fly them around, they had 11 pilots with two helicopter companies. It was busy and fun and interesting. Everything was just *fine*, until the start of 2020 when tourism got the wobbles, and then fell off a cliff.

Austin was worried about the drop in tourist numbers due to the blanket coverage of the horrendous bushfires a few thousand kilometres away in south-eastern Australia. They were a three-hour jet ride away, but as far as overseas tourists knew, Australia was on fire and so they stopped coming. 'We were dealing with what we thought was an avalanche of cancellations,' he says. 'And at the same time news was starting to come out of China about the emergence of Covid, but I didn't think that would affect us in particular. Then the Northern Territory government announced that the border would close in two weeks' time. There was a frantic upheaval. Everybody knew they were going to be out of work. Most people were given a letter of dismissal, except for me as I had to look after buildings, vehicles, and choppers. The whole resort was like a mad rush with people packing their cars to get back to their homes interstate. People departed expeditiously and those "grey nomads" who did escape from the southern states heading north were not allowed into the National Parks.'

The farewell was swift and Alida posed with a couple of dozen friends as a setting sun turned Uluṟu blazing red. She posted it under her handle @li.li.pink on Instagram with the following caption.

> 26 March. The rock is closed. The country is shut down. Our group photo barely fit everyone in as we tried to maintain distancing. No tourists, just a bunch of locals saying goodbye

with a final toast 🥂 Loved living and working with all of you guys! The Yulara crew are some good eggs 🥚

Austin and his son went out to the airport to say goodbye to Alida, who flew a helicopter home to its Melbourne base. 'She had the Bell 206 Jet Ranger jam-packed with all her belongings and we waved her off. That left just my wife and me and our two children at Yulara. There were no tourists and only one of every five staff members remained. It was a daunting and uncertain time. I dealt with customers and the thousands of advanced seat bookings we had from travel agents. After such a fast exit, I also had to clean and hand back the houses that the company rented, then put their furniture and goods in storage. I had to manage the fuel and do weekly engine-runs and monthly half-hour flights in both the choppers. I also drove to Kings Canyon weekly to do the same out there. We had thousands of litres of fuel to look after.'

The six-leg trip to Melbourne went 1100 nautical miles (2037 kilometres) from Ayers Rock Airport, in a near-straight line southeast through Leigh Creek at the northern end of South Australia's Flinders Ranges, finishing in Moorabbin. Below her on the first leg, a single narrow road sliced the hazy ochre and olive desert. The blue sky was patched with cloud cover and a rain shower presented ahead. Crocodile-shaped watercourses sprouted intertwining lines of green, and a tiny square dam waited for stock from who-knows-where. Further along, tonal shifts of yellow clay swirled like batter, with a verdant watercourse meandering to the radiant white of Lake Eyre. Alida was just getting comfortable at the silent Leigh Creek Holiday Park when the police confronted her with a knock on the door to check her transiting forms. It was an ominous sign of the times.

First thing the next morning she was flying over the Flinders Ranges, their peaks standing up like stiff whipped cream. A side view of Wilpena Pound was glorious, red and green layered Rawnsley Quartzite. With a dusty black elastic-sided boot in the corner of her next photo, some Mallee scrub passed below as she made for Horsham in Victoria for fuel. One of her girlfriends managed to get to the airport with some supportive hot coffee and muffins.

Tullamarine Air Traffic Control granted permission for Alida to overfly the normally busy international airspace. Commercial aviation had ground to a trickle, and this was a rare opportunity for smaller aircraft to land there without the hassle of the constant inflow of jet traffic. Over the course of lockdown, a few times a week the under-utilised air traffic controllers would gladly interrupt their Scrabble to grant permission for a fly-over, a touch-and-go, or a full stop. The terminals, shops and car parks were desolate; the only regular activity was the freight planes, carting things, not people. Private aircraft were taking advantage of the empty skies and the chance to land at a major airport was a blessing. Even one of the air traffic controllers, Kingsley Just, did his private pilot's annual review with a flight into his workplace. Bored by the slow plane and the lengthy Tullamarine runway, he joked that he'd have preferred to do it inverted in his high-performance aerobatic aircraft. Up in NSW, the Stooge Formation team, a group of four friends who learnt the art of flying in formation a few metres apart from each other, did a landing at Sydney's main Kingsford Smith Airport. The four home-built aircraft, flown by private pilots, touched down simultaneously, did a press conference, then departed in formation like a flock of birds. Before any of these events, however, there was Alida in a Jet Ranger helicopter blowing out the red dust.

'Call us at the 30-mile mark and track 1500 feet direct to Tulla', they said. She flew towards the tower, with no requirement to enter a circuit pattern and descended to 1000 feet down runway 09, did a 70-degree right turn and flew along runway 16, the main runway. She waved goodbye to the air traffic controllers. Melbourne's empty airspace was eerily silent. Down below, aircraft were parked up, as they were all over the world. She continued a few kilometres on to

TAKE FLIGHT

Essendon Airport. There, she flew at 800 feet up runway 17, which was also idle.

Enjoying the private scenic view of the city she reached for her phone once more to snap the CBD, the rail network and the almost empty freeways coursing past Docklands' giant ferris wheel.

Getting closer to Moorabbin, an airport that is normally buzzing with student pilots doing circuits, and General Aviation activity, Alida reported to their tower. They told her to just come straight in and go to where she needed to be. In front of the parked helicopter, she lamented that now reality would surely kick in as she got comfy in a house of six during school holidays and isolation.

Back in Central Australia, astonishing photos from the Asia Pacific Aircraft Storage Facility in Alice Springs showed rows of Singapore Airlines and Cathay Pacific A380s baking in the dry heat. Almost 100 wide-body jets lay like toys nose-to-tail in a grid, divided by lines of smaller aircraft. The anxious world waited and wondered.

Farewelling the few staff at the hangar, she hung up the keys on her longest solo flight and went home to her sister's house to wash out the red dust and contemplate her position. Her mum describes the sisters as being 'incredibly close, like twins. Alida helped with the kids and the cooking and keeping people sane. She's a lot of fun also'.

To maintain her spirits, she continued to share images from the outback. Included was an interesting visual of the day she landed on the north wall of Kings Canyon to collect a hiker who was paralysed by fear. After three hours of trying to coax him to walk on, the helicopter was called and he was back at the base in minutes, where he stood straight and walked without trouble. His only problem then was the cost of the rescue. Sharing images was the best she could do to stay motivated and positive, which was no mean feat when living in the most locked-down city in the world.

Melbourne's 5.5 million residents were issued with stay-at-home orders and only essential workers were allowed to leave in 262 days of lockdown. Public galleries, churches, sporting fields, swimming pools and schools were hauntingly empty. Fountains flowed and public gardens bloomed with nobody to see them. Escalators cycled through their day without a footprint and ghost trains kept to schedules. The seasons changed and the city's industries, once so bright and bustling, grew dark with the night. On all-seeing security cameras, we watched a growing cohort of wildlife step meekly out of hiding to experience a freedom we were coming to envy. Society was divided into vaxxers and the much smaller but growing number of anti-vaxxers. Like the rest of us, Alida began to yearn for what she had lost, posting:

> It's possible to be surrounded by people I love at home and still feel less alone in the middle of the desert. There's always plenty to do at home, but nothing is as fulfilling as time in the sky. Looking beyond the next few months is tough but life always manages to deliver amazing eventually. 😁 🚁 👮 We got this 💙

It was a hopeful message and she did at least manage a few local maintenance flights, and a sling endorsement to add to her licence. A sling is a cargo hook that is slung below a helicopter to enable carriage of external loads and it requires special training to be able to use it. This endorsement was another useful step towards flying a Firebird helicopter, used especially for firefighting, and carrying the firefighting Bambi bucket (a specialised firefighting water-carrying bucket) in the future. For much of the time, however, everyone had way too much exposure to the online news cycles. Reflecting on how far she had come in her career and how it might pan out, her usual sunny disposition dimmed with the weather on the coldest day of July 2020:

> One year ago today I was living my best life enjoying a sunset walk at Uluru. Today the world has gone mental and I'm not

loving life, but I can be thankful for good health and hope for better days ahead. We got this 😊 (... I hope 🤞)

Having arrived home right on the start of the first Melbourne lockdown she was back on Jetstar the day after the second lockdown ended at the end of October 2020. The return was sweet relief. 'There is a feeling you get when you see Uluṟu. When you're flying along and you get this glimpse of it, you can't help looking at it. When the dry heat hits you after the door opens, it's *BOOM. I'm home!* Melbourne had been cold and rainy, and I needed the heat. To me it was welcoming, though it doesn't always feel like that to the tourists.' Austin agrees. 'The weather is fantastic, but during the NT's hottest summer on record – 2018–19 – we had 60 days above 40 degrees. I remember reading the helicopter's outside air temperature gauge at 47 degrees. The coolest I recall was minus 4 one morning just before sunrise.'

As Australia tried to get back to pre-Covid routines, some of the pilots didn't return to the Rock, so by a process of seniority, Alida was senior base pilot within a year. The flying was now 'really interesting' and she started by taking a geologist, a financier, and an anthropologist to survey for oil and gas. 'Consulting with proposed fracking maps, we'd land at potential anthropological sites where they'd search for any signs of human habitation including cave paintings, tobacco plants and figs. The team also noted locations of endangered tree stands, and nesting trees of the vulnerable princess parrot. These areas can now be protected. I was fully loaded with four men. I'd drop them off, return to base for fuel, then return and move them around. It was my first proper job aside from scenic tours.'

Working at Uluṟu means an inevitable intersection with the Aṉangu people and Australia's colonial descent upon them. An interesting survey job came in from the local Central Land Council and Alida flew them and an anthropologist on a well-researched track to try and follow the journals of the 19th-century English explorer Ernest Giles. In the middle of the 19th century, Giles and his camels crossed from Port Augusta in South Australia to Geraldton on the west coast, down to Perth and back again following waterholes. From August 1873 to the winter of 1874 Giles travelled from Beltana, north of Port Augusta, up through the centre to Uluṟu and Kata Tjuṯa. He claimed to be the first explorer (in 1872) to see Uluṟu. He must have wondered what he'd come across! Surveyor William Gosse, the following year, named it Ayers Rock after a former South Australian premier, Sir Henry Ayers.

The Australian Dictionary of Biographies concludes that: 'Giles is among the more interesting Australian explorers by virtue of his journals … His culture, perception and imagination were no less marked than his skill and determination.'

The anthropologists were trying to find the last of the wells, where Giles's diaries record that he watered his camels before continuing on to Uluṟu. 'It was important for the Aṉangu people to find information about the exact location of the well, so they could pass that information along again. Just north of Yulara is Lake Amadeus. They were flying just to the north of it looking for a particular well. Giles had dug a trench to try and get down to some drinking water, without much success.' They were searching for a limestone pool, north of Lake Amadeus, that was a couple or a few metres deep. 'To find it from the air a century later is difficult and we'd gone out a few times looking for signs', says Alida. 'We'd park the chopper and walk around; the lead researcher would explain how they knew this area was like a highway through the desert. I was chosen because the manager and I are qualified to fly at low level. Tracking and mapping for local Indigenous people is from the height of the sand dunes. You can see from higher up, but you lose shadows on the dunes. One indication for middens was the shape of the dune. You can see that the winds prevail from one direction creating the shape of the dune. We'd look around there and see tools and seeds and change in the vegetation from where food had been consumed. We searched about 10 square miles from ground level up to 500 feet high. I spent a whole day doing three flights. We'd refuel at the airport and go out again. There were five Indigenous people and one Caucasian anthropologist. It was a new way of honing thousands of years old skills. Whenever we saw white limestone patches in the red sand, they'd signal for me to land and shut down so they could investigate. Most of the conversation was between the Aboriginal Elder and the anthropologist in the front of the chopper. I could hear them very clearly through my headset and I'd walk with them to search. It was another pilot flying when they finally found the well they were looking for. Earlier we'd visited a different well they'd already found, and it was shown to the younger men. It was a men's business area so I remained in the heli with the blades turning.'

Because they now had a female pilot, Aboriginal women were able to access women's areas by air. Alida flew a group of them to survey the boundary of a township where there was overlap with Indigenous lands. With English as a difficult medium, some of the staff from the Land Council and Parks helped with translation. In that short, targeted trip they were able to confirm where the overlap occurred and how they could best manage ground access in the future and protect it.

Over her time working at the resort, Alida took advantage of the tours that staff could access. In partnership with local experts, one tour company ran a trip to some of Australia's oldest preserved cave paintings at Cave Hill, South Australia. She had a special place in her heart for people like Sammy Wilson, an Anangu man who is a senior custodian of Uluṟu and, as Chair of the National Park board, was instrumental in the fight to have the famous Uluṟu Summit climb closed. The board members voted, and it closed in late 2019. His knowledge and connection to the area intrigued Alida, who enjoyed every chance she got to speak with him. It was a wonderful and fascinating time.

After being back out in the centre, four years in all, the thought of going back to Melbourne didn't appeal so much. Some friends had moved on to bigger machines working overseas and Alida was now keen to spread her wings beyond Australia; to see how far she could take her career and on what adventures. When a former colleague contacted her about a job in Borneo, she jumped at it. The working environment would be completely different, flying in jungles and in an iconic twin-engine machine: the BO105. The Bolkow is a German twin-engine helicopter first developed in the 1960s and famous for its speed, agility, and incredible aerobatic ability. It is also strong and, with its high-mounted tail rotor, able to land in confined areas. Most importantly, it operates well in extreme weather conditions. Some call it a 'beast' as it is so durable and reliable.

In early 2022, she packed the same 20- and 10-kilogram suitcases and small daypack that she's travelled with since Melbourne and threw $18 000 at a new helicopter rating. If she passed the course, she would get the job. If she didn't, she'd be $10 000 down in her super, and $8000 poorer from her savings, with no result. It paid off, though, and she joined a crew of six pilots: three Kiwis, one Malaysian and two Australians in Borneo. Because there are settlements lining the coast and the shores of the hydropower dams and reservoirs inland, she treated herself to a birthday present – a one-day Helicopter Underwater Escape Training (HUET) course, which prepares aircrews to cope with a ditching – when the aircraft enters the water unplanned.

They learn how to escape from the helicopter, which, horribly, will usually roll upside-down. Two years prior, Australian firefighting pilot Lachie Onslow escaped from his pink Huey 'Lucy', in a dam in southern New South Wales after suffering an engine failure while refilling the craft's bucket. With little time to respond, Lachie credited his survival to his recent HUET renewal course.

TAKE FLIGHT

The training begins with classroom theory and a briefing, then goes to the pool for a few staged escapes from a helicopter simulator. Alida recalls, 'we practised with and without breathing apparatus, and jettisoning the windows underwater. It's a scary feeling having to wait for the aircraft to completely submerge and roll before escaping. If you don't wait, then you risk becoming completely disoriented'.

Her first week on the job was 'awesome'. Every day was invigorating, with many new experiences. Each carved-out landing site, remote village, steaming mountain, unique tribe and tasty meal heightened her senses. Each rickety bridge, concrete classroom, palm-fringed playing field, blazing sunset, and post-work tinnie brought its own dimension to her days.

Mostly, the company she flies for acts as a flying doctor service, transporting a medical team and supplies to remote villages and, when necessary, as an emergency medical service on standby for patient transfer. Their outreach operations include overnight village stops. Some large villages may have clinics staffed with nurses and medical assistants, but sometimes they require a doctor with specialist equipment like a portable ultrasound. It means the company can get to the communities they regularly service, as well as flying to extremely remote areas. Building hours as the 'multi-engine pilot in command' is crucial and will be at the forefront of her résumé when applying for new jobs.

The helicopters cross into the inaccessible interior, traditionally only reached on foot or by river. Any road in is, unfortunately, usually in poor condition due to flooding, and the drive may be upwards of ten hours. In one instance Alida was flying over mountainous jungle as far as the eye could see. A breathtaking waterfall dropped steadily in the midst of it before the landscape gave way to waterways. And cloud. There's almost always cloud. Tropical storms are as threatening as some of the exotic insects and venomous snakes. Her focus, though, is the people she gets to meet from many different tribes and locations.

Alida Soemawinata, helicopter pilot

From routine clinic rounds to emergency retrievals, the many success stories blend together. However, there is one instance that stands out from the rest, when help came too late. She started up the engine to transfer an infant to hospital, then heard the alarm sound on the monitor as the medical team signalled for her to shut down – the baby was dying. The team performed CPR but it was not successful – she was sad at both the loss, and that the cost discourages some families from accessing their medical services, or asking for help too late. The helicopter transfer to hospital is provided by the government for free, but the trip home, which can be as basic as hopping on a bus, is still beyond some people's financial reach.

Cost is a factor for pilots too, and a helicopter pilot's wage starts at the lower end like many industries. Safety is always at the forefront of operations, though, and the $6500 cost to upgrade from a simple headset to a full-face helmet came as a shock to Alida. While not compulsory, helmets save lives, and flying in this new environment and role made it a priority. Somebody suggested GoFundMe, which thankfully many of her friends, some of her 5000 Instagram followers, and most of her family responded to. Coupled with her savings, she was able to afford a brand-new helmet. She chose a dark-tinted outer visor and a yellow inner visor that helps with highlighting contours of the terrain, which is especially good during deteriorating weather or low light. As someone who wears glasses, it helps rest her eyes.

On overnight stops, the medical teams can be hosted in the villages and while much of that experience is new, some of the food is not. Familiar smells and flavours hark back to her childhood and there is much to discuss with her parents when she calls home. Margaret adds, 'Sometimes after shut-down in a remote spot, the team must walk half an hour on muddy tracks. Sometimes they land on a soccer field, or a patch of grass cleared with a scythe. We love her portrayals of village life that Eddy would have experienced as a child. He loves traditional history and culture, so we really like that she's seeing that first-hand while it still exists.' Alida agrees that she enjoys learning about Borneo's many different cultures and eating the traditional cuisine. Though Borneo and Australia are near neighbours, Borneo is such a world away from the job she left behind.

Professionally, Austin now watches from Queensland and admires her grit. He saw when 'mostly older guys would make sexist remarks' while she was learning. As a close friend, and a married father of two, he found it confronting to see her encounter the 'regular stuff that guys just don't have to deal with'. But Alida didn't let it stop her; she was always heading on to bigger things. Austin was impressed by the risk she took in upgrading her qualifications and moving overseas, when she'd stayed almost twice as long as most pilots out in the Centre.

'It's quite a large step to go from single-engine daytime flights to multi-engine medical transport overseas. It's pretty cool. She also took the financial risk of outlaying for the multi-engine endorsement, because you don't have the job until you have the qualifications.'

From Borneo, Alida's encouraging daily Instagram updates continue to be upbeat and excited by life, and she recently shared the story about watching a villager in a straw hat make their way up the hill through the jungle, led by an excited little dog. Somebody was coming to see the clinic staff at the helicopter. Her friend replied, 'It still blows my mind that you're flying one of the coolest helicopters ever made!' She replied, 'Me too'. By being open and sharing her life, she inspires those who are interested in following the accounts of her job. Her Instagram inbox revolves with questions about how she achieved her flying goals. One such Malaysian follower recently signed on to flight school. There will inevitably be a next step in this story and one dream for Alida is to fly Parks Conservation and Safaris in Africa, and Kenya looks like an ideal place to start. 'However, I think I'll have to pause that plan for a few years and look at working back in Australia before I can afford the licence conversion and extra training required.'

She is remembered well by those she's encountered. She was encouraging to young Tia McVeigh, who helped with a spinal injury rescue. 'I was volunteering at Kings Canyon while I was still doing my helicopter licence. Alida and I spent a lot of time together. She taught me so much about the industry and made me realise that I really wanted to work in that operation.' Tia is now flying helicopters around Uluru in Alida's former seat.

Jessica Van Der Meer was grateful for the help from everyone at Kings Canyon and fundraised to upgrade the equipment for their medical staff. There is now a plaque to remember Antony and there are two extra permanent defibrillators along the Kings Canyon Walk. Rob Mengler is managing a 300 000-hectare cattle station midway between Alice Springs and Mount Isa. He fondly remembers Alida as outgoing, approachable, and focused. Alida takes it all in her stride, and there have been some big strides, including the loss of her friend Dean, as well as one of her instructors, in separate accidents after she left Australia. Aviation is an unforgiving innamorato.

Cadets developed her leadership skills and confidence, and barista work provided her most of the funds. The rest has been hard work, flexibility, and determination. By the permanent smile on her face, though, the small winged one wouldn't change much since the day she determined, 'I'm going to do this'.

3
FROM THE TALLEST MOUNTAIN

HEATHER SWAN, WINGSUIT BASE JUMPER

'We'd taken three weeks to climb and three minutes to get down. I felt small but enormous and so much more than this little human shell.'

Heather Swan

In a tiny tent on a frozen mountain high in northern India, Heather Swan peered out into the dark. It was 2.30 am and today she would make her final attempt to achieve her six-year goal: a world record BASE jump down Meru Peak's 2000-foot cliff. She would land in the glacial field below. The launching point was located 21 661 feet up, where the air is so thin that it's hard to think. Where the frontal cortex of your brain stops working, leaving you unable to effectively solve new problems. You need to work from memory; your training needs to kick in and your activities should be second nature. It's an extreme place to pursue your dreams: tough on both the gear and the climbers. If this attempt failed, then Heather and her husband, Dr Glenn Singleman, would have to relinquish their plan. There was no arguing with the weather.

Meru Peak in India's Uttarakhand region is one of the tallest peaks in the Garhwal Himalayas. At around three-quarters the size of its giant cousin Mount Everest, the difference seems academic, but to the climbers, every step was a hard, hard win. They were not using bottled oxygen, which was effectively the same as being atop Everest with bottled oxygen. The most immediate problem on Meru was that the exhausted team was now out of food.

They set out from their high-altitude camp at 4 am and climbed anyway. Step by agonising step and focused on the destination, their perseverance was rewarded when, in a 30-minute window of early afternoon sunshine, the ground crew instructed them to immediately suit up. In minus 25 degrees at 2 pm on that freezing Saturday, 16 May 2006, Heather stood with her husband on the edge of a granite cliff. Impossibly quiet, it was surely one of the most remote places in the world. Observed by only a dozen or so carefully positioned team members, Glenn jumped and Heather followed like a shadow.

Seconds later, a couple of expert Nepalese Sherpas, Mingma Sherpa and Samgyal Sherpa, balanced precariously atop the same skyward ledge. Having kicked their crampons into the ice, they crouched on the slippery 70-degree uphill slope and peered over the cliff in shock and disbelief. Heather and Glenn, the people they had spent three weeks climbing with, inching their way along steep inclines with ice picks, and surviving in snow caves with ever-diminishing rations, disappeared into the abyss like a couple of rag dolls. The Australians flexed their every muscle against the force of the fall and their wingsuits finally inflated, rocketing them away to a world record. Their return to earth, 2000 feet down and 1000 metres out, took a splintering 180 seconds. The footage is unsurpassed. The Sherpas were wide-eyed at the horror of it.

A condensed story like this belies the preceding six years of devastating setbacks and exciting advancements. The expedition took Heather from her lounge room, where she'd blithely announced after a long day in the office that she'd like to give BASE jumping a go, to the Hindu 'Centre of the Universe', this icy granite point that placed them halfway between sea level and the altitude of an airliner.

IN NORMAL LIFE 'THE OFFICE' WAS HEATHER'S LATEST CAREER location, where her uniform was a corporate power suit. It was a quantum leap from her policewoman's boots, her flight attendant's silk, and her journalist's pen – all jobs she'd previously held. By 1995 she was the national manager of Harry M Miller's speaker's bureau. His agency had secured some of Australia's most interesting and high-profile champions and rascals, detailed in his book, *A Not So Secret Agent*. If you were looking for a world-class speaker, Harry M Miller was the go-to and Heather was the one to talk to. Behind her professional face, though, was a busy single mother. All that she worked for supported the ideals of Sydney life: beachside living, a BMW, and a fulfilling job to pay the bills. On weekends she caught up on anything she'd missed, and sometimes took time out for creative pursuits. It was a full diary, which shifted its focus late that year after meeting Glenn, the man who would eventually become her husband.

Glenn was booked to speak at a corporate function, and he was late. Heather paced the hall, as much as her blood-red stilettos would allow, while trying to centre herself. *Where is this guy?* He was caught in traffic. The crowd's expectations weighed squarely on Heather's expensively tailored shoulders. It was worth the wait, though, because when Glenn eventually fronted the audience, the room was stunned into silence. He took them through his life as a practising emergency-room doctor to his alter ego as an extreme sportsman and documentary-maker. He had tales of deep-sea diving, of forming part of the team that flew a hot air balloon across Mount Everest, and of rock climbing and mountaineering. In 1991 he had led a mountaineering expedition. Together with Nic Feteris, they set the world BASE jumping record from the 19 300-foot (5880-metre) Great Trango Tower, in Pakistan. The first ever BASE jump in the Himalayas, at that time they also believed it was the highest cliff in the world. Their record stood for 14 years and the resulting film, *BASEClimb*, was seen by millions of people internationally and won more than 21 awards. It was all about understanding and harnessing your fear, he told them. Glenn had seen plenty of fear, because most people approach an emergency room with a healthy dose of it, and he felt it because he sought it out deliberately.

The screen showed terror-inducing footage of him trying to control his fall, while a helmet camera recorded the Trango Tower's granite cliff screaming past in horrifying proximity. As the highlight reel played through again, Heather, who had never even been camping outside of a caravan park, sat back in her chair, awestruck. 'Wow!' she thought. 'What have I done with my life?' She needed to know more so she nervously asked Glenn out for a coffee. They were married three years later, and when he took her to see the beauty of wild places, it shifted the way she thought about everything. She began walking, jogging, mountain biking and weightlifting to get fit. She has prioritised her physical fitness ever since, and as she became physically stronger, her mental toughness improved as well.

In spring 1999 Heather came home from a long day at work, exhaled and kicked off her shoes. Glenn was full of beans and couldn't wait to tell her what he'd just learned. There was a vertical cliff in Nepal higher than the one he'd set the record from. It was on a mountain called Ama Dablam. Glenn was off and Heather would be left behind; she could already see it. With scant consideration to what came out of her mouth, she responded with a proposal that seemed to develop as she was formulating it: she'd like to go too. He could train her to climb the mountain and fly off it with him. The 37-year-old reasoned it could be 'the perfect opportunity to prove your theory that anyone can do it'. Suddenly, there was an unexpected twist in the story of Heather and Glenn.

In a *60 Minutes* interview years later, Glenn enthuses that 'everybody has what it takes to—' and Heather interjects confidently with 'nooo, some people don't'. They laugh and their interviewer Liz Hayes comments, 'she is right!' Perhaps his point was that everybody has the potential to do better.

Did Heather have what it took? The pros and cons ping-ponged between them. Most people thought it suicidal. She thought it would be romantic and eventually found plenty of benefits to the project. She had faith in Glenn's leadership and experience, and the more she thought about it, the more convinced she was of its success. She would acquire the skills, shake herself into readiness, and they would make a documentary. How divine to fly off a beautiful mountain with your husband! The goal was set: to climb the highest cliff and jump off it together. And that's no mean feat for somebody with a crippling fear of heights.

To their joint amazement, the Australian Broadcasting Corporation (ABC) and the Film Finance Corporation Australia (FFC) took up their offer to make the documentary. By Christmas they had a contract, and Heather had a severe case of the shakes. What in God's name was she doing?

HER DETAILED TO-DO LIST AT THE START OF JANUARY 2000 would be, frankly, a bad joke to most people. It felt overwhelming to Heather too because while maintaining 'normal life' and advancing the project, she would have to learn four extreme sports: rock climbing, mountaineering, skydiving, and BASE jumping. Later they added wingsuiting to the list. She'd need to reduce body fat from 36 per cent down to 15 per cent and get to a point where she could run 10 kilometres in under 50 minutes. She also had to raise $150 000 in sponsorship. Aaaand learn to 'deal with or ignore ongoing criticism, be open to change and be prepared to look foolish, which would also be ongoing, not to mention difficult'. Glenn wasn't mincing his words when he wrote that list.

Suggesting to the average person that they skydive 200 times will abruptly halt a conversation. Heather understood that. It terrified her. But education is key, so she read a book on the subject to prepare. It went some way to softening the risk perspective. She should have left it there, but she dived deeper and watched a fictional drama that climaxed with an ugly tragedy due to a parachute malfunction. Reiterating that there is merit in monitoring what you consume, Heather was now justifiably terrified. 'I had already set myself up to fail.'

Everything about the skydiving course was confronting: the unfamiliar surroundings, the unorthodox people, the crazy act of jumping from a plane. Her tattooed and dreadlocked instructor was great at his job, but his hard-earned wisdom fell on increasingly deaf ears. There was too much to take in: the theory of exiting the aeroplane, the terror of doing it, arching her body, opening the parachute, sorting out wind direction – her natural fear of what she had signed up for clouded everything. The night before she started the course, she didn't sleep, couldn't eat breakfast, and felt sick. She woefully explained to her husband that she was about to fail her first item on their list. While everybody kept telling her to relax, she just wanted to vomit.

The tightly fitted skydiving suit that they zipped her into had stitched-on handles so the instructors could keep a grip on a student in the freefall. Over that, Heather fitted an altimeter, goggles, and the bulky skydiving rig (beginners use a bigger parachute). She tried to remember the emergency instructions for if the thing didn't open. Learning to control her fear felt like a pipe dream and climbing to 10 000 feet in the light aircraft eased nothing. Combatting that was the distant ghost of some instructions that may as well have been shouted into the wind – everything would be OK if she could relax and control her emotions.

Relax? Tell it to somebody else, because the aircraft door had just opened, and Heather was dead scared. The distant earth was horrifyingly present; her head kept spinning and her stomach kept lurching. Against every grain of intuition, she edged towards the roaring outside and crept out onto the wing strut. Her instructors were close behind her bearing huge smiles. Issue any expletive you can think of here, because Heather was thinking it. Were any of these people normal? With her instructors reaching for the handles either side of her jumpsuit, they all fell away from the plane. Freefall was sensory overload. She was trying to rationalise plummeting towards the hard earth when the canopy finally opened with a bang. She inspected the spindly lines holding it above and pleaded to the sky-gods for integrity in the equipment. As that hard earth came dangerously close, her mind raced with all the landing instructions, particularly the wind direction. Where was it? Which is upwind, crosswind, downwind, and what was she meant to do? Trying for the first time to judge her approach speed and angle, she and her bright pink canopy landed inelegantly and her knees buckled beneath her. She got up, thankful that it was over. It's fair to say that the ecstatic enthusiasm Glenn was feeling was a world away from his wife's emotions in that moment.

There were just 199 more jumps left to do. She continued to question the attraction in the sport, and gradually went from sheer ignorant terror, to rationally understanding it, though still terrified. 'Acceptance' was a long way in the distance. Her skydiving contemporaries were on a totally different wavelength. They were a tight-knit bunch of young blokes. Fearless, the lot of them. Heather was without peer or partner and the fortnight ended with only two-thirds of her training done. Surely this was the worst of it. She felt like she'd totally failed; however, there was no time to dwell. She now had to learn abseiling and bungee jumping. She went to New Zealand for this, where the landscape would add an element of the extreme.

Heather drew on her long-time practice of transcendental meditation. Learning to be present, to control breathing, and to visualise the whole challenge beforehand helped enormously with being centred and focused. Her abseiling/caving expedition was a world away from skydiving and she stared it down. Her fellow cavers shrugged; you'd never get them skydiving, but they were excited to take her underground, on this occasion into Harwoods Hole, a 183-metre sinkhole that is the deepest in the Southern Hemisphere. She put her trust in their skill, and in an isolated paddock, out where the stars shine brightest in the night sky, Heather learnt how to rappel (abseil) on a 200-foot rope, control the speed to avoid breaking her legs, and to change ropes midway. Swinging from the rope, Heather descended into a deep dark hole. It was a long way down and even longer to try and crawl up if she couldn't bring herself to go into the cave. Sliding down, she found it surprisingly beautiful, and the cave was spectacularly adorned with crystal-clear pools of water and a luminous limestone floor. Over the long day, she negotiated waterholes, holes, rocks, and hills, squeezing and contorting through impossible corridors to navigate this wild landscape. It was difficult and exhilarating.

The next activity was terrifying.

BASE jumping is the act of jumping from a fixed object using a parachute. BASE stands for Buildings, Antennae, Spans and Earth. So, that includes skyscrapers, radio masts, bridges and cliffs. The added level of risk is that the jumper has no emergency parachute and little or no time to deploy it anyway. There is also the real risk of falling back into the cliff face, or not deploying the parachute quickly enough; you usually have about three seconds. It is possibly the riskiest of the extreme sports, but infinitely exciting and skilful. Skydivers will tell you that BASE jumping isn't for everybody (including the skydivers).

To simulate a BASE jumping launch, as they'd be doing off the Ama Dablam cliff in Nepal, Heather had to learn how to launch and control her body in the still air, as opposed to jumping from an aeroplane into rushing wind. The launch, or 'exit', is the most important part of the jump and she'd have to get it right, because if you are angled in the wrong position, you can tumble out of control, either unable to release your parachute, or keep yourself away from the cliff. The best practice for a BASE jump launch, pushing out from the base with enough strength and technique to fly safely away from the structure, is to launch from a platform, something that doesn't have a wall for you to smack into. From a bungee platform, you are firmly attached to a bungee cord, leaving you free to focus on your technique – arch your back, choose your point on the horizon, and practise your launch. If you muck it up, no problem. The bungee cord will bounce you back to where you started, and you can have another go.

Heather stood knock-kneed at the edge of New Zealand's second highest bungee platform and stared down through 500 feet of crisp

Kiwi air to the distant river rapids below. Horrified, she reeled back from the edge and refused to jump. *What, how, oh my god!* With all eyes upon her, the camera kept rolling. 'Relax', she was told again. She was here to be de-sensitised to falling. Shaking her blonde ponytail, she reasoned, 'No. I can't. Look at it. I can't do it; I can't do it ...' But she did.

She sucked in a deep breath and took one brave, terrifying, almighty leap forward with the bungee cord secured at her ankles. As adrenaline surged through her body, she shrieked with every emotion and decided afterwards that it was fabulous. She did another. Then there were only 18 more to go, but this time they would be done forwards, instead of head first, with the bungee cord fitted to the centre of her back, and the belt buckled at her front. That would leave her feet free. With her arms spread wide, her back arched and her mind steeled for the task, she flew from the platform in a near-perfect arch, weightless like a bird. 'Good job!' the onlookers exclaimed and noted pleasingly that she'd already started moving her legs appropriately to maintain a symmetrical body position.

Their excitement was cut short when at the bottom of the fall, the full *g*-force generated by the bungee exploded a hole in Heather's small intestine. In excruciating agony, she lay back up on the platform squealing, confused and crying with acute pain. Trying to explain through tears what was wrong, she tugged at her shirt and lightly hovered her hand above her abdomen.

Glenn rushed his vomiting and delirious wife to hospital, where she was diagnosed with a ruptured duodenum. With medical directness, he explained that the contents of her bowel could leak into her system and poison her to death. The successful emergency surgery left the 40-year-old with an angry scar from her breastbone to belly button, and a lecture from the surgeon, who told her never to do anything so extreme EVER again. This was the end of the project, and her mental recovery was as big a hurdle as the physical one.

The couple agreed that Heather wasn't strong enough to go on and there was a real chance that another injury could be a fatal one. They set about bringing it to a close, and spoke to the insurance assessor underwriting the project.

How quickly things change.

The insurance assessor wasn't keen to pay out, and addressing Glenn as though Heather wasn't in the room, said, 'Well, if she can't do it, just find another female who can'. At this inflammatory statement, Heather doubled down, determining that if she were scrubbed from the project, it wouldn't be simply because she was frightened. And she wasn't sending her dearly beloved off into the mountainous extremes with another woman. There came a deep shift after that, and Heather zeroed in on her goal. Anybody who didn't have anything positive to say would have to tell it to someone else, because she wasn't listening. 'That negativity can come from a lack of emotional intelligence, and it is absolutely no help to the person who is trying. My advice is that you should not listen to people trying to discourage your dreams. It's really just an alarm that they are not living their own dreams and are projecting their own fear onto you. It's not about you at all.'

With two out of her three tasks on the list unfinished, she began meditating twice daily and expelled the hovering dark cloud of fear. Her fitness slowly returned. She watched skydiving videos repeatedly until she knew every minute and every step of the process. Educated and empowered, she travelled to Coffs Harbour for more skydiving with a calmer head and a champion's attitude. She stepped onto the wing with quivering legs but jumped with purpose. Her instructor was smiling; she signalled her goodbye and pulled open her canopy. Her feet touched gently on the ground and she cried with joy while he marvelled at her transformation. 'When a thought is not serving your goal', says Heather, 'don't judge the thought as right or wrong: simply interrupt it, challenge it and change it for something that will support your goal'. It seemed to have worked.

To complete the massive number of jumps required, Heather bought her own lighter parachute and pushed on with her training. She was no longer spinning out of control and began formation jumping in groups. Even a fractured ankle didn't slow her up. She'd rather strap it than lose more time being restricted in plaster. She was truly on a mission to get these things sorted out before her trainer Marta Empinotti, the world's most experienced female BASE jumper, arrived from the USA. When she did arrive, in August 2000, Heather had skydiving, bungee jumping, rock climbing and mountaineering skills in hand.

'I was blown away that there was this person who had such a big vision for herself and wanted to pursue it', says Marta. 'As a teacher, I felt honoured to be part of the project, and of course to do my best to train and prepare her for BASE jumping, and for her to be in love with it. Heather's were the biggest goals I've ever encountered, and at the end of the day it would depend on her. We became great friends and joke that we were sisters in a past life.'

The two women clicked straight away and Marta, whom Heather describes as a 'beautiful soul', enthusiastically got down to work. It started in the popular ballooning centre of Canowindra, a few hours' drive inland from Sydney. From a large hot air balloon, Heather, Marta, and Glenn planned to parachute from a purpose-built platform fitted to the outside of the basket. 'Ballooning has the characteristics of BASE jumping', says Marta. 'You're more in touch with nature and there is a focus on the purity of the jump, the freedom of quietness. It's a very safe way to start. Heather was accustomed to meditating and so I didn't think the balloon would be a foreign place for her.'

As a balloon will only puddle along at the pace of the breeze it rides on, Heather would launch into quiet, sub-zero-temperature air, just as the sun was rising. The difference from jumping from a plane is that the balloon is only a few thousand feet above the ground; a plane will usually be three times that altitude. This meant there was no time to reach around to pull the ripcord. BASE jumpers need to launch with the parachute in their hand and throw it after three seconds. Heather gingerly put one leg over the side of the basket, then the other, and stood on the platform. She launched, counted 'one two three', threw her parachute and landed in a boggy field without hurting her weak ankle. Glenn and Marta landed either side. Success! She finished the week excited for further training in the USA, learning the broader and specific BASE jumping skills she'd need.

At Twin Falls, Idaho, the Perrine Bridge is an ideal BASE jump teaching option. Heather and Glenn walked across the expansive structure, which straddles the Snake River. The cars roared past, and the bridge rumbled in response. Heather doubted she could ever climb the high, rattling railing to make a steady launch from the other side. Unhelpfully, a nearby sign recalled the efforts of another adventurer, the stunt rider Evel Knievel, who had failed his attempt to jump the Snake River canyon due to a parachute malfunction (he survived). However, he was trying to jump across it on a motorbike, while Heather would fly down lengthways under a perfectly good parachute custom-made by Marta's company. It sounds good in theory, but her fearful voice made excuses. The risks are many and with a churning stomach she watched Glenn climb over the railings, holding on with one hand and holding his parachute in the other. In no time, he was almost 500 feet below and packing up his rig. She watched many more jumps until she could normalise the process and get her eye in. The bridge seemed so low. 'This is the real deal', says Marta. She believed Heather was ready for it. 'She was just scared enough to respect life, but not enough to shut down. It was a good balance.'

In fine weather, Heather was yet again reassured, 'You'll love it' by the old hands around her. She focused on her breathing, keeping it nice and steady, which would set the rhythm for everything else. Out on the bridge she maintained her focus, and as she prepared to jump, everything was silenced – the traffic, the people, and the insecurities in her head. She let go of the bridge and pushed off into the still air, flying like never before into the rich, enveloping space between herself and the ground. She felt like she was floating for an interminable three seconds before her canopy opened. It was beautiful! She landed gracefully and finally accepted that now, after all this, anything was possible. It was a hugely satisfying breakthrough moment. Now that she could BASE jump, she had to learn to do it from a cliff.

For the next step, the team went to a cliff in Moab, Utah, for a 'hard earth BASE jump', meaning a jump from a naturally occurring high point. The area, coloured like Central Australia, is peppered with names like Punk Rock, Stinky Sock, and Boulder Rush. This is extreme sport territory. The beginner's jump is 'Tombstone'; the name makes sense when you see the cliff's flat rock face and rounded top. With the perspective of physical distance, it looks like a big red rock tombstone – only the chiselled names of the departed are missing. It is surrounded by lurching red cliffs, tumbled boulders, and jutting ledges, through which the Colorado River meanders in the shady green depths. It is the area where the final scene of *Thelma and Louise* was filmed, simulating the Grand Canyon.

To Heather's horror, the almost 500-foot cliff of Tombstone had boulders and obstacles on the way down, and Plan A, the sandy landing area, looked impossibly small. Plan B, to try and land on the winding dirt road without getting run over, was less appealing. After careful assessment and a nervous wee, Heather gathered herself, steadied her breathing and ran for the edge of the world. Unassisted, she flew out, away from the cliff, out into the clear air with the freedom of an eagle. 'I can flyyy', she hollered, then out went the pink pilot chute and the main white chute; whoomph, it fluttered to life and gave a jolt as it took flight, and her legs swung beneath her as she guided it down to an ungainly but safe landing. She let out a big scream. Marta knew it to be quite a spiritual experience once you commit to the exit and detach yourself from the cliff. 'BASE jumping is very powerful that way', she says. Heather returned to Sydney astonished at her own abilities and the leaps and bounds she had taken. Plenty before her had baulked.

There was a noticeable shift in her personal life then as she realised that she was not actually indispensable. The family and the office had continued without her hovering presence, and this freed her to pursue the next skill – mountaineering. She'd been training at a climbing gym and when she'd built enough strength in her arms, she went to the Blue Mountains. She looked like a tiny doll spider-climbing up the straight-edged, golden cliffs, clinging to divots half as deep as her fingers. Shortly after, she flew with a small team to Lukla in Nepal to test out her own and Marta's high-altitude adaptation and to check out Ama Dablam. The team consisted of Glenn, Heather, Marta, Adam Darragh, an experienced guide and high-altitude instructor, Russell Brice, the Kiwi mountaineering instructor, and Ken Baily, their American climbing cameraman.

They hiked for a few days to Syangboche Airstrip. Up at 12 500 feet, the thin air played havoc with Glenn's lungs. It took eight days to climb another 3000 feet to the exposed and windswept village of Chukhung. The whole team were starting to succumb to altitude mountain sickness.

A framed photo of spectacular Ama Dablam had hung above Heather and Glenn's bed for the past year. As they got closer, they determined that it was not quite high enough for the jump, and was in fact dangerous. However, Russell decided Marta and Heather could still start the basics of mountaineering on the ice cliffs near the bottom of it.

The first task was to learn about crampons, a system of 12 metal spikes that fit to the bottom of mountaineering boots. The spikes dig down into the ice to provide traction. The two spikes at the toe end face forward, so that on an ice cliff – where Heather currently found herself – you can kick forward, dig into the ice and stand up held in place by the bits of steel on the end of your toes. To add to this, she then had to learn how to swing an ice axe and jam it into the ice. 'It's all in the swing of the axe', said Russell as Heather fell a short distance with a splat. Fortunately, her altitude sickness abated quickly, and soon she was in love with climbing on ice. Every aspect of Ama Dablam presented a problem, though, and reluctantly, the group agreed that another mountain with a better and cleaner cliff face would have to be found.

IN THE INTERIM, THERE WAS MORE TRAINING. FROM BASE jumping off a cliff such as Tombstone, Heather had to try something bigger – something more akin to where she was heading. Marta, of course, knew just the place, and it was in northern Italy. Mount Brento is 1170 metres high above the ground, with a cliff of around 800 metres. Upon arrival, the jetlagged and astonished Australians parked themselves at a café opposite while they checked out the other people jumping from it. On first inspection, it seemed like the jumpers coming down from the top took an uncomfortably long time to open their canopies. There was no more 'one, two, three' like in the US. This was a long, long drop from a windswept plateau that required a drive up a single-car road to the most breathtaking views and a launching point. The landing spot was on the other side of the pine forest at the bottom of a steep ridgeline. They made the journey to check out the cliff a couple of times before finally jumping on the third day. The wind was still, and Heather got into her knee and shin guards, boots and rig, sunglasses and helmet. It was a cumbersome outfit, far more so than her usual cotton pants and T-shirt. Here at the top of this incredible mountain, she nervously toed the ledge. What a place. She was filled with gratitude for the privilege of what she was about to do. She spread her arms wide and pushed off into clear air.

TAKE FLIGHT

Momentarily mesmerised by the whooshing landscape behind her, she pulled out her pilot chute and hurled it aloft. Whoof! Everything slowed and she enjoyed the ride down to a perfect landing. She'd done it! Her first big wall jump. By the end of the week, Heather had around 20 jumps as the team honed their skills with their equipment and camera gear. She was claiming her power, she was ready, and the team arrived in Pakistan for the first of their three attempts at their record.

The Great Trango Tower is one of the world's highest granite spires. Glenn knew it well, but Heather had never seen it. They planned to spend a couple of weeks gradually ascending and making three camps, which would allow everybody to acclimatise.

Together with a dozen large black barrels of climbing gear and food, they arrived at Skardu, the largest town in Baltistan. The desert town had expansive rock outcrops and a river to the north, dunes to the west and a lake to the south. As they were here just ahead of the main throng of tourists who come for the climbing season, the group almost had the place to themselves. This team consisted of Heather and Glenn, Marta, Adam Darragh, Kiwi mountaineer Dave Vass, and one of Australia's best rock climbers, Mark Baker. Entrusted to the camera work was one of Glenn's good friends, Mike Dillon. Mike is a highly respected and multi-award-winning cinematographer, director and documentary-maker. He works on a world stage and is the go-to guy for this type of expedition, having done seven documentaries with Sir Edmund Hillary to Everest. 'I was very happy to be invited on this expedition and it was great to work with Heather and Glenn', he says.

The four-day trip to the staging point for the Great Trango Tower started along an achingly narrow road that at times could only accommodate three of their vehicle's four wheels. Over the sheer cliff edge, a white-water river raged by at the bottom. Through fascinating ancient villages, across swinging steel and wood bridges, and edging along perilously narrow roads, they arrived at the final town on the trail – Askole. Porters were employed from a gang of around 70 people who turned up to apply for the jobs, and the cook provided a beautiful meal. Under a brilliantly lit sky, they slept soundly before walking out of town the next day. They were off to a good start!

A necessary part of climbing such high mountains is acclimatisation. You don't just chuck on an oxygen mask and shoot to the top. Acclimatisation must happen slowly, about 1000 metres at a time, and happens naturally when carrying gear up to various staging camps.

The walk from Askole was across the dusty grey field of rocks that were strewn like rubble from a collapsed building site. There was no trail. On eight-hour days, they crossed shallow rushing rivers on boulders and badly eroded riverbeds. At the Baltoro Glacier, their dust became ice. On the final ascent to base camp, they climbed an extraordinarily steep hill of loose gravel, before descending into a glacial moraine of unstable ice, mud and water. Up at 13 400 feet, the team camped beside a crystal glacial lake. The surrounding mountains reached as high as 25 256 feet, which is slightly higher than their highest practice jump had been (24 000 feet) from a hot air balloon.

The following two days were spent exploring the jump site; a sheer, ice-topped wall that stretched skyward from a perfect sandy landing site. As they surveyed the wall, a thunderous avalanche shattered their thoughts as, 'tonnes of ice and snow plummeted off the top, crashing to the glacier below, exploding on impact into a torrent of ice blocks flying in every direction'.

The shock of the avalanche terrified Heather, who reckoned it was a great time for her and Marta to head back to camp and leave the men to continue with their jump site investigations. She mistakenly presumed she'd be able to find her way; however, their footprints had been washed away and as they precariously hopped from one ice block to the next, Marta had to rest. She readily admits that she's not a mountaineer. Heather pushed on ahead to rally some food and water for her but got lost again. It was a long and distressing day. When they made another attempt to climb the mountain to set up the first camp, Heather recalls that the intense summer heat created instability in the rocky, icy, scree-covered, bouldered landscape. The view from the camp was incredible, with an infinite snow-capped mountain range emerging from behind giant rock ledges. They returned to base camp and then had to climb again, beyond camp one, to establish camp two, carrying 'everything but the kitchen sink'. On that next ascent they found that everything they'd previously carried up, was now buried under snow, which had to be shovelled away.

These efforts were all captured on film by Mike, an integral crew member, not only for his mountain experience, but because the documentary underpinned the funding. One of the challenges for them all, including the photographers, was to try and keep their wits about them. Mike acknowledges that with less oxygen to breathe, there is around a 40 per cent loss of cognitive functioning, and that can lead to mistakes. For the camera operators, that means triple-checking their gear: are the camera batteries warm enough to work? Batteries don't last as long in the cold and so they are usually tucked into sleeping bags to keep warm overnight. Did they go back into the camera? Is the camera turned on? There was a lot riding on this footage.

After a couple of days lugging gear up the mountain, the team of seven set off once more on a push to the second camp. Heather was feeling stronger and happier, but Marta had to return to base camp. Mike went with her, but not before he filmed Heather and Glenn climbing hundreds of metres up an ice wall with crampons, ice picks and enormous backpacks full of gear. As she hauled herself up on to a huge snow slope, Heather gasped for breath in the hopelessly inadequate thin air. The climb continued through stunningly beautiful landscape so harsh and high that it made her question the sanity of their expedition and caused Glenn to almost collapse under the pressure of his struggling lungs. At the top of the climb, two of the team welcomed them with hot tea. Their packs were unloaded, and they completed their seven-hour round trip back to the first camp.

Resting there after a few days up and down, they noticed some people walking towards base camp. In the group was Vonna (Von) Keller, a young American climbing guide, registered nurse and film student, who had begged Mike to be allowed to join him as his camera assistant. It was her first big trip, and she was amazed by everything she was seeing. Tucked in her bags, she also had emails from home, and the telephone that, for reasons unexplained, had been confiscated from Heather at the airport back on arrival in the country.

With her fresh energy, Von hopped into work straight away, helping to carry gear up to camp one. She also quickly summed Heather up as someone who wasn't afraid to do the work required and who could go the hard yards. 'You could see the fear in her sometimes, but she pushed through. A healthy sense of fear keeps you alive and it's how well you can swallow it that makes the difference. Heather accepted me immediately. She was super friendly. When I arrived, they radioed down and sang me a silly song. They were a good lot to be with.'

Heather packed all her belongings for the move to camp two, expecting to summit and jump within a week. But it was a good lesson in 'hurry up and wait', as a three-day storm blew in, confining her and Glenn to their tiny dome tent. In fear of getting blown to smithereens, she snuggled in with her husband and peppered him with questions and strategies. Every couple of hours they emerged to clear the snow from the tent. When the sun came out, they climbed down to camp one to find everything there buried under snow and the whole set-up torn and strewn about. They silently cleaned up, and then returned down to base camp where Heather collapsed into her tent. Peace at last.

TAKE FLIGHT

'Avalanche!'

Higher up the mountain, collapsing ice and snow from a thundering avalanche whipped up an apocalyptic wind. The camp was ripped from its pegs and sent flying into the lake. There was another avalanche the next day, followed by snow and gales for a week. The mountain was talking, and Glenn was forced to listen. The end, when it came, was his radio call from camp two proclaiming the place a death trap. It was over and now they had to carry three weeks' worth of gear back down the mountain. It was a crippling disappointment, but the right course of action.

'Getting there was brave', says Mike Dillon. 'We had lots of bad weather and snow. It was an extraordinary attempt on their part.'

Back in Sydney, the couple had to front the ABC executive producer who had commissioned the documentary. Safely back in the harbour city, they pleaded their case. The footage was exceptional, and they could still splice together a great documentary. Just as the insurance guy had been, the producer was unenthusiastic about leaving it there. The film had no ending. Why not pop back for another go? She suggested their completion guarantee insurance would cover the cost of a return trip. Could they be ready in a fortnight?

Heather reeled. Another attempt at achieving the world's highest BASE jump? Absolutely. Another trip to Pakistan, after all the effort and setbacks they'd endured? She wasn't so sure about that.

Within a couple of short weeks, a regrouped team was back on the mountain, pushing for the summit. Heather had a flu, and Glenn was struggling with his breathing. Filming continued, and the area around Trango put on its best display, with the colours ranging from a beaming blue sky, through the greys of the granite cliffs, and dazzling white powder snow. Then when it went bad, it went really bad and rendered the humans powerless, huddling in minuscule tents at camp one and waiting for days to be able to go outside. Cooking was done bent double in the entrance to the tent using melted snow that was unavoidably laced with sand. They lived on a meal replacement powder, chocolate and cheese. Heather was not cowed by the challenges. She was feeling fit, acclimatised and keen for a result. As they pushed on up the mountain one day, Glenn began struggling with his lungs, as well as debilitating diarrhoea. He had to rest that day, but he urged Heather to go on. He handed over his pack and watched her set off, struggling under its weight. She attacked the ascent five steps at a time, trying to sustain her breathing. Von was with her on this difficult climb.

Heather was almost spent when she hauled the burdensome pack into camp two and collapsed. The team were already set up and the cook handed her a hot mug of tea. Von arrived in much the same state. Once they'd regained some strength, they pushed on for the top. When Heather stopped to collect herself, she looked around and realised she had reached the summit of the Great Trango Tower. Beyond them stretched divine views of K2 (the world's second highest mountain, after Everest), and a carpet of other high-altitude mountain peaks. What a moment! All their senses were alive, and Heather hollered down the mountain with joy. Even if she never got to make the jump, she had at least made it to the summit of this spectacular place.

That joy was tempered with physical and mental exhaustion when, gasping for breath, the women made their slow and cumbersome descent down back to camp two. 'We were dehydrated and sunburnt, and had headaches, but we later learned we were the first women to summit Great Trango, and that was a great surprise', says Von.

Glenn made it to camp two and brought with him two harrowing weeks of bad weather. The team did their best to stay buoyant and it was a relief when the weather finally cleared. Heather was raring to go and felt like she could sprint to the top. She would finally get to jump. The only clouds, in her opinion, were in the dark sky around her. However, she pulled up very short when she saw Bruce and Adam coming down towards her from the summit without their packs. She stopped in shock, but the story that followed was beyond shocking.

An ominous 'crack and zipper' had opened in the snow. This is when the sheer weight of the icy sheet covering the mountain tears it away from its upper reaches. It means the swift beginnings of a deathly avalanche and an unlucky mountaineer on that spot is doomed.

Inexplicably, just as the men digested the situation, the zipper stopped. It had not separated. In disbelief and terror, they gingerly edged away. They were deeply traumatised and flatly refused to go back. They were sure somebody – maybe everybody – would die. No person on earth was ever more serious than those two men at that moment – one of them in tears and unable to speak. Sitting in the snow against a cinematic backdrop of granite mountain peaks and frozen glacial rivers, Heather fell to her knees and put her head in her hands. She was the picture of a shattered dream.

They briefly tossed around the idea of another last-ditch jump site, but unknown to them, away from the isolation of the high-altitude camp and immediate decision-making, the outside world was falling apart. The day was 11 September 2001 and the reverberations of '9/11' were powerful enough to reach even the Great Trango Tower and affect the aspirations of the people on it. Apart from anything else, they were only 500 kilometres from the northern borders of Afghanistan and at that point it felt like any-bloody-horrible-thing could happen. They had to get out.

BASEclimb2: Defying Gravity was released into the world. Some of the messages Heather received were heart-rending, especially from women who took inspiration from her bravery. It was the best outcome given the state of events, and the team were immensely proud of their achievements. However, Glenn's agile mind could never rest and while continuing to train and pursue extreme sports, he and his wife kept searching for the world's true highest BASE jump. They planned an expedition to Meru Peak in India, this time with new technology: wingsuits. Instead of falling off the cliff, they would fly. Safety was greatly improved as the wingsuit allows the jumper to fly away from the wall of the cliff. The downside is that it adds an extra layer of gear. A young Australian named Jimmy Freeman, a world-leading wingsuiter, trained Heather and Glenn, and Heather immediately loved it. 'I knew this was what I was here to do. It is true personal flight.' Jimmy accompanied them back to Italy, where they trained to jump as a trio. He would be an extra cameraman on the way down Meru, and an important part of their preparation.

Funding for the Meru expedition came unexpectedly when they were well into the planning. Glenn was on the other side of the world and had been offered a once-in-a-lifetime opportunity to dive the *Titanic*. In re-jigging his commitments at home, Heather took on a big engagement that he was booked for, addressing a room full of investment bankers. She felt inadequate for the task, but with her inimitable flair, delivered the presentation. In return, she was stunned when the CEO pledged $100 000. 'It was a completely nonsensical sponsorship for him', she says, 'but it meant the expedition could go ahead'. What a gift, and what an effect her story and presence had on those people.

MERU PEAK WAS UNTESTED. PLANNING BEGAN AFTER A reconnaissance trip in 2005 and was hampered by all the pitfalls of negotiating bureaucracy. The year-long visa marathon ended the night before departure from Sydney. Heather was excited about Indian cuisine and began planning fresh food for the start of the trip, and stacks of dehydrated and powdered meals for the rest, including plenty of mood-elevating chocolate, lollies and nuts. It was another task, and an important one; however, their decision to outsource that job (on trusted advice) later meant they almost starved.

TAKE FLIGHT

Heather packed her long list of equipment. Broadly, it was two sleeping bags, mats, clothes (casuals, plus layered thermals, wind breakers, and an outer layer of down jacket), boots, toiletries, medications and vitamins, communication and imaging gear, and all the gear for the actual jump. This time it included her wingsuit. They weren't going to take any chances on this untried side of Meru: they had 2000 metres of rope, hardware, climbing gear – and a full field hospital and a bone-saw for emergencies.

The small team arrived in India in April 2006, and this time Heather had more female companionship – Elise Vale (one of Heather's skydiving instructors), Sophie Ward (a friend), and Lauren Swan (Heather's daughter) who would be at the team's landing camp, and Tove Petterson, who was their high-altitude cinematographer.

The first day of the all-important trek to Meru was a hard five-hour slog through unseasonal thick snow. While the team had soldiered on to the camping point, many of the porters had given up, leaving only a small handful to arrive at dinner time to a frozen, hungry, and increasingly unwell climbing team. The following day Heather got a stomach bug and trudged to Tapovan, a picturesque campsite in the shadow of the enormous east face of Mount Shivling, which neighboured Meru. What had been a grassy meadow on their recce trip the year before was now a freezing, pristine snowfield.

The next arduous day heading around the west side of Shivling and up to the base of Meru was through deep snow in ominous weather, ending at one of the most beautiful places in the world. Meru had somehow become more intimidating up close; however, the vertical jump cliff was a vision to behold. It went straight up in a smooth line.

A few days later, the rest of their stuff arrived and all the gear had to be carried 12 kilometres in driving snow to establish base camp. The team now consisted of five tough high-altitude Nepalese Sherpas (Samgyal Sherpa, Mingma Sherpa, Norboo Sherpa,

Mingtemba Sherpa, and Thinless). The climbing team consisted of Heather and Glenn, Tove, Mick Hill (a trusted professional skydiver), Jimmy Freeman, and Mal Haskins (a registered New Zealand alpine guide). With 700 kilograms of gear, it would be a hard first leg, and leave precious little energy for the final assault up the mountain. Thankfully, at the last minute, 23 porters were secured to transport the goods to the next camp and snaked their way in a long line around the mountainous paths. They arrived in the thin air at 16 400 feet (5084 metres), where the cook produced a strange meal of boiled eggs, dried bread fingers, curried chickpeas, and sultanas. After washing this down with an all-important large amount of water, the team then pushed on to 'rock camp'. With a rock wall on one side, it looked down a large snowy slope to the other. They spent the next few days ferrying equipment back and forth from Tapovan. By the 16th day they were only half as advanced as they'd planned. The jump was within their grasp, but it was starting to slip as the food was quickly running out, the climbers were losing weight, and snow kept falling.

Glenn, Mick, Mal and the Sherpas set off in search of a route to the top of the mountain, leaving the rest of the team to carry the ropes, tents, food, camera gear and BASE jumping equipment. Heather was feeling strong and fit as she jammed her crampons and ice pick into the mountain and climbed with a pack on her back. They pulled up at the next campsite, which was at 19 302 feet (5885 metres) and higher than the Trango Towers. She returned to base camp in five hours. Down the mountain, Heather could see the other half of the crew pack up and move around to the Meru Glacier landing site. Their communication was now cut until the jump crew reached the top of the mountain. Hopefully, that would be soon.

The team continued to be plagued by food shortages and after a difficult climb in snow to their knees, Heather made a comment to Glenn. The meal was distressingly inadequate and that evening at camp two, he quickly inspected the distressingly tiny food supplies. Not yet halfway into their eight-week expedition, they made some tense phone calls to their supplier. It appeared the food had either been stolen, not ordered, or simply had to stretch too far between the scattered teams. The climbers were burning about 6000 calories per day, which was being replaced by around 1000 calories. They were rapidly losing weight. The Sherpas were likewise alarmed, and the endlessly cheerful cook was mortified.

More difficulties arose soon after when, on the journey to camp three, Jimmy collapsed in the snow and vomited. He had to get off the mountain; the three-way BASE jump from Meru would now be two-way, with just Heather and Glenn. Weak, distressed and barely able to talk, Jimmy needed to get to a lower altitude quickly. He launched himself off the mountainside at 5880 metres and flew in a straight line back down to 'advance base camp'. In less than five minutes, he was standing before the astonished kitchen staff and the following day joined Lauren, Sophie, and Elise at the landing camp.

When Mother's Day came Heather couldn't speak to her daughter around the other side of the mountain, but she was able to speak to her sister in Australia. She felt terribly homesick, and her Mother's Day lunch didn't help. It was a miserable bowl of noodle soup and a small KitKat. After another ripping storm that night, the cook brought dinner with a smile. Heather envied his buoyancy.

The summit was only 400 metres above camp three, but in keeping with the theme, it was difficult: a broad sheet of barely penetrable ice covered most of the mountain, which inclined at a 70-degree angle. On the first two days as various team members climbed in the hope of surveying the jump and landing sites, weather forced them back. Everybody was tiring.

The following day the storms abated and clear skies allowed Mick and Mal to ascend to a point on the hazy ridge that Glenn and Mingma had surveyed the previous day. They were on a col, which is the lower part of a ridge between two peaks. In this case they were between the south summit of Meru and the middle summit, known as the Shark's Fin – the jump site. It was a simple single run from where they stood on the ridge to the Shark's Fin. The radio reverberated with the team's excitement. Not only was the wall down straight and agreeable, but it was also topped by a small ledge from which to launch. The place was perfect. It also had an ideal filming site. But just as they thought they were about to conquer the mountain, the mountain responded with a deep dark snowy storm that forced the team to do a dangerous descent in the dark. The following day they returned down to advance base camp to get some decent food and sleep, and more breathable denser air. It was there, having a wash, that Heather reeled at how skinny Glenn had become. His ribs were now sticking out. She knew that without adequate food they couldn't hold out much longer. They were within a hair's breadth of the finish, yet it was still in doubt. They returned up to camp three in one day, while some of the team back up at the jump site cleared snow and ice away from the ledge. This mountain was made for them, and the jump felt like it was finally within their grasp. Heather's mood-meter spiked at the possibilities and after an excruciating five-hour climb, they were rewarded with a stunning vista. Heather says:

> The cliff rose like an arrow shooting for the sky, so vertical it looked like the rock had been smoothed clean by a giant sculptor. The whiteness of the snow and ice, the golden tones of the rock and the blueness of the sky came together in perfect alignment to create an image that looked as though it had been made with a photo-editing program.

Mick's ledge at the top of the cliff was about a metre wide – wide enough for a person to spread their arms. It was only deep enough for Heather to stand diagonally behind Glenn, not directly behind him as planned, and so the next day the team chipped away a little further to expand the ledge. Heather wasn't much help. She was severely calorie-deprived and exhausted.

On her final call, 2.30 am for a 4 am start, the breakfast was black tea and runny dhal, apologetically offered by the cook. In the blur of step after step and yanks on the ropes, for six long hours hauling herself up, Heather hoped for success but wondered if she'd have the strength to execute a jump. Below her, cloud filled the valleys. Above her, mountain peaks poked up through it. For a mountaineer, the summit would spell success. For a BASE jumper, it was just the launching point.

As Heather, Mick and Glenn discussed the situation, both Heather and Mick agreed they'd given it their all and this would be the third, but last time they stood atop this mountain. Poor Glenn. He changed the topic hopefully, to ask what they thought about the cloud that was marching over the summit. Before they could answer, the radio erupted with some startling news from the team on the Shark's Fin.

There was a break in the weather. Heather and Glenn should get into their wingsuits and prepare for the jump. In total disbelief, they confirmed the news with the team at the landing site and the others who were partway up the Meru Glacier. Tove commanded them, 'Just trust us and get ready'.

Heather nodded and, anchored to an ice screw a few centimetres from the edge of the enormous cliff, tried to kneel to unhook her crampons. It was difficult and adrenaline, emotion, and practicality all collided in the thin, minus 25–degree air. She struggled to get dressed, but with Mick's help, put on her wingsuit and rig, jump boots, and altimeter. She adjusted her sunglasses and wriggled the camera helmet on over her hat. She was weak and it was heavy. She carefully turned on the cameras and stood there like a penguin, zipped into the wingsuit, hobbled at the feet and arms by the wings that would spirit her away. Getting the feel of Jimmy's heavy cameras on her head, she noticed that her weight and balance were different to what she was used to jumping with.

Glenn edged closer to the ledge and she helped him slip his last shoulder strap on. After checking his camera gear, he pulled his own helmet on over his thick hat. With a click of his chinstrap, he gave the thumbs-up sign, smiled at Heather and asked if she was good to go.

The cloud started lifting in front of them. Heather sensed the sun and in the gaping space beneath her, the dazzling Meru Glacier beckoned. A short distance away, Mingma and Samgyal were stunned into mumbled conversation. Mick revealed that it had just dawned on the Sherpas that Heather and Glenn were actually about to jump off the edge of this gigantic mountain. Mick felt equally confronted. The enormity of the undertaking was suddenly as clear and dramatic as the rock hard ledge before them.

Heather and Glenn did a final gear check on themselves and each other. The command went down to the rest of the teams. 'Turn on the cameras and be ready.' Tove, 300 metres away, would film the exit. Elise, down on the landing area with a giant lens, would film the whole jump. Lauren and Jimmy, further up the glacier, would capture the landing. There would be no Take Two. Mal Haskins leaned down into his radio. Against the white-grey background, he drew breath: 'Be prepared for [the] two-minute call'. He looked up to the distant mountain top as if expecting to see them respond.

Time ground to a stop as Heather stood untethered, precariously close to the edge of this two-kilometre drop. It makes my stomach churn just to write it. From the very edge of the ledge, Glenn trusted that Heather, mere centimetres behind him, could remain balanced and not push him off.

Ahead of them, Mount Shivling rose like a phoenix. Heather stood side-on to the ledge, with a large ice overhang behind her. She had a mounted Canon 20D and a Sony Hi-8 film camera on her helmet. Glenn had one film camera on the back of his helmet. The helmets hugged tight and came down around the chin, leaving only the bottom lip to above the eyebrows exposed. It perfectly framed Heather's trademark big smile. 'Have a good one', Glenn said as they performed a playful pre-jump ritual tap, a fist bump, and a joined flutter of their fingers that mimics flight. Taking their eyes off the ledge, they looked each other in the eyes and blew a blue-lipped kiss. The connection between them was iron-clad. Glenn stretched his neck to one side briefly. Heather glanced down the cliff and momentarily reached to him.

The menacing cloud rolled and drifted across, darkening one side of the valley and throwing a shadow across part of the glacier, which ran directly away from them and then curved to the right, around another mountain, and out of sight.

From where Tove stood on the Shark's Fin, the scene was cut into perfect vertical thirds. On the left was blue sky, made grainy with thin cloud and cut clean by the straight edge of the golden grey Shark's Fin cliff. The other vertical third had a wavy intersection cut through by the peak where Heather and Glenn stood, before it drew back like a ribbon and continued upwards. The grey, brown and gold granite was topped with a five-foot-high layer of snow and ice. The third to the right of the image was pure uninterrupted white.

With only a sliver of light between them, Glenn arched forward like an eagle about to launch. Heather did the same. Mick announced to the team that there was 30 seconds to jump. He picked up his camera to film the exit and caught Glenn, who said to the camera, 'Six years of work; this is it! Woo!'

In the remaining seconds, Heather focused on her feet, tightened her stomach, tensed her arm wings and raised her head for the launch position. There was no room for error, and she had to fly perfectly in synch with her husband. 'Okayyy. Ready-Set-GO', said Glenn, who took one step – a single, brave, confident, giant step – and was gone. Heather stepped forward, so focused on what she was about to do that she didn't notice the warning on her camera go off – there was condensation on the film, and it was now unusable. They'd find that out later. The Himalayas is hard on people and their equipment. It's hard on their dreams and forces people to resolve problems in the present. Now. Now, in perfect time and a split second after Glenn, Heather launched herself out into a patchwork of blue and white sky. There it was. The culmination of all that work, a lifetime away from the woman in the BMW concerned about office life and peak-hour traffic. A world away from the naysayers, and in a world so much bigger than she could ever have imagined at that first meeting when she impatiently paced the hallway in her blood-red stilettos.

Now freefalling in her bright red synthetic suit, she dropped for about four seconds and had a moment of alarm when things didn't feel right. The heavy cameras, the wingsuit that now bagged around her thinned body, the air so thin that she was falling through it at twice the usual speed. She adjusted her balance and fought to get control of her outline. Concentrate. Focus. Her wingsuit inflated and adrenaline filled her body as she started to fly. Look at her go!

Keep it together, Heather, she told herself as for the next few splintering minutes she flashed across the sky at up to 200 kilometres per hour through cloud, past granite cliffs and over the concrete-hard glacier. Glenn shot away like a bullet. Heather clenched her stomach muscles harder, opened her leg wing fully and tried to point her toes more. She was dragging every fraction of performance out of herself and of her equipment to keep up with him, but his course was deviating slightly from what she'd anticipated. She couldn't catch him.

Her level of engagement was so profound that it shut off the part of the brain that registers time. Everything slowed and each second was imperative. At these extremities, you understand what one second really means, and here it was happening in split-second slow motion frames.

From the top of Meru, Mick struggled for words. 'Wow! Look at them go across the valley! Woooowwww!' They looked like little red darts.

The overwhelming beauty of this surreal environment made Heather laugh with exhilaration. The landscape was rocketing past as she chased Glenn. She pinpointed her landmark, the south-east ridge of Shivling. At 500 feet above the glacier, she pitched her pilot chute, the canopy opened but the lines were twisted. She kicked out the twists and flew perfectly. She navigated to a landing site that was free of deathly deep crevasses, and told herself, 'Don't land your arse in a hole where no one will ever find you again!'

Glenn came in for a perfect landing, breathless and exhilarated. He looked over his shoulders. 'Where's Heather? Where's Heather?' he asked in genuine distress, desperately trying to find her. Had she made it?

'When I landed, Heather wasn't anywhere near me, and I literally didn't know whether she was dead or alive. It was very traumatic and heart-wrenching', says Glenn. 'Jimmy came up and I said, "I don't know where Heather is. Did you see her?" "No, I didn't", he replied. "But she'll be on your camera."

'"Can you look at it, because I don't think I can look at a video of my wife dying."'

The radio team announced, 'There's a canopy landed dead centre on the glacier in the snow, but we've only seen one canopy'. Mal radioed anxiously up to Mick: 'Mick, did you catch sight of the second canopy?'

Mick: 'Yeah, roger. I ... certainly can't, but the two Sherpas definitely can.'

In the cavernous empty valley, Heather shrieked with exhausted, exhilarated, overwhelmed relief, fell to her knees and sobbed. Her voice echoed back to her and she suddenly realised that she was completely alone. But where? The cliff was at least a kilometre behind, and the team were somewhere below. She couldn't see them because she had landed too far up the glacier. She was all alone.

'It was quite a spiritual transcendent moment that was honoured by being completely alone in this vast environment, looking back up at the cliff where we'd taken three weeks to climb and three minutes to get down. I felt small but enormous and so much more than this little human shell. It was a spiritual feeling.'

She de-rigged and packed her gear for the soggy walk down through deep snow. It wasn't over yet as there was the risk of falling into a hidden crevasse. Before long she saw the team coming towards her, fell into Glenn's arms and thanked him for taking her on this wild adventure. The team were whooping and rejoicing from their various vantage points, and there was indescribable joy at finally achieving the highest BASE jump in the world. From 21 661 feet in altitude, they flew two kilometres down the cliff face in three minutes. Glenn was astonished and proud of his wife, who had gone from a standing start to a world record holder in one of the world's most extreme, male-dominated sports. It was incredible, and he knew it. Wow.

BACK IN THE CITY, THEY WERE BOMBARDED WITH MEDIA requests as the world came to learn of their achievement. From the USA, Marta sent Heather flowers. 'I wanted to congratulate her on this amazing feat. I knew how huge it was. I am their biggest fan. I was so emotional, so happy, and knew that it was so deserved. When somebody works so hard: physically, training, gaining permits, getting a team together, finding and managing money, the enormous amount of time! It's no wonder that not a lot of people do this stuff. As a couple, it's an amazing adventure that binds you together.'

Glenn is more philosophical. 'It was the expression of all our being and engagement with the environment, each other, technology ... That to us is an expression of our creativity, and what is possible for us. We have a profound connection to that environment, the winds we ride on; we have a responsibility to protect and restore it. Science says we must plant more trees, and we are starting a carbon farming project. We'd also like to make one last documentary that covers all our adventures. (If the Chief Content Officer of Netflix is reading, please call Glenn.)

It is almost 20 years since those first mighty leaps. Heather and Glenn continued to push their boundaries, and wingsuited over Antarctica, across the Grand Canyon, over Central Australia, and Melbourne, Sydney and Brisbane. In 2023 they were awarded *Australian Geographic*'s top honour – the 'Lifetime of Adventure Award'. Now in their early 60s, they have retired from jumping, and immersed themselves in country life at Yackandandah, Victoria. Heather also recounted her story, in much greater detail than I can, in her book *Love Flying*.

Surrounded by nature on their idyllic 100-acre property, 'Dark Horse Farm', the couple engage in carbon farming, with an intensive tree-planting program and a vegan lifestyle. They also host wellbeing retreats for women, and events that promote a holistic, empathic approach to horsemanship. It's a whole new direction and life is still busy. Away from the work, though, a part of Heather's soul will always be centred on that distant granite peak in the sky – the centre of the universe. She is still the only woman known to have BASE jumped the Himalayas.

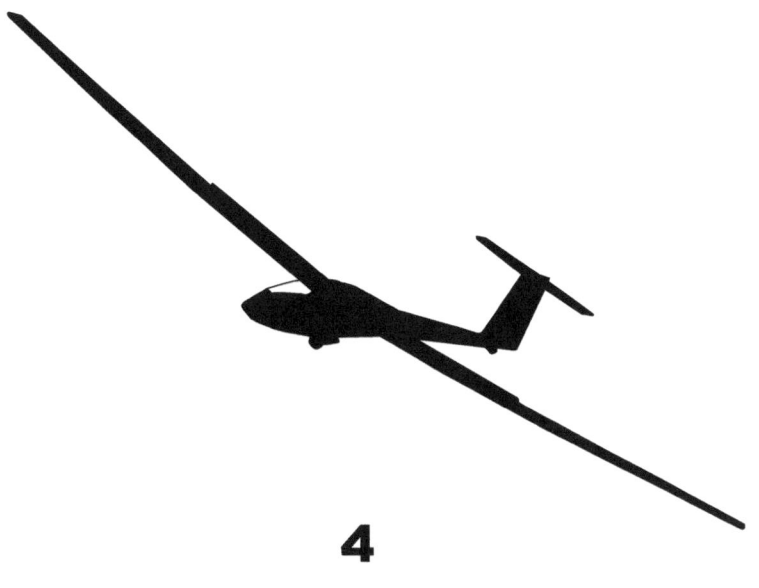

4

SOARING TO GREAT HEIGHTS

CATHERINE CONWAY, GLIDER PILOT

'I've been privileged to share the sky with eagles and had them ride my wingtip vortices. I've flown amongst them on the ridge, watching their play and aerobatic antics.'

Catherine Conway

TAKE FLIGHT

A 1957 *Women's Weekly* advice column listed The Queen Victoria Maternity Hospital in Rose Park, among other institutions, as a place where teenage girls with an 'unwanted pregnancy' could go for help:

> There are a number of places in Adelaide where unmarried mothers are cared for and you should visit them ... One of the wonderful qualities common to all these places is the sympathetic help that is offered free. Don't be shy about seeing the people concerned, they deal with similar cases all day.

Around lunchtime on a boiling hot Australia Day in 1966, the 'sympathetic help' erected a restrictive screen to block a birthing mother's sight of her emerging child, lest she bond with it. In the previous days, the young mother had let slip that she might consider keeping the baby if it was a girl because she felt that society might treat a single mother more favourably if she had a daughter. Keeping the baby would be difficult, but because she had a job, she could support herself and thought maybe she could manage. Only a few years later, social, legal, and economic changes, particularly the introduction of the single mothers' pension, would have made all the difference, but they didn't happen in time for her.

They told her she'd had a son. Without her seeing him, staff on the other side of the screen at the hospital, a stunning historic building that also acted as an adoption agency, removed the baby, and separated 25-year-old Jude Lynch from her first-born child. They had maintained this practice for many years, and believed that the 'bond was broken' immediately. As tough as it was, they reckoned it was better for everybody, that the mother would recover, and the child would be fine. It was a hard landing, and fortunately the child *was* fine in the end; however, in reality, the mother never really 'recovered'. She held the loss close.

Around the same time that day, half an hour away, another mother waited in vain for her three children to return from Glenelg Beach. The story of the missing Beaumont children received blanket news coverage for months and years. Life changed that day for Australian parents. An age of innocence was over, and the community believed that children were no longer safe to be out alone. While all hell broke loose in the newspapers, Jude was presented with adoption papers. In a postpartum fog of shock and confusion, she learned that the baby was a girl, but she was too stressed to argue the case for keeping her. When she could get someone to listen, she asked for the baby, Jane Lynch, to be placed with a Catholic family. Only the mother and child were listed on the birth certificate. Back home in Western Australia, Jude's infuriated father made sure that the baby's father, John Walmsley, would never become his son-in-law. According to John's next wife, Jude's father 'pointed a rifle at John and ordered him off their farm and said if he ever saw him again, he would shoot him. They were a very devout Catholic family'.

When they had discovered she was pregnant, her family had apparently gone into damage control and sent Jude to the care of Catholic nuns at St Joseph's Refuge, a home for unmarried mothers that Sr Mary MacKillop co-founded in the late 1800s. In 1966 it was at 82 Wattle Street, Fullarton, a few kilometres straight up the road from the Queen Victoria Hospital.

The impressive, handcrafted sandstone building stood to the fore of its 4.5 hectares, fronted by a small circular drive. She would have walked through its arched entry – the doorway dwarfed by oversized leadlight windows throwing a soft hue across the wide reception hall's mosaic tiles. Those earthy-coloured tiles, now chipped and worn in parts, must hold the emotions of the many pairs of shoes that shuffled across them, heavy with child and weighted with sorrow.

In the January heat, Jude would have climbed the 29 stairs, perhaps not noticing that they are slightly smaller than standard height, possibly to make it easier for a Victorian nun in a bulky habit, or a pregnant mother, to climb them. On the second floor, in a large dormitory, she'd have lain heavily pregnant in a room that is still impossible to cool. It was a far cry from her life on the farm.

A fortnight after the birth, Jude and another woman lobbied to see their babies – just one look? A moment? Some closure? Staff relented and showed the women to a large viewing window. They saw a myriad of coloured bumps in rows of steel cots, and were told, 'it's one of those'. It was a small victory in her mind, but really it was a placebo because baby Jane had already been gone for a week. With a practical sense of resignation, Jude returned to Western Australia with empty arms and, no doubt, instructions never to mention the whole sorry episode. And she didn't – not even to her future husband or kids. Jane's birth certificate was locked away in Adelaide so there was no reason, provided the few in the know kept their silence, to think the secret would leak. Her life returned to some kind of normal after the 'holiday', but those around her couldn't see that, like thousands of other Australian mothers, she constantly wondered what had happened to her baby.

A 2012 media release by the Australian Institute of Family Studies says that in the following couple of years (1968–1969) almost 7000 children were adopted in Australia. Legislative changes in the 1970s tightened secrecy provisions to ensure that a child's birth certificate could be 'sealed forever'. It was deemed in everybody's best interest to make a clean break straight up by starting the baby's new life as soon as possible. It was also illegal to adopt privately, and so agencies had a captive market in a rapidly liberating society. Plenty of babies, and plenty of business. Following protocol, Baby Jane's identity went into an ever-expanding filing cabinet.

By 1972, 'forced adoptions' reached their peak of 10 000 in one year. Jude was not forced by the hospital per se, but rather by circumstance: the people around her and the times they were living in. Her misery might have been tempered if she'd known how well the baby was going to be loved and cared for by her ecstatic adoptive parents.

When Jack Hehir, a hospital administrator and trained accountant, got the call, he might have sprinted up the hall to tell his wife. Jack was fleet of foot – he had won the Bay Sheffield in 1953 by about half a body length, racing over the line with his chin thrust full forward. The prestigious 120-metre race has been held on the Glenelg foreshore since the late 1800s and with his prize money Jack bought an engagement ring for Norma, his Italian sweetheart. The couple married two years later but sadly were not blessed with any children. It took years for them to be offered a baby and as soon as Jack laid eyes on the newborn, he didn't hesitate to accept this precious gift. 'Yes, we'll take her!' he said excitedly. Then he remembered to consult his wife. A new birth certificate was drafted, and to Norma and John Hehir, their daughter Catherine was born. An accompanying letter shared some background information, but nothing to identify who she really was.

Catherine didn't make it easy on her new parents. She screamed for six months, only quietening when baptismal waters kissed her forehead. The family always joked that it was a miracle, but Jack reckoned she was worried she might be drowned if she didn't shut up. Two years later a brother entered the household and the family moved to Novar Gardens, about a kilometre from Glenelg.

Once the settling-in problems were sorted, Catherine got on well with her parents. Her father's joke was, 'What are you if you're half Irish and half Italian? You're Catholic'. She was well and truly enmeshed in the culture of the church and to alleviate the tedium of mass, the teenager signed up to be an altar girl, then graduated to the church band. She still plays her guitar, which brings her great joy.

Norma and Jack happily indulged her as far as their finances allowed. Her education included learning piano, and signing on to

Catholic school. After initially attending the local Catholic primary school, in Grade 4 Catherine went off to an all-girls school attached to an imposing three-storey, Gothic-styled convent. Adelaide has some stunning architecture and this school's bluestone facade reaches to gables and peaks that stand proud in the landscape. The raked verandah runs between two gabled wings and there you will find a statue of Our Lady. The school was established a century before by seven Irish Dominican nuns who arrived at the invitation of the Bishop of Adelaide to 'provide education for the young who were destined to hold a more prominent place in society'. A place for the local Catholic population to get a decent education. It was an admirable ambition and the building remains one of Adelaide's prominent and beautiful buildings.

'School was shit.'

OK. Not one size fits all. Catherine was a sensitive girl with unruly dark hair and no particular interest in 'fluffy' hobbies. She was a self-confessed loner who didn't look or play like the other girls and went about her days with only a couple of close female friends. The teenage years can be excruciating at best, and the pain of social isolation was only eased slightly in Year 9 when she met a 13.2-hand-high cremello pony named Ben, on the reserve at the end of her street. He was owned by a local man, who despaired at his son's disinterest in riding, and asked Catherine if she'd like to take up the cause. She sure would and she joined the Southern Districts Riding Club on Ben for a couple of years. That single kind gesture was her childhood saviour. 'It made a huge difference to my life, and I put my energy into that pony. It was a segue into the equestrian world, which I'd always longed for.'

Catherine only grew to about 5 feet 4 inches, but she did outgrow Ben and traded up to Danny, a graceful 15.2-hand-high dapple grey. He came at the right time as her high school years were almost unbearable. She and a friend would race along the beach on their horses, timing themselves against the apprentice jockeys exercising their racehorses. The freedom of riding and having an animal to indulge was a saving grace, and her love of horses and dogs has been lifelong. It was by chance that aviation came into the picture, because Danny's paddock was near the main runway of Adelaide Airport. Even though the weather balloons launched each day and aircraft flew overhead, neither Catherine nor Danny paid much attention. The weather would be vitally important later in her flying life. Her attention was on the Metropolitan and District Showjumping Club, of which Catherine was a founding member. It was just off the end of runway 23 and she credits showjumping as her introduction to flying, when she and Danny flew over the jumps a few feet in the air. The take-off and landing time was a lot shorter than her future endeavours. There is a freedom in horseriding; it's great for decision-making, teamwork, and patience. Sometimes it also requires bravery, and without question, there is always something new to learn and to manage.

One day, when an Air Force jet flew low over an event, an extravagantly priced horse had a tantrum while tied to an expensive float. It pulled back and manoeuvred the float into the side door of an even more expensive Range Rover, leaving a large dent. The furious owner, trying to calm her steed, turned to Catherine paddling past, bareback with a halter on docile Dan and asked, 'Is he deaf?' Danny was completely calm, and the overflying aircraft made as little impression on the horse as it did on his rider. He remained a constant from the end of high school right through university, passing away from complications associated with colic when Catherine was about 23. After he died, her interest in gliding picked up and horseriding tapered off. And though her parents mostly understood the horse world, what came next was a world away from the family who 'couldn't even spell aviation!' Though she was always close to her parents, Catherine's natural left-brain inclinations were at odds with them, and Norma was known to say in exasperation or mock desperation (depending on the situation), 'Sometimes I just don't know where you came from!'

Norma wasn't the only one exasperated when trying to decipher her daughter's psychological makeup. English and History were lost on Catherine – she considered them 'airy fairy' subjects with no logical rules – but she took unwavering pleasure in maths and science. Catherine might not remember your name, but she will remember your phone number! A kind and understanding nun, Sister Patricia Brady, nursed her through the arts subjects and explained the nuances of the language, getting her through to Year 12. She passed Year 12 in Physics, Chemistry, English, Geography and most unusually for someone of her abilities, S1 (simple) Maths. The school had told her that her marks weren't good enough for Advanced Maths, but she topped the class and attended a reunion a few years later with a bachelor's degree in applied maths and computer science.

She was primed to start veterinary studies at uni, motivated by her equine enthusiasm and the recently published writings of celebrity Yorkshire vet, James Herriot. But Norma wasn't so keen to let her go away to study yet, as she was only 17, so Catherine enrolled closer to home at the University of Adelaide. 'I didn't know what engineering was at that stage and so I didn't apply for that. I'd never heard of it. Then while studying science, I became interested in computers, and veterinary studies fell by the wayside. It was the dawn of the computer age.' She changed to a degree in Mathematical Sciences, majoring in computer science and applied maths. Her interest in computers went back to Year 9 when she joined the after-school computer club. 'I've still got the *Byte* magazine that Mr Leidig, the teacher, gave me. It launched an IT career.'

Uni life suited her well, and she fell in with the computer crowd, who showed a dedicated interest. 'I worked for the engineering department and the computing centre and had various other jobs, and stayed on at the uni as a system programmer after finishing my course.' Finally, she was no longer the outsider, and quite soon she was encouraging her new friends to try gliding.

It was by pure happenstance that she got airborne. At a neighbour's 21st birthday party, another guest, a PhD student, asked her on a date: would she like to go for a drive to collect a glider? Who knows what the sleeping neighbours thought when a Regency Green XC Falcon sedan pulled up out the front of the Hehirs' at 5 am the next morning and 20-year-old Catherine hopped in and drove off into the rising sun. She had practical skills to offer in this venture: she knew how to drive a large vehicle and how to reverse with a trailer. She was used to towing a horse float, and a glider trailer isn't such a huge stretch from that. On that trip she also had her first lesson in driving a manual car.

For five hours they drove east towards Mildura, through sheep and cropping country, across the Riverland and the citrus and wine regions, arriving at Sunraysia Gliding Club by mid-morning. Her new friend, a gliding instructor, asked if she'd like a joy ride in the glider they'd come to collect. Unlike regular light aircraft, a glider, or more correctly a sailplane, is lighter, streamlined, and has extremely long narrow wings to sustain itself in flight. Without an engine, it is generally towed or launched, and then seeks to climb using thermal lift created by rising warm air. They will circle in an updraft like a bird on a wing.

Not knowing quite what she was in for, she climbed into the front seat of the blue and white Bergfalke IV and fitted the four-point harness. She was sitting only a foot or two off the ground. He climbed into the back, then pulled the perspex canopy forward until it clicked shut. The cockpit is far forward and the Bergfalke IV has a short nose. For the passenger it can feel like the front car on a carnival ride, where everything is happening in your face.

The glider has a tow release, attached to a long cable that is laid the entire length of the airstrip. At the far end, the gliding club's powerful

V8 winch starts to take up the slack, controlled by the launch crew. At the command of 'All Out' the winch opens the throttle, and the glider has a short ground run across the grass strip until it becomes airborne and then rapidly accelerates to a 45-degree climb, which is maintained for less than a minute until the aircraft reaches 1500 feet. As they climbed higher Catherine gripped, white-knuckled, on to the glider's round tubular structure. 'Oi! Open your eyes!' she heard from the back. The view outside was superb and once she did as instructed, she was entranced by this new perspective. As they banked to turn on a wingtip, Catherine felt like she was going to fall from the sky. In 40 years, the wonder has never dimmed, although she's stopped feeling so nervous in the turns. Up at 1500 feet, Mildura to the north was surrounded by what looked like December-dried scrub, a large dry salt lake and country defined by the snaking Murray River. There were no thermals to bounce them around, but there were definitely butterflies in her stomach. It was over in seven minutes, and though her feet were back on the ground, she was still floating as they de-rigged and loaded the glider into the trailer for the long drive home in time for dinner. They then went to see the latest aviation documentary, *Top Gun*. Cath had been converted.

Her attention was then turned towards Adelaide University Gliding Club, where, after nearly a dozen flights, she was brave enough to try taking the controls. It had all been new and scary until then. That was it: a lifelong love was born. On weekends, it was a joy to escape from the city. The Gliding Club leased a paddock from a farmer in Lochiel, in the mid-north of South Australia. The flying up there was brilliant as the western face of the Hummock Ranges provided reliable ridge lift in the prevailing westerly winds. 'We became accomplished ridge pilots and years later when I needed a low-level endorsement [a formal stamp in her logbook that allows pilots to fly below the standard minimum height allowed], that experience stood me in good stead. We got used to picking topographical features and paddocks in case we ever needed to do an out-landing. We flew from there for a decade.'

There are around 3500 glider pilots in Australia and around 1000 aircraft who take to our summer skies. It's an old sport that formed the foundation for modern aircraft; it deserves our respect. It goes back to the earliest days of experimental flight, leading up to the Wright Brothers flying the first powered flight at Kitty Hawk Beach, USA, in December 1903. After the First World War, the Treaty of Versailles severely restricted Germany's Weimar Republic from making or using single-seat powered aircraft. Without power, they were effectively reduced to soaring. In the ensuing years, as the rest of the world refined the powered aircraft, Germany did the same with gliders, increasing their efficiency and range. By the outbreak of the Second World War there were 50 000 glider pilots in Germany, with one man flying a (then) incredible 272 kilometres, freakishly riding on the wave of a storm front. The current record is over 3000 kilometres.

After the war, gliding designs and materials evolved in line with the increasing demand for higher performance as the sport and materials grew more sophisticated. Glass and carbon fibre provided lighter weight and structural integrity, wings and aerofoils became more streamlined, electronic instruments aided the pilot's awareness of conditions and the Global Positioning System helped them get home safely. Of course, giant advances in forecasting have enabled pilots to accurately predict weather and to seek it out, leading to a greater number of records and endurances. The most expensive glider ever built would have to be the space shuttle *Discovery*, which was designed to glide back to earth and be reused. One of the things that has vastly changed with technical advances is the distances that can be flown. Initially 300 kilometres and 500 kilometres were considered great achievements, but now a 1000-kilometre flight is a regular distance, with some even managing a whopping

3000 kilometres. Altitude records, however, while still being broken, are not being smashed.

It was inevitable that she would buy her own glider and in 1988, a couple of years after her first flight, Catherine bought a single-seat wood and fabric Boomerang glider as part of a syndicate with three other people. 'The Boomerang was designed and made by a German man, Harry Schneider of Edmund Schneider Pty Ltd in Adelaide. They were the only people making gliders in Australia. Schneider moved to Australia after the Second World War, when their part of Germany became Poland. The Boomerang performed well and was ideal for competition in its day, but it was overtaken a few years later by fibreglass designs brought in from Germany.'

By now she had met her future husband, David Conway, through the Gliding Club. While flying itself was fun, Catherine yearned for more structure and challenge and so bought the glider to fly in competitions. With practical application to the task, she worked with the syndicate to restore and re-cover it and flew about 800 hours in it. The couple were married the following year and continued to fly together. There was so much about gliding that Cath loved: science, aerodynamics, weather and engineering. Although she was competitive, she also found it relaxing to circle in a thermal, chase the rising air and enjoy views of the world that people seldom see; a world in which she floated, lazily circling on the end of a long, slender wingtip, and perfecting her techniques. Without an engine, she could still stay up there for as long as the energy from the rising air, and the enthusiasm of her beating heart, would sustain her. There was always something new to learn and a new badge or skill level to pursue.

JUDE MUST HAVE HOPED THAT HER BABY WOULD TURN UP ONE day, and she did. Behind a closed door on a lunch break at Telstra, where she was now working, Catherine handed a West Australian phone number to her friend and left the office. She had always been curious about her birth parents and South Australian legislation had recently changed to allow the unsealing of adoption birth certificates. It was big news. Policymakers had realised that children had a right to know about their birth family, and likewise, that some parents grieved endlessly after the loss of their child.

With Jack and Norma's support, Cath had made the appropriate enquiries and when a packet of paperwork arrived, its small amount of identifying information started the trail. After a fair bit of detective work involving official records, and the White Pages, she had what she needed. The woman on the other end of the phone excitedly agreed to take the call. After leaving Adelaide empty-handed, and 25 years of wondering, Jude spoke to her daughter for the first time.

'Hello! How are you?' she asked.

'I'm fine, thanks', replied Catherine.

'Do you like flying?'

Taken aback, Catherine replied, 'Yes, I'm a glider pilot'.

'Ah, so not real flying, then', was the quick retort. She immediately regretted the joke, which are fighting words to the gliding community.

In the ensuing conversation, Catherine learned that her mother held a pilot's licence, and that her long-absent but recently deceased father, John, had been a 20 000-hour Tiger Moth and Winjeel pilot, and an instructor with the Royal Australian Air Force (RAAF) at the end of the war. Jude had completed her licence in 1968, and flew until the 1980s, working in various roles, one of which included flying night freight out to Kalgoorlie.

John's personal story deserves a book of its own, meandering through a string of relationships. He had come to Perth in 1964, 'poached' from Melbourne's Royal Victorian Aero Club to manage and run a fledgling charter and air training company, Millard O'Sullivan Aviation, at Perth's new Jandakot Airport. He and Jude flew together (presumably with John as the instructor) in a Piper Pacer; however, her parents were having none of this union between their daughter and a divorcee 17 years her senior. John then married for the third time, eventually settling happily with his last wife, Leslie, and their four children at Geraldton. Some years after returning from Adelaide, Jude also married and had four children, bringing Catherine's half-siblings from both parents to 19.

Not long after the phone call, Catherine was in Perth for work and met Jude for the first time. It was an awkward meeting at Perth Airport where Catherine, a reserved and quietly spoken person, was greeted enthusiastically by a complete stranger. 'I was very introverted and didn't know how to take this person who was really into wanting to be close to me. I didn't know her. She was bubbly and talkative and wanted to know all about my life. She wanted to be much closer than I was comfortable with, but once the waters settled, we got on very well. She was practical and down-to-earth. She had tried her best in 1966 to get around the situation with John and didn't succeed, [and] she didn't escape unscathed.'

To counter the difficulty of explaining to her family the sudden appearance of a fifth child, Jude introduced Catherine as a friend from the Australian Women Pilots' Association. They talked at length when they could over a weekend at her home and discovered a mutual love of horses. Their strongest connection was aeroplanes and Jude was keen for Catherine to experience powered flight, so she arranged a Tiger Moth joy flight at Jandakot. The pilot handed over the controls and they did some aerobatics, which Cath had learned in gliders. But aerobatics are different in a Tiger as the required climb is very slow in the old machine. The pilot said, 'if you want to do aerobatics – you're a glider pilot – find a thermal and climb!' And so, they did, circling in the thermal lift, before rolling and looping high in the sky. Catherine loved it and it was the first powered flight entered in her logbook. It reads DH82A VH-FAS. Jude was grinning happily when they returned, pleased at their reunion and their shared interests.

While Cath was reserved, her two mothers got on quite well. There must have been so many questions to answer from both sides. A few years later, Catherine's sons Michael and Peter Conway were born in 1995 and 1997. Jude joined Catherine and six-month-old Michael for a day at a gliding camp in West Australia's Stirling Ranges, a few hours' drive south of Perth. It was the last time she saw her for quite a few years.

Spurred on by the joy flight, Catherine won a scholarship from the Australian Women Pilots' Association, who in 1994 granted her some money, matching each dollar she spent with their own, to the value of $800 each. The scholarship was to train to solo standard in a powered aeroplane. She soloed in a small two-seater Skyfox, but then put powered flying aside for a while. It was expensive!

On the work front, the maths and science were holding her in good stead as her career continued to develop in ways she couldn't even imagine when she was at school. She was working for a defence contractor at Defence Science and Technology Organisation (DSTO) on the Jindalee Over the Horizon Radar project. She had a brief stint in the IT department of Telecom Australia (later Telstra) in 1989 where she put the first internet connection into Telecom House in Adelaide, before re-joining the Jindalee Project when Telecom won the contract. In 1997 at the end of that project, Simon Hackett, a friend she had met as a university student, invited her to help start Agile Communications, which would focus on building rural wireless broadband in South Australia and that also deployed optic fibre cables in strategic locations in Adelaide.

In 1991 Simon had left his first job, at the University of Adelaide, to start Internode. Over the next two decades he grew it into one of Australia's largest privately held Australian national broadband services companies. Internode built and managed its own broadband infrastructure in Telstra exchanges. By the time he sold the company to iiNet in 2011, it had around 450 staff and 200 000 customers.

In 2002, Catherine and David moved their two kids and a Ventus B high-end glider 45 minutes east up the freeway into the Adelaide Hills. The children joined the local scouting movement and then the Air Force Cadets. Catherine's involvement with teaching and mentoring children began when both organisations asked for more parent helpers. With about 13 years as a gliding instructor under her belt, she put up her hand to help with both organisations – first as a scout parent helper and then as an officer in the Air Force Cadets, teaching aviation theory and flying (both in gliders and powered aircraft). Taking her own glider, she would park it on the side of the parade grounds to bring an aviation presence to end-of-year parades and presentations. She helped run camps, at RAAF base Edinburgh in Adelaide, up at Gawler, and across South Australia.

The family spent most weekends on a gliding field, competing and advancing skills for the parents, while the boys were left on the ground with their bikes and an Xbox. Inevitably, they wanted to learn to fly; according to Michael, 'Mum never tried to push us into it. We had to organise our own hours and training when we needed to go solo. Peter and I used to make pocket money by washing the gliders for competitors in the morning for $2 per aircraft.'

Catherine and David would often return to find that the kids had sidled up to an instructor and asked to have a lesson. Both boys went solo in gliders when they turned 15, and in powered aircraft when they turned 16. Michael says, 'Mum has always been very selfless about supporting our interests, and about sharing her time and skills. She has always gone out of her way to help people. Later, we had a family holiday in Germany when Mum was managing the women's gliding team.'

Competition was important to Catherine, whose first event was at Mildura in the old wooden Boomerang she'd purchased with the syndicate. 'It was a little bit off the pace from all the others, although I did get my first 300-kilometre flight in that one. I also landed-out [an out-landing means the glider was not able to return to the airport and landed in a paddock somewhere] almost every day and at the closing ceremony they called me up to the podium.' She knew she hadn't done well in the competition, so she was nervous when she stepped forward. They presented her with a stick. 'You fly a Boomerang, but we're going to give you a stick because that's a boomerang that doesn't come back', they joked. She took it in good humour, but she discarded the stick. She's had many out-landings in her time, but only one bad one. She misread the wind and in a rocky paddock spun the glider around on one wheel in a ground loop. Generally, landowners were pleasant and helpful at the sudden arrival of an interloper, and it was not uncommon for an old farmer to call their grandkids out to see the glider. On one occasion she was flying a wooden Arrow from Monarto a couple of hundred kilometres north-west up to Lochiel, passing Adelaide on the way. 'The ES59 Arrow glider is a wooden glider design from the early 1960s. It had a 13-metre one-piece wing. Adelaide University Gliding Club used it as a first single-seater conversion due to good handling and docile characteristics.'

The route to Lochiel bypassed the airspace at Gawler and she ended up having to land in a small paddock at Marrabel. Of the town's 200 residents, it was the postmaster and his wife who spotted what they thought was a plane crash and hurried to investigate. This unorthodox introduction led to a roast dinner and a few hours' wait for the team to arrive and de-rig the glider for towing home.

Gliding competitions are held from club level all the way through to world championships. Catherine has captained several Australian teams at world championships, in competitions in Lithuania and Germany. She has also represented Australia in competitions in New Zealand and Australia, and had the opportunity to fly in Italy, Austria, Slovenia, the USA and England. According to the Gliding

New Zealand website, one of their annual competitions is the Tasman Trophy, which is 'contested between selected pilot(s) from New Zealand and an equal number from Australia at the National Championships of the host country. The two countries host alternately, and aggregate scores decide which country retains the Trophy'.

Catherine was selected to represent Australia for the Tasman Trophy in New Zealand in 2003, flying from Omarama. During those three weeks she fortuitously took another woman for a fly: 'She had been with a male instructor, and she'd had a knock to her confidence, so we went up together and she obviously enjoyed it'. The night before Catherine was due to leave New Zealand, somebody came into the bar and said, 'The wave is on'. The bar emptied; everybody went to bed anticipating the morning's flight.

Wave is formed by wind hitting the side of a mountain, and setting up a standing wave behind the mountain, which is often many times the height of the mountain.

The ripples of that standing wave can be exacerbated as the layers go higher and a glider pilot can 'ride' these waves like a surfer. It is something power pilots avoid, and glider pilots seek. Glider pilots can often see the lenticular cloud and position themselves on the windward side of it, then surf the rising air to great heights. As pilots scrambled to get airborne, the husband of the woman Catherine had flown with the day before offered her his LS3 15-metre high-performance glider. It was a kind offer, and she soared to 22 500 feet on the wave, something difficult to achieve in Australia. Pilots usually get this type of result in the mountainous areas of New Zealand or South America. Having already completed the 300 kilometres and 500 kilometres components of the 'Diamond Badge', she was able to use this last-minute flight to satisfy the third component: the height challenge, being a gain of 16 800 feet. Once on the ground, the flight log was downloaded, and she dashed to the airport, with a Diamond Badge in her logbook.

A glance down the list of famous glider pilots shows that she is in good company. Author Barbara Cartland, singer John Denver, actors Christopher Reeve (*Superman*) and Steve McQueen, pilots Amy Johnson, Charles Lindbergh, and the Wright Brothers, and astronauts Alan Shepard and Neil Armstrong. In Australia there is Matt Hall, Red Bull Air Race World Champion (see Emma McDonald's story, chapter 7). But before Matt became a household name, Australia secured the services of Ingo Renner, a German immigrant who settled at Tocumwal. He flew almost 38 000 hours and won four world titles. When asked about her inspiration, Catherine instantly cites a flight with Ingo. 'He was just so good; so inspirational and so unassuming. He was a legend.'

Her flying continued to evolve and as her career progressed it was a useful skill to have. In her roles with Agile Communications and Internode, Catherine – who got her powered licence in 2000 – flew around rural regions in South Australia to meet with councils and assess the possibilities for establishing broadband in their localities. 'I'd been flying gliders all over South Australia and so knew the country like the back of my hand. When I came to do my private pilot licence test, the instructor joked, 'If you don't look at the map, I'm going to fail you'.

Simon Hackett, in the meantime, had been flying gliders almost as long as Catherine, after she invited him to the Adelaide University Gliding Club in their student days. He was bitten by the same gliding bug, and he progressed in his own flying endeavours in parallel to hers, flying many types of gliders over the years, though not with the same degree of competitive dedication that Catherine has always had. After buying and flying an old 'Motorfalke' motor glider (a touring glider that can self-launch, and then operate with its engine on as an aircraft, or off as a glider) for some time, Simon progressed to a Cirrus light aircraft and a Stemme S10-VT. After he sold Internode to iiNet, he bought a brand-new Pilatus PC-12 turboprop aircraft, his long-term 'dream' aeroplane. They cost between four and five million dollars today. He routinely jokes that Catherine has cost him a lot of money over the years in terms of his flying habit.

After Simon sold his company group, Agile was closed and Cath found herself looking for a new job. Despite having been instrumental in installing the first internet link into Telstra's South Australian offices, she was told by a senior recruitment company that she was too old and too female to be taken seriously in telecommunications. She wondered if she could turn her substantial flying hobby into a career, and aged in her late 40s, set about gaining her commercial pilot licence and multi-engine command instrument rating, and an instructor rating.

After assisting with establishing the Air Force Cadets glider training program in Adelaide in 2013, the following year she got the chance to combine her technical and aviation knowledge with a job at Airborne Research Australia, based at Parafield Airport. They were very keen to employ her, as her technical and gliding background suited their scientific operation, where special-build motor gliders were used as airborne sensing and research platforms. Her aeronautical skills and engineering qualifications meant she could also help to maintain these motorised gliders.

By 2015, Cath was flying various aircraft, including the PC-12. On a trip to Perth, supporting the Royal Flying Doctor Service (RFDS), she sat with Jude for the final time. Although Jude was an old woman by then, she was still living independently. In wandering, and often difficult conversations, Jude talked about her early days at Newmarracarra, her family's large country estate near Geraldton. She showed Catherine a photo of herself standing on the steps of a ten-seat Navajo aircraft and mentioned that she'd done some work for the RFDS, though it has been difficult to obtain details on that. Records are incomplete and back then apparently the RFDS sub-contracted some of its work. She handed over some of her old flying maps, which show long track marks bearing in from the west, including one in black crossing South Australia's Spencer Gulf at Cowell, and another in red transiting Whyalla and Port Pirie. The pencil lines then go off that chart and presumably lead on to Adelaide. Catherine and Jude's flight paths must have literally crossed at times, in parallel worlds 25 years apart. That was their last meeting and Jude passed away in February 2016.

In the same year, Catherine contacted the extended Walmsley family – her biological father's side – and was subsequently invited to meet the whole gang when one of John Walmsley's offspring pulled everybody together. An ancestral document cataloguing his background and his life, his career and his loves was compiled. It's a fascinating read as you piece together those involved and how their lives panned out. Each of his sixteen children's mothers were written about and the kids all wrote about themselves. At the gathering, somebody said to Catherine, 'So you're the lost child!' She was warmly welcomed, and delighted to meet her new-found relatives, many of whom were mechanical, mathematical, and aeronautical like herself. If only she'd known that as a teenager … Norma (her adoptive mother) also went to the picnic and was jokingly 'reverse adopted' by the relatives.

In 2005 Cath went in search of her own (adoptive) great-grand-parents, Norma's family, and visited the ancestral home in an Italian village. When in 2018 she went to a trade show in Germany, she looked them up again. She was in Europe to look at an aircraft and then at a couple of models of electric aircraft that her old friend Simon was interested in potentially buying. She had to drive from Austria to Slovenia to view the aircraft and, on the way, she took a detour via Italy to visit her great-grandparents' home in the picturesque Valtellina Valley. Not one to do a bus tour, she hired a motor glider with an instructor and flew up the wide verdant valley, taking it in as she was most comfortable doing – from the air. From the village of

TAKE FLIGHT

Berbenno, the valley winds along the far northern Lombardy region on a 132-mile axis to the town on Tirano, part of the mountainous Swiss–Italian border region. Lush mountains – some with permanent snow caps – hold terraced vineyards, winding mountain trails and roads, bike paths and rock-climbing sites. Tiny villages sit alongside modern ski and spa resorts, with farmland producing wine and cheese. It was so removed from her usual Australian landscape. 'We could see the whole valley from the air. My mother, Norma's, grandparents came from a tiny little town there called Boalzo, and they emigrated to Broken Hill, presumably in search of work. I was agog at the contrast of this gorgeous, lush place and the life they must have gone to. Nanna's parents founded San Remo pasta in Adelaide after emigrating first to Broken Hill, where some of the children were born.'

Travel is a wonderful side effect of flying and during the first waves of Covid, people around the world were reflecting on their holidays. They shared photos with friends, and planned their next escape, waiting for borders to reopen. Catherine continued working, maintaining and repairing gliders, but also joined an exciting team venture exploring electric flight. Together with pilots Barrie Rogers and David Bradshaw, she undertook an electric-powered aeroplane flight around South Australia. The team, 'Eyre to There' battled strong winds, rain, and early morning temperatures below zero on a multiple-flight-leg distance record of 1350 kilometres for an electric aircraft, in a little two-seat Pipistrel Alpha Electro named 'Bobby'. They broke the German record set the year before, along with other world records for electric aircraft, including longest over-water flight (30.8 kilometres); furthest distance in a 24-hour period (330 kilometres); and fastest speed between waypoints (177 kilometres per hour ground speed). They flew to 18 stops, from Parafield, returning to Adelaide's main airport.

The Alpha has a small electric motor bolted directly to the propeller. It is powered by two lithium batteries, which needed to be recharged about every 30–45 minutes of flight time. Recharging takes about 90 minutes, and in that time the team met with local children and adults. As yet, there are no aircraft recharging stations. They finished the flight back at Adelaide Airport and again Catherine created a record, by flying the first electric-powered aircraft to land there. They put it away in the Pilatus hangar, pleased with their groundbreaking achievement.

At the start of 2023, Catherine had come full circle in employment terms, and was back working with Defence, this time on Project Wedgetail E7a. She is employed by Boeing on this project, working as a system engineer. In a serendipitous moment, she learnt that one of her Walmsley brothers, Mark, was the Commonwealth Chief Test Pilot for this aircraft when it was purchased in 2005–06. Aviation and engineering continue to dominate this story, with Mark, and Catherine's son Michael, getting to know each other when Michael was at the Australian Defence Force Academy in 2017. Both Michael and Peter are aeronautical engineers and Michael is now a Navy Seahawk helicopter pilot. Peter went the civilian route and is working on Boeing's Ghostbat project, based in Melbourne.

Catherine has lived single for about a decade, and when not working or flying, she is with her adored border collies. She has a home office stuffed full of engineering, maths, and flying books. Nestled inconspicuously among them is a box with a blue ribbon and an Order of Australia medal, awarded in 2018 for Services to Gliding and Youth in Aviation. She smiles and is a bit stuck for words. 'I am proud to be recognised for my achievements, but it was all done for the joy of the doing, rather than any thanks I'd get.'

She is one of the few women ever to be involved in the Gliding Federation's National Airworthiness Administration, and the only woman currently on the team. She holds a commercial pilot licence and a multi-engine command instrument rating. Guinness World Record holder Phil Frawley endorsed her to fly an L-39 military jet trainer. She has owned multiple powered aircraft and gliders over the years, including four Schneider Gliders from the Schneider factory in Adelaide. Edmund Schneider, hosted by the Australian Gliding Federation, was invited to set up a factory in Adelaide by the Australian Government after the Second World War. More than 100 gliders were designed and built in the 20 years after 1952, and for 17 years these gliders held most of the podium places as Australian pilots set new records.

Initially the Schneider factory was at Parafield Airport, yet to Catherine's annoyance, nothing is mentioned about it at the airport museum. She met Harry after purchasing her Boomerang and restoring it and stayed good friends with him until he passed away. The factory had relocated to Gawler airfield by that time. She is dedicated to the restoration of some of their wonderful sailplanes and preserving their place in Australian gliding history. She has become the Type Certificate holder to ensure their continued operation.

The sport has taken her over some of the world's most beautiful landscapes and mountain ranges, all around Australia, and some cool places close to home.

Contrary to Jude's initial offhand comment, probably blurted out in a nervous moment, gliding is definitely real flying. Europeans see it as an essential introduction to powered flight. It teaches pilots great stick and rudder skills, and about the fluidity and movement of air. To glide well, you must truly understand aerodynamics and weather, and be able to operate in that environment without the luxury of an engine. Americans see it as another form of aviation that holds its own. In Australia, however, many see it as the poor cousin. In 2016 Catherine fulfilled a dream of opening her own school at Parafield Airport with a Diamond Super Dimona motorglider. Her mission was to teach these important skills to powered pilots, making them safe and sharpening their knowledge. It still is, and her desire to pass on the finer points of glider flight remains, as strong as ever.

Gliding certainly focuses the mind and harnesses the power of flight in its rawest form. For Catherine, competitions bring purpose to her endeavours and a goal to strive for, but in the race to do well, there is also great peace and solitude, circling alone on thermals with just the whoosh of air outside and the world at your feet. It's a world that has revealed itself to her over time, grounded in her affinity with science, technology, engineering and maths. Aviation was an integral part of her makeup and even though she entered the world as a baby needing a soft place to land, she taxied out with the unique combination of John and Jude's DNA. What a gift they gave, particularly to the sport of gliding, including the many young people who have benefited from Catherine's knowledge and gentle guidance.

5

TWO CRAZY IDEAS

STEF WALTER, WING WALKER AND MOOMBA BIRD(WO)MAN

'To turn a crazy idea into a worthwhile idea requires energy, courage, and perseverance. It can seem silly only because we cannot see beyond it. I believe success depends on asking "what if?" and allowing ourselves to explore ideas.'

Stef Walter

Stef Walter, wing walker and Moomba bird(wo)man

You won't hear anybody say, 'The Yarra River was crystal clear today'. It just never happens, because since European settlement it has slowly gone from clear to brown and is now ingloriously known as the river that runs upside down. It appears that the muddy bottom is always on the top, but Melburnians love it, especially from beside a barbecue on its banks or from onboard a floating device. Every March during Melbourne's four-day Moomba festival a select few that enter the Birdman Rally get much closer to the water than a floating device. Moomba, which began in 1955, is run by the City of Melbourne. Millions of people flock to enjoy the four-day carnival of music, fireworks and watersports by the Yarra River. In 2017 one of those people was a fixed-wing private pilot, Stef Walter. She is always up for an aerial adventure, but there is nothing in her flight manuals to suggest she strap on a giant set of butterfly wings and leap into the Yarra's clay waters. Nothing at all. In fact, Stef's logbook would indicate that she didn't have to leap from anything. She is qualified to fly almost anywhere in Australia. But on a drought-baked autumn day in 2017 there she was, lined up with the rest of them, wearing a crazy outfit that denied the four forces of flight: Lift, Thrust, Drag, Weight. The lift is usually provided by an aerofoil (a structure with curved surfaces, such as a wing) and the thrust comes from an engine, or in this case, from Stef pushing off the ledge. The weight of the aerofoil and its occupants is the naturally occurring opponent to Lift, and the Drag comes from any non-aerodynamic parts that push back and slow the aerofoil – the giant butterfly wings being a perfect example. Backlit by a magical Melbourne morning, Stef ran for the edge of the Birdman platform and took a mighty leap, carrying plenty of drag and weight and precious little of the other two.

Let's retreat from the action for a moment and zoom out to the crowds that line both sides of the river. There, the city's neatly defined edge runs stock straight east-north-east along Flinders Street, while the Yarra parallels it with a lazy upstream S shape until turning abruptly east-south-east. On the outside of the bend is Birrarung Marr, a park whose name originates from the Wurundjeri people whose ancestors knew this river when it ran clear. The name translates to 'By the side of the river of mists'. And in the chilly southern climes of Australia's second largest city, the winter river earns its name.

The Yarra is still central to Melbourne's vibrant life and since 1976 has hosted the Birdman Rally competition where entrants jump from a raised platform into the water, and are judged on (mainly) how long they can stay airborne, how far they can fly, how exciting or imaginative their costumes are, their performances pre-jump and the amount of money they raise for their nominated charity.

Birdman came to Australia in 1972, the year after the Brits invented it, and for four years the Glenelg Jetty in Adelaide was awash with craft such as homemade gliders, hang gliders and any other type of human-propelled aerofoil you can dream up. The competition came to Melbourne in 1976 so there's been almost 50 years of inspiration to draw from. Eyeing the other competitors, Stef's team reckoned that her giant butterfly wings were the best in show that day. They were a visual feast of the Spanish persuasion.

The vision for her design came after she entered the basilica of Barcelona's La Sagrada Família, a large, extraordinary church that is one of the most visited sites in Spain. Begun in 1882 it is the largest unfinished Roman Catholic Church in existence. The part of the building that was designed by Catalan architect Antoni Gaudí is considered his masterpiece and is now one of seven UNESCO World Heritage sites to his credit. He was nicknamed God's Architect, and so it's little wonder that Stef was immediately taken by the unsurpassed glory of windows that famously subvert the conventions for the use of coloured glass windows. Normally, the most spectacular part of a stained-glass window is far beyond direct viewing as they are brightest at the top where there is no obstruction from buildings or trees outside to cast a shadow. The Sagrada Família, though, has the clearer glass at the top to draw unfiltered light in and highlight the upper reaches. Down lower, the intricate coloured glass details, words and images are sited to enable people on the ground floor to view them directly. Gaudí wanted the colours and textures of the glass to gel, with 'light gliding over the windows like water over pebbles'.

Stef stood transfixed at the foot of this masterful work and committed the images to memory. Could she lightly glide the windows over water?

'In the back of my mind I'd had the vague idea of competing in the Melbourne Moomba Birdman competition. I now imagined launching off the platform carried by a pair of giant colourful "stained glass" butterfly wings. Back home when I sat down to design them, I marked out simple designs on butcher's paper. Obviously, I couldn't make them out of actual glass and so I spent many months carefully cutting out the wings from corflute.' Working with corflute, the hard plastic cardboard substitute used for real estate signage, was a natural choice for the bones of the structure. The lightweight corrugation gives it strength and it is affordable and fun to work with. Stef knew the stuff well because her father, Rob, had used it in his real estate dealings. She joined a variety of coloured plastics and cellophane to create the stained-glass effect. The design evolved organically, but she never imagined they'd end up being so *'majestic!'*

From a pile of craft supplies, the project eventually took over the living room as it evolved from an idea into a 3-metre-high, triple-jointed, two-part multicoloured monstrosity. Her daily challenge was to pick her way through the unit without disturbing or damaging the laid-out parts. They looked like nothing anybody in suburban Ballarat had ever seen before and may even have given Gaudí himself cause for pause. But unlike a cathedral that relies on bricks, mortar and a good solid foundation, Stef's creation had to be portable, durable, and believable. It required innovation.

'How could I attach the huge, 3-metre wings to my back, have them look realistic, and survive the rigours of me launching?'

The answer was just up the road at the Holy Church of Divine Creations – Bunnings. 'Bunnings people get some weird questions and requests, but this stumped them. They were so puzzled when Dad and I explained what I was trying to do. Dad finally came up with the solution; he would donate his trusty European backpack. Its adjustable shoulder straps and waist belt would provide a firm and rugged fuselage. With a bit of modification, we were able to attach the wings and then it was back to Bunnings for plastic tubing, nuts and bolts and duct tape.'

The problems continued. The wings were too big for Stef's Toyota Camry. They had to be redesigned so they could be disassembled at home and reassembled after the one-way trip to Moomba. After more time in the Bunnings aisles seeking extra fasteners the Bird of Paradise was born around the due date, pushed out of the nest and driven down the Calder Freeway.

Rob, excited by this great adventure, had also introduced Stef to aviation as an 18-month-old when he took her to the Point Cook Airshow, a three-hour drive away from their home at Horsham in Western Victoria. He was a huge aviation enthusiast, a love that he inherited from his own father.

'Grandpa was a pilot instructor in World War Two. He instructed on Tiger Moths and flew Avro Ansons [two training aircraft widely used in the Royal Australian Air Force at that time]. From that, Dad became fascinated by aviation, and he indoctrinated me by taking me to airshows. I loved spending time with him and having him share his knowledge. He is in love with engines, and he can hear a plane and know what it is even before he races outside to look up! Now he has the scanner so he can tell us all about an aircraft and its flight details as it passes overhead.'

From these early experiences Stef also became fascinated by flying, formations, aerobatics, the whole lot. She was in awe of how it all worked but never imagined that flying would feature in her own future other than on a jet to Europe to visit her mother's family for a holiday.

'Mum is Swiss and the first of many flights to Switzerland was when I was a toddler. One time when I was about twelve, I went into the cockpit and one of the pilots let me wear their hat and hand out chocolates to the passengers. That was my "job" for the flight! It was so lovely that they included us kids. I think it may have been a Swiss Air flight from Singapore. It made me believe that maybe I could become a flight attendant.'

Well, that never happened. Stef left Horsham at 18 and went to live in Zurich with her ailing grandmother. She learnt to speak German at work, and Swiss German at home while she trained and worked as a nurse for 18 months at a Zurich Hospital, which was just a ten-minute walk away. It seems incongruous now, but Stef wasn't drawn to any aviation hobbies while she was in Switzerland, an attractive place for aviation enthusiasts; it's the home of the pristine Pilatus factory, and a birth place of paragliding. She enjoyed the spectacle of paragliders soaring around the Swiss Alps but nobody, including Stef, assumed she'd be interested in it. 'It looked like a lot of fun, but I never assumed I would be up there in any capacity'.

Back in Melbourne, Stef began her formal nurse's training at LaTrobe University and the northern training hospital at Bundoora. The nursing assistants were well paid for their work on the wards and so it made a smooth transition while studying for her Registered Nurse qualification. During this time she would fly with an old school friend in his two-seater single-engine Tecnam aeroplane. It was her first foray into light aircraft, and she couldn't believe how much fun it was when he allowed her to take the controls. She says with a laugh, 'We will blame Rowan. He got me into flying and it was exhilarating and rather unbelievable that someone in their twenties, as young as we were, was allowed to just fly around in a little aeroplane!'

They often flew over the Grampians National Park, 50 kilometres south-east of Horsham. The park's five craggy north-south sandstone ridges rise around 1000 metres to face the morning sun, with slopes falling gently away to the west. Wildflowers dot the dramatic landscape, which features the towering MacKenzie Falls, the Elephant Hide climb, The Balconies lookout and well-worn hiking trails. Flying is a great way to get around, but it still didn't enter her head to get a pilot's licence. She just liked being a passenger and occasionally steering; however, that changed on a holiday to the Gold Coast. She was working in Ballarat, Victoria, as a mental health nurse. For the quietly spoken woman with a ready smile, it was busy, fast, wild, and fascinating. It also required a bucketload of empathy and patience. She loved her work and the people within it. During her annual leave, she and her sister took a holiday to the Gold Coast where, finally, the idea of flying took hold.

Now 27 years old, Stef coaxed her sister into a seaplane. As they waded towards the bobbing aeroplane for a joy flight, Stef was impressed by the beautiful white craft gleaming on the water and the grey upholstered seats within. Her reluctant sister, with a fear of flying, was relegated to the back seat while Stef apprehensively made herself comfortable up front.

'The pilot, in a moment of faith, handed over the controls to let me fly. That was it! While holding the control column, I looked back at my sister. White-knuckled and pressed hard against her seat, she wasn't sharing the enthusiasm, but up the front I couldn't believe my luck.'

Back home in Ballarat, Stef met her partner Mick and was soon commuting the hour and a half to Bendigo, shuffling between houses and two jobs. She never really settled in Bendigo but, looking for a way to feel comfortable in a new town, she volunteered at Bendigo Animal Welfare and Community Services (BAWCS). An animal shelter that relies on volunteers and donations.

No conversation was too silly for the cats, whose company she adored, and though Stef shared her dream of flying with friends she had to overcome her first hurdle, which was her mindset about booking a lesson. She was scared she'd be laughed at for coming in so fresh-faced. Would they accept a woman? Would anybody take on the task of trying to teach her? She sat by the phone for a month but when she finally called, she received a warm welcome from Colin Hokin, who subsequently taught her to fly in a Tecnam.

'Colin was a really nurturing, lovely person and I needed that. I needed someone to ease me into it. He'd reassure me that the cockpit might seem overwhelming, but he would continually follow up with, "you are going to get this". Bendigo Flying Club is a fantastic and inviting club.'

Colin delighted in her determination, her sense of humour and ability to laugh at herself. 'She was a good student, but she had one funny day when she departed on a solo cross-country flight. The wind on the ground was still but it was a fierce headwind up high and 45 minutes later when she returned, I asked how she went. She answered, "I never found the place. I feel so silly!" I think her ground speed was so slow in the little Tecnam that she never actually got there in the first place!'

A year later, Linda arrived. Linda Beilharz OAM is the first Australian woman to successfully trek the South and North poles and she is a kind and calm soul. It was wonderful for Stef to have another woman at the club. A kindred spirit.

Her basic flight training finished at the end of 2016 and Stef then transferred back to Ballarat to complete the navigation component. Her only hindrances now were the reliably unreliable southern weather and coordinating her own roster with that of her instructor who lived some distance from the airport.

On her non-working, non-flying days, Stef raised funds for the animal shelter by doing bake sales, and then turned her efforts to the next Birdman Rally, unable to shake this crazy butterfly idea.

'I was working night shift and in my spare moments I would start designing the wings. I do a lot of painting, sewing and woodwork and am very much into aesthetics. I wanted something artistic and beautiful rather than practical. I shared the idea with Mick, and he replied, 'OK, but just try not to get too carried away'.

She had some cathedral window photos for inspiration but soon departed from those blueprints and let the design evolve organically, leaning a little towards costumes from *The Adventures of Priscilla, Queen of the Desert*.

For reasons unknown, her application for the Birdman Rally was rejected. Well, that was a setback! Stef quickly replied, 'I've got this massive set of wings in the lounge, and I can't possibly wait until next year because I'm going to Nepal to live'. She thought if she added an extra layer to the wings, that would show how keen she was. She doubled their size, and it worked. In the six-month window to finish her wings she also needed to raise funds for a charity of her choice. It was an easy decision to donate to BAWCS and support came from all corners. She went into the event with $2359.92. That should buy a lot of cat food and equipment!

The night before the event Stef packed her black exercise pants and a brightly coloured running top, and headed to Melbourne with her team. The next morning around 40 000 people lined the banks of the Yarra, stretching from the rowing sheds on the south side, down to the Princes Bridge and back up the north side, past Birrarung Marr, to enjoy the 2017 Moomba Birdman Rally. Like any good comedy, the entertainment was in the joyous ambition and predictable misfortune of the performers. Then it dawned on Stef. All those people would be watching, and it would be televised, and she'd been to and seen how high the Birdman platform was and now she was terrified and too nervous to eat.

As the 90-minute competition got underway, the guys on the microphone revved up the crowd like a variety show. The excitement was palpable. Enjoying the spirit of the day, Stef's team helped hoist the brightly coloured translucent butterfly wings with the ambitious name onto her back. They secured them over her shoulders and around her waist. They fitted them snugly and then Stef balanced the wings above her and smiled for photographers, videographers, newspapers, and news stations.

Her father stood back with a mixure of pride and astonishment. Now he recalls, 'The apparatus was just massive when she had it on. She wouldn't have been out of place at a fashion show. The huge crowds were hooting and hollering and suddenly it dawned on us what she'd put her name down for. I couldn't help thinking, "Gee Stef, you're in the big league here!"'

Dizzy from hunger and with the magnitude of the event now crystal clear, Stef suddenly felt light-headed. The air was electric as she and the other eleven contestants prepared to walk the plank, or run the gauntlet, knowing they couldn't avoid a watery end. Many would be separated from their apparatus before they hit the water, and some would end up stuck beneath it waiting for rescue. Some of the media and promotion seemed so professional that Rob reckoned the Walter team looked like rank amateurs. With matching uniforms and a shimmering goddess in their midst, the others might have looked back at Stef and thought the same thing about themselves.

The launch platform was fixed four metres above the river and backed by a large screen onto which was flashed an oversized image of the brilliant butterfly alongside her name, her charity, and the name of her craft. Despite her nerves, she walked gloriously towards the base of the stairs. Her crown, pinning her mid-length blonde waves, blended with the crepe and cellophane wings. She was an angel before a cathedral window.

Against a deafening roar and cheers from the crowd, the friendly announcer broadcast, 'First-time flyer Stefanie has made the trip from Bendigo to support the Bendigo Animal Welfare Centre in the Penguin Category. She took inspiration from stained-glass windows to create colourful wings'.

The music began and a super-sized Stef was beamed to the audience, her broad smile masking her nerves. As she entered the stage, ascending the stairs like Miss America, the wings filled the entire screen. Off camera somebody in the crowd exclaimed, 'Oh wow!'

Further east along the bank, her family watched with many emotions: pride, excitement, nerves, concern. They were right there with her.

'Stefanie has raised money for BAWCS giving her an additional 18.6 metres for charity jackpot' – results are calculated using distance flown plus money raised, which is converted into distance and added to the total. The announcer continued to bellow, 'but first ... heeeere's Stefanie!'

Adjusting her vest and harness over her left shoulder, Stef turned, squared up for the crowd and spoke to the microphone. The announcer told her she looked marvellous. She thanked him with a laugh, and that's when you noticed the comical goggles on her helmet rimmed by pink flowers.

'What made you enter the Birdman Rally this year?'

With an assured stage presence Stef replied, 'I've been watching the Moomba Birdman Rally for years and I just always thought I'd love to be a part of it and here I am today! So ...'

'And how did you train for this today?' he asked.

'Ummm, it took up a lot of our lounge room space so I'm happy to have our floor back, but not much training went into the actual diving or soaring.'

Stef Walter, wing walker and Moomba bird(wo)man

In front of thousands of people, on live TV, she admitted she hadn't practised.

She explained that she'd been volunteering with BAWCS for two years and seen the wonderful things they achieve, and that they're Central Victoria's only no-kill shelter. A zoom out revealed the full extent of her magnificence being buffeted by a 10-knot breeze (judging by the flapping flags at the side of the blue and white platform). The commentator didn't need to point out how huge the crowd was as Stef stood knock-kneed before them, overwhelmed by the blaring music and pyrotechnics. He ramped up again as his voice went up a couple of octaves and the camera panned to placard-waving supporters across the water.

'Oh, here we go! Give us a big cheer, guys! Stefanie they're all cheering for you in that incredible costume that is *Birds* [sic] *of Paradise*. How stunning is that? It seems such a shame that it's going to go into the Yarra Riverrr. WHAT DO YOU THINK? DO YOU THINK STEFANIE IS GOING TO BAKE OR SIZZLE? WHAT IS IT?' A resounding 'sizzle' boomed across the river and, facing Stef, he continued, 'All right, Stefanie, they're all on your side. Let's see you TAKE OFF!' A faux air traffic controller came on the radio and three seconds later his guttural voice advised, 'This is Ground Control. You're clear to take off'.

The expectant crowd leaned in as the announcer dramatically asked, 'Final words, Stefanie?' He flicked the microphone towards her, and her unrehearsed reply was, 'Umm. I think I'm just going to WING it'.

She wiggled her eyebrows at the silly joke and then laughed and took her departure position. Her stomach was doing cartwheels, but her legs were doing a little dance. The screen behind her, still filled with stained glass, flicked to a cartoon of a penguin and an eagle, then began the countdown. Five. Four. Three. Two. One. JUMP!

Stef was determined to put on a good show and as she tested the wires connecting her wrists to her wings, the announcer belted out, 'All right, this is Stefanie with the Bird of Paradise. LET'S HOLD OUR BREATH THAT SHE CAN FLY INTO THE YARRA RIVER OH LOOK AT HER GOOOOOOO'.

The crowd let out a deafening roar. With thirteen running steps and a few determined flaps of her arms, she fought the resistance of the most unaerodynamic flying contraption ever to see Moomba. The 'glass' roses on her crown bobbed as she raced to the edge of the platform and got a split-second glance at her immediate future. Undeterred, she took a herculean cup of bravery and offered herself to the river gods. Carrying about 10 kilograms on her back, Stefanie Walter, caring lovely mental health nurse, recreational pilot and lifelong cat lover, raised both hands to the sky in the spirit of healthy competition and sacrificed her creation to the cause.

Owing to a design flaw, the precious wings immediately folded flat and vertical behind her, providing absolutely no aerodynamic stability or lift. Wishing that she could soar like an eagle, Stef twisted slightly to the left and in less than three seconds had dropped 4 metres into the cold, salty river. It was fast and furious. She probably screamed, recalling that the organisers had said to try and keep her mouth shut – not to quell the screaming, but so she didn't take on any water. She was frantically treading water, and that's why she was in the Penguin Class, because she was never going to fly and dressed the way she was, she was barely able to swim. Actually, she needed help.

As the judging cards flashed up 'Sizzle', Stef took a few horrid gulps of Melbourne's unfiltered drinking water and scanned desperately for the rescue boat. They took five seconds to reach her; only just quickly enough. The boat's crew cut away the string and wire and the complex contraption that was dragging her down. They asked her how she was feeling and how the river tasted.

'Disgusting.'

The cameras turned to Stef's colleagues from BAWCS who thanked the supporters and their now infamous volunteer whose donation would support 'the care of so many animals that come into our care every day, including those that are in crisis situations such as domestic violence.'

The large screen replayed the Bird of Paradise jump, then replayed it in slow motion as the flightless bird made her way to the dais for a post-flight debrief. The announcer congratulated her and asked how it felt.

'Oh, it was saltier than I expected!' she said with a big laugh.

'Welcome to Melbourne', he replied. 'What are you going to take back to Bendigo after the experience of doing that in front of the great crowd here at Moomba?'

'Well, I think I have definitely boosted my immune system ... I'm gonna take home some pretty fine memories.'

Her jump distance was confirmed as 2 metres, with a charity jackpot distance of 20.5 metres. Despite not flying any great distance, Stef took out the first prize gold cup for most inventive craft. That was no mean feat, considering that some of the other entrants came adorned with hang gliders in various forms, cardboard aircraft, a seahorse made of blue and white balloons, and a trembling bride. Stef's leap was closely followed by a single wing-shaped aerofoil, which was then followed by a cantering pterodactyl. There followed another pair of plastic-covered aeroplane wings, and a man in white leggings with a shredded white cape. True to the spirit of the Birdman Rally, most people cry with joy as they go over the edge and many separate from their craft; some craft separate from themselves, and one craft was separated from its pilot and lobbed over the edge while she stayed firmly planted in dry dock.

The overall winner, with a fundraising total of $25 000, was *The Secret Life of Us* and *Rush* actor Samuel Johnson who, though scared of heights, abandoned his multicoloured bra apparatus, put his hands over his ears and gritted his teeth. Wearing pink shorts and T-shirt with a pink cardboard batwing mask, he threw caution to the wind, forgot his fear of heights, and made a determined run for it. After an impressive one and a quarter forward somersault roll, Samuel executed a painful face-plant on the water. It was the extra quarter that was the problem.

'I came just hoping to etch my charity into the annals of Australia's cultural iconography, but it turns out we might have won the Birdman Rally as well, so I'm flipping beside myself', he said.

His contraption was called 'Titty Titty Bang Bang'. The charity, 'Love your sister' was started after his sister Connie's third breast cancer diagnosis. Sadly, she passed away six months later, but the charity continues still. And so does the Birdman Rally.

Though the deceased wings were sadly fished out of the river and bundled into a rubbish skip, Stef quietly wandered with her team through the streets of Melbourne wearing fresh clothes and a stunned look. She was exhilarated for weeks. Each year she is invited back to compete and if she ever does take up that offer, she expects to create something more aerodynamic (she's been chatting to the engineers). Stef is proud of her efforts to join the exclusive club of penguins: that group of bird people who jumped into the river not realising how far down it was.

With the excitement of the day still fresh in her mind, she joined Mick on a backpacking trip through Asia before undertaking an 18-month stint in Nepal, which included a nine-month nursing placement.

In August 2023, six years after her Birdman Rally effort, Stef went head-on into another challenge, this time in the United States. After she got home, without any fanfare, she popped a rather startling video onto her social media account:

Stef Walter, wing walker and Moomba bird(wo)man

One of the best (and most challenging) weeks of my life!
Completed my wing walking training at the world's only academy!
Finally fulfilled a lifelong dream, absolutely exhausted, bruised
and sore, but ecstatic!!

Ten years prior, Stef had seen the Breitling Wing Walkers, a British group, perform at the Avalon Airshow. It sparked an interest, and while her father said, 'Who would ever do that?', she thought, *maybe I would like to do that* ... People have done it since the early days of aviation, when Hollywood stunt people would walk out onto the wing of an aircraft and perform for the crowds, or the cameras.

Stef's online research revealed that Mason Wing Walking Academy in Sequim (pronounced Squim), Washington in the US, was the only place to train. She quietly made enquiries and was told there was no space. The one-day courses sell out in a flash, and they only trained during the three-month good weather window. She continued to enquire, on the quiet, every year. In 2023 she got her break; there was a high chance they could book her in for August. They gave her some tips and tricks on how to get wing-walking fit. There was a big disclaimer to say there's no guarantee at the end of the course that she could do the wing walk. The thought of paying all that money, training and being rejected was more anxiety-inducing than the actual event. They told her she'd need a lot of upper-body strength and flexibility. Many people who had trained had still managed to fail the pre-flight test.

Now with a date and the task of packing her bag and buying a ticket, she decided she'd better tell her husband about her plan. Then she had to explain what wing walking was, but he quickly put his hands over his ears. He didn't want to hear anything about it until it was over. Her parents and sister were justifiably concerned, but not surprised.

Undeterred, Stef trained in earnest, flew to Seattle, then caught the bus out to Sequim to meet Mike and Marilyn Mason, who have been in the business for 40 years. Luckily the weather was good, and training began early. It was vigorous – repetitious instruction on how to climb out of the cockpit safely and secure yourself onto the tether (a steel cable clipped to a belt around the waist), and then how to climb onto the top wing, down to the bottom wing and walk out. 'When strapping myself in, I kept wondering what would happen if we fell off?' Nobody brought it up and neither did Stef. Apparently, nobody had ever fallen, of the more than thousand people who had done it. The wing walking is done from one of two Stearman biplanes, which are extremely precious. Stearmans were first produced in 1926, ceased production in 1946, and were primarily used as a military training aircraft. Owners treat the wood and canvas machines gently, like vintage cars. With this in mind, there were extremely strict instructions about where to put your feet, including keeping your toes from rubbing on the canvas, what you could touch and how you could move about without causing damage.

 An obvious question from Stef was about the force of the wind. 'Like a leaf blower', they said. How hard could it be? A 60-mile-per-hour leaf blower.

 At the end of the day's training, when it was time to actually go up and do the walk, Stef was exhausted on many levels. Apparently, the training was only half the job. 'I felt almost no emotion – I was ready to do it. The flight was around 15 minutes. We became airborne and climbed a few thousand feet. Michael Mason gave me the signal, banking left and right a few times, which meant it was time for me to go out. I unbuckled my seatbelt and re-buckled it beneath me. I stuck my left hand up to reach the handle to pull myself up and it shot back from the resistance of the air. We were doing about 60 knots and I freaked out, thinking I'm not physically strong enough to combat the drag. But I'd come all this way, and it was one time I had to power through any fear I might have had.

And I had it. Every movement was so physically challenging getting onto the top of the wing, directly in front of where I had been sitting. I screamed with every movement. I climbed past the support pole and the wire stays that help hold it in place, edged myself in front of the pole and buckled myself in. I was so relieved. I gave the thumbs-up signal to the pilot, and he started to perform the first of six aerobatic manoeuvres.' They were two each of a loop, hammerhead, and barrel roll.

Michael pushed the nose down into a dive and then eased back up into a loop. Stef was screaming with every emotion, while her face streamed with tears. Her arms were out wide like she wanted to fly herself, and for that heart-stopping, breath-taking, terrifying few moments, the ground disappeared and the sky filled her view. At the top of the loop, Stef hung suspended, upside down, disoriented and fully alive. As it rolled out of the loop, he then went into the hammerhead manoeuvre – a climb straight up, followed by a sharp turn on the vertical axis, and then flying straight at the ground. Stef's arms were blowing back from the force.

As the aeroplane turned vertical to the mountains and forests below, she was a starfish once more. After the six manoeuvres, she got the signal to climb back down into the cockpit. It's one thing to look up at where you're going, but another thing completely to have to look down a couple of thousand feet at the earth below.

Back in her seat, they climbed again to gain altitude and then Stef executed her next move, which was to step out of the cockpit once more and gingerly take four steps across the wing, carefully stepping on the taped markers, and mount a javelin fixed between the flying wires that brace the wings. She lay prone, while hanging on for dear life, and put her hands forward of the leading edge to clutch the wires, before wrapping her legs in a pre-determined lock at the ankles around the other end of the wires. Hello Superman. Or Tom Cruise – he turned up a week later to do the same thing.

TAKE FLIGHT

After she gave a thumbs-up to her pilot, Mike Mason, Mike repeated the six aerobatic manoeuvres. The aircraft went into a loop and Stef was screaming like there was no tomorrow, because ... well, it felt like that. As the wires bounced beneath her and the sky came clearly into view again for another six manoeuvres – this time without the seatbelt – she didn't hold back.

'When I got back into my seat, we did a bit of a joy flight around the beautiful local area, over the beach and the national park. It was a moment of absolute relief that it was over and that I had done it. I can't describe the feeling.'

She quietly slipped back into Ballarat a few days later, safe in the knowledge that she'd never have to climb out of a cockpit ever again. And the Birdman Rally? That could be on the cards.

'Performing in the Birdman Rally helped me realise that to turn a crazy idea into a worthwhile idea requires energy, courage, and perseverance. It can seem silly only because we cannot see beyond it. I believe success depends on asking "what if?" and allowing ourselves to explore ideas. The Birdman Rally taught me that I'm more courageous than I gave myself credit for. And that if people don't understand my dreams, then that's OK. We can achieve great things if we put ourselves out there.

'These life lessons, Birdman and wing walking, have taught me resilience and enabled me to challenge myself. As a mental health clinician, I can see the importance of leading a well-lived life by striving to achieve dreams, no matter how small they might seem. Throughout my nursing career I've witnessed many clients facing significant challenges. Many run from them, or assume that someone else will solve the problems in their lives. Despite the anxiety I felt competing in Birdman and learning to wing walk, I was able to learn that facing obstacles head-on can yield the best results.'

Stef is very committed to her work as a practising mental health nurse, and as an academic at Australian Catholic University teaching mental health nursing. Outside of work, she continues to pursue her various artistic interests, and to fly as a recreational pilot, with a role as Secretary of the Ballarat Aero Club. She absolutely loved the aerobatic component of the wing walking and says she wouldn't mind the exhilaration of stepping out of the cockpit again, or of trying aerobatic flight herself. See? That's how it starts.

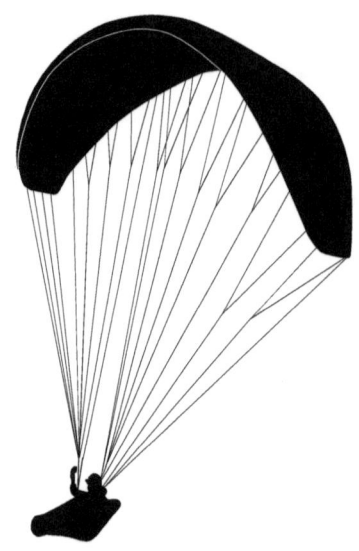

6

ON EAGLES' WINGS

KIRSTEN SEETO, PARAGLIDER PILOT

'I've thermalled wingtip to wingtip with an eagle and watched the unique patterns and individual feathers move as it feels for the strongest part of the core.'

Kirsten Seeto

In that lull between Christmas and New Year when the focus for most people is on socialising, and nobody's quite sure what day it is, Kirsten Seeto carefully packs her bright red and white 'wing', the name for a paragliding canopy that most of us would identify as a parachute. Into it, she folds her lightweight harness, her sleeping bag, and her one-woman tent and its poles. She divides up some cooking gear, sesame baguettes, ham, cheese, salami, and breakfast porridge. She knows exactly what day it is.

At 160 centimetres tall and a featherlight 52 kilograms, Kirsten heaves on her pack. It weighs more than a quarter of her body weight, but she is undeterred because the mountains beckon. The town of Bright, her new home in the foothills of Victoria's High Country, is one of the most picturesque places you could choose to live, and is the perfect salve for the challenges of 2020.

Kirsten had fled her home in February during the out-of-control bushfires that roared around the nearby mountains. The small tourist town was evacuated for a week. No sooner had the smoke cleared than the region was shut down by Covid. This forced the difficult decision for Kirsten, as club president, to cease paragliding operations. Having spent the long winter living and working in her tiny house on the edge of town, by the following summer she is on shifting personal and professional sands. It is time for a new perspective, and she will seek it on that nearby mountain as she has many times before. But this time she won't walk back.

Lucy Legget, an equally experienced English-Australian paraglider pilot also living in Bright, is able to get childcare for her two young children and at 4 pm the two women do the one-hour trip to Mount Beauty to drop off a car and continue to the car park at the trail head. By 6 pm they are on their way 1000 metres up to one of Victoria's highest summits.

Their usual haunt was Mystic Launch, a flat, manicured custom-made spot atop an 800-metre (2200-foot) mountain, 2 kilometres out on the road to Wandiligong, in the foothills of Mount Hotham. The pine forests that sprawl across its surrounds are crisscrossed with busy mountain bike trails, tourists, and a narrow but well-trodden dirt road that winds up through the forest with a herculean drop on one side and switchback turns to keep drivers alert. It's no problem for experienced paraglider pilots. They're just eager to launch, but it's a gut-wrenching ten-minute trip for a newcomer like me.

In contrast, on this day the two women take a different trip. They hike alone for three hours up Mystic's untamed neighbour. The narrow gravel trail terminates at a memorial cairn and Kirsten and Lucy are filled with wonder: the sun is setting over layer upon layer of blue mountains unfolding before them across mottled green granite, dotted with white summer daisies. They can see as far as NSW from up here and as they zip their jackets against the chill, they count their blessings.

The final task is to erect their tents and then, with baguettes and wine (in cans, as they are lighter to carry), they sit carefully observing the fluidity of the clouds and how they move around the mountains, for clouds, the greatest of storytellers, will dictate the next day's activities. A spectacular full moon casts a comforting glow across this remote hilltop campsite. Both women are experiencing major change in their personal lives, and this moment of peace and supportive connection with each other is deeply restorative. They retreat to their tents excited and hope that the promised weather will transpire.

The next morning Kirsten sleeps through as Lucy watches the sun usher in a crisp clear day. It is a good start, but during breakfast, disconcerting clouds form just as a couple of their friends crest the hill to share the last hour's walk to a distant peak. The clouds rise menacingly and then settle high enough to fly under. No paraglider pilot wants to launch into cloud. A perfect day requires calm conditions, a little bit of warmth to create 'lift', and a lazy breeze crawling up the mountain face. The group plans to fly over the parallel mountain ranges that create the wide Kiewa Valley and a convenient passage to Mount Beauty.

Kirsten unpacks her gear, slides her harness over her shoulders like a backpack, and fastens the nylon straps and clips. At the top of the harness, she sorts a pair of ten multicoloured cords that attach to the wing. The single brake lines connect the trailing edge of the wing and the handles. Taking a grip on each handle, Kirsten steps up to the launch spot and turns to face her wing spread 10 metres wide on the ground behind her. She is intently focused. She rechecks her lines and buckles, and she listens. What is the wind doing? Is it so strong that she will have to fight it? So weak she will need more runway than she has? She feels the breeze with her face, watches the movement of foliage, listens to the ripples on the other wings lying dormant around her; she senses a pressure change between cycles and monitors it.

The lightly pulsating breeze is strong enough to puff the elliptical wing and after getting into the rhythm of a few cycles she gives a couple of tugs to coax it into the air. The silky canopy ruffles and balloons into life. She steadies herself then deftly lifts and uncrosses her arms, turns to face the valley, and runs towards the edge of the mountain, guiding the elevated wing above her head, fighting its resistance. Five, six, seven steps and it rises high, making her feet light on the ground. A couple more steps and the air inflates each individual cell in the wing. Taut and ready to fly, it lifts on the rising breeze and carries her aloft. The fine wing shines a burning red under the sun and her friends watch in earnest. Is she rising? Is she sinking? Is she circling?

Testing and teasing the air and the thin thermal lift, Kirsten dispatches her earthly concerns and focuses on the task at hand. Across a patchworked green landscape, her light wing, appropriately named 'Fire', doesn't disappoint. Though its performance will never set the world alight, its beauty is that it only weighs 2 kilograms, as opposed to the usual 5 kilograms. It is light enough to haul up the mountain, yet versatile enough to fly off it.

TAKE FLIGHT

Kirsten settles into the moulded seat to enjoy the ride and makes for the Mount Beauty Airport, circling around in a warm thermal when she can, to gain height so she can stretch the flight. This is the best part of the day. She has successfully escaped the earth and hooks her feet into her pod, creating a warm pocket for the lower half of her body. She is focused on tracking the lift and the most efficient flight path. Each frequency of her 'vario' instrument (a tool for measuring height) beeps to indicate whether she is rising or descending. She relies on it in shifting weather and it is telling Kirsten that she is in light lift. The air is rising around her. It confirms what the swirling clouds just above are indicating. She cruises across to Little Bogong and hopes she can gain enough height to be able to glide to Mount Beauty. Her vario beeps that the air is 'sinky'; she will be losing altitude, but intuition and experience tell her that it will lift on the smaller peak. Just in time, it does, and she knows that her friends will be relieved. As she circles up the thermal, she sees her friends preparing to launch.

Up at 1900 metres, the wetter air of the wispy cloud chills her face but she now has enough height to complete the flight. For the next 20 minutes she glides peacefully down the valley reaching speeds of up to 40 kilometres per hour. She descends for a beautiful landing and turns to see two of her friends taking their time to enjoy the ride. She checks her satellite tracker, which indicates that Lucy is thermalling and sightseeing back up on the mountains. With her higher-performing wing and a slightly later launch (in warmer weather, providing more lift), Lucy can make the most of this opportunity. Kirsten smiles; she's happy that her friend is having such a great flight and they collect her on the way home a couple of hours later.

In her 15 years and 1000 hours paragliding, there has always been something new to learn and after mastering cross-country, coastal, mountain and competition flying, Kirsten has just found her new love: 'vol biv' – the French term for hiking and camping to paraglide.

Kirsten Seeto, paraglider pilot

BEFORE LEARNING TO PARAGLIDE, KIRSTEN HAD BEEN A FIXED-wing pilot. She had also tried parachuting on her way home from a trip to England, when she joined an overland tour from Nairobi, Kenya, to Cape Town, South Africa. She was the eldest in a group of 20 young people; in a four-wheel-drive bus, they camped, shopped locally and learned how to get along for six weeks. They tried it all: quad bikes, beaches, safaris, sandboarding and canoeing. She toured Victoria Falls in a microlite – a small powered buggy-like vehicle that flies under a hang-glider-style wing. She then took up an option to do three bungee jumps. She reckoned it would take her all of the three goes to get the hang of it. She never did; she didn't enjoy the freefall. The skydiving package, however, was a popular addition to the tour and in such an exotic setting, Kirsten thought it might be a fun thing to experience again (she'd tried it once in Australia).

Up at altitude, she was positioned in the open doorway of the aeroplane with her arms folded across her chest. She tilted her head back and on the count of three rolled out of the aircraft with the instructor attached behind. They somersaulted, freefalling and tumbling through the air. He then threw out his first chute, which stabilised the fall, and with her arms outstretched and her body arched, she screamed towards the ground, spread-eagled as the velocity contorted her skin. The golden sands of the world's oldest desert sprawled below her like a bad dream.

After 60 seconds the main parachute opened and her legs dropped into a familiar position; forcing her body upright in the harness, she relaxed into the ride and enjoyed the slow descent to earth. By the time she had run to a stop and the parachute had settled onto the sandy dunes, Kirsten realised that she only needed to go paragliding to have the experience she enjoyed. Skydiving was amazing but she still hated the freefall. She needed the canopy and with great reports about Cape Town's paragliding, she booked an extra week there at the end of the tour and hooked up with a local paragliding guide.

TAKE FLIGHT

She did her first cross-country flight of 9 kilometres and was told to be careful where she landed. A potential problem was the chance of landing in a shanty town, where she could be mobbed by over-enthusiastic locals who, depending on their experiences with tourists, could be extremely friendly or not. She was mostly met by adorable, excited children.

Kirsten's love affair with aviation began as a 13-year-old in Sydney, at the movies watching a formation pair of Grumman F-14 Tomcats (military fighter planes) blast over Miramar in the California desert. For the first time, specially designed camera mounts and lenses were fitted on the inside and outside of the aircraft bringing us not only into the cockpit, but right under the pilot's helmet. A pulsing bass beat thumps in our chests, raises our adrenaline and lifts us off our seat. The kinetic thrill is real for earthlings who dream of hurtling through the sky to the intoxicating beat of 'Danger Zone'. The music is a call to action and the cutting-edge photography brings it home. Thirty years on, Tom Cruise believes the photography in *Top Gun* to be the best aerial footage to date. The film brought us aviator sunglasses, obligatory nicknames, and the enduring one-liners, 'You can be my wingman any time', 'Talk to me, Goose!' and of course, 'I feel the need for speed'.

The film's full-throttle patriotism was so inspiring that the United States aviation forces had a 500 per cent increase in applications. No movie had ever done that before, but no movie had ever been *Top Gun*. And while the film sparked every boy's dream of the best career you could ever have, there were only two significant female characters: Kelly McGillis as an instructor/love interest and Meg Ryan as a pilot's wife. It was 1986 and while the young Australian men in the audience dreamed of donning a flight suit and buying a motorbike, the message for women was to hope to be serenaded in a bar. Change was afoot, though, and would happen within the next decade.

In Sydney, Kirsten was wholly enamoured with the idea of flying. She watched the film ad nauseam until she knew every song and sequence in it. For the girl from the northern suburbs who didn't play beach volleyball, aviation entered her life. It has been intoxicatingly enduring, but it brought some harsh early lessons.

Kirsten joined the RAAF Air Training Corps. While the weekly parades were held in the inner western suburb of West Ryde, weekends were spent out at Camden Airport, an hour's drive from the city. Through the Air Training Corps she was able to access affordable and structured flying lessons. The organisation was full of teenagers, with a ratio of 80 per cent boys to 20 per cent girls, who were all equally keen to get flying, whatever form that took. Kirsten took the chance to complete a week-long static parachuting course at HMAS *Albatross*, the Australian Navy's main naval air station, near Nowra, NSW. The excitement of it made her want more and she embarked on her powered licence. As a young teenager, there was nothing more fun than these weekends, camps and excursions. That is, until things went horribly wrong in December 1990.

It was the end of a camp and, disappointed that she wasn't going to get another flight in, Kirsten helped instead to prepare for that evening's large formal dinner by peeling a big plastic tub full of potatoes. Others in the student group waited to fly with the two instructors. As the afternoon slipped away, one of the two-seat Cessna 152s returned from a flight over nearby Lake Burragorang. The other had crashed and sunk, but that was not apparent until the end of the next day. As concerned conversations made their way to the kitchen, Kirsten pieced together the story. A friend was missing.

Her parents, John and Sue Derrett, will never forget that weekend. When Kirsten called with the shocking news, Sue withdrew for a rare moment of prayer. It was her only comfort in this dark and conflicted time – so relieved that her daughter was safe, but devastated for those who weren't. They arrived at the camp after dark and Sue stepped out of the car. In the gentle breeze, the only thing to break the stunned silence was the continual hopeless clanging of ropes and metal clips on a flagpole. Distraught leaders and students hoped for good news that wasn't coming. In fact, it got worse.

On the silent drive home, Kirsten offered only minimal snippets of the day's events, and barely slept that night. In a tragic continuation of the story, a search aircraft late the next morning suffered an engine failure. Four more people were killed, two of whom were Kirsten's friends, and two passengers were seriously injured. Aged only 17, Kirsten had no idea how to process the huge events of this horrific weekend.

Sue eventually turned off the repeated news cycle and over the following weeks, put the newspaper cuttings away, for a time when the family might be able to cope with it. They slowly accepted that they had been very fortunate and never forgot those who hadn't been.

The Australian Transport Safety Bureau (ATSB) report concluded that two contributors to the crash were unauthorised low flying in an environment conducive to visual illusions and an inadequate level of supervision exercised over the conduct of flying training operations.

As all activities were then suspended pending inquiries, (and a whole change of culture and personnel), Kirsten was determined to finish her restricted private pilot licence, and moved her training to the Richmond RAAF base flying club. She sat her theory exams alone in a city building and passed her practical exam in a whole new environment, with a different aircraft and instructor. She grieved for all she had lost in those accidents just before Christmas 1990: her deceased friends, her social group, her flying, and the structure that brought it all together.

The following year she passed initial RAAF testing but learned she was too small to be a fighter pilot. Without a second option – she couldn't think past flying – she missed out on the RAAF altogether and so began a mechanical engineering degree at the University of New South Wales. She was one of eight women and 192 men doing the course. Mechanical engineering was not quite the thrill that flying had been, and Kirsten struggled to maintain focus. After failing a few subjects and feeling like she was on the wrong path, she transferred to a Bachelor of Science, majoring in meteorology to finish her education. She settled for a financially responsible business career, continued studies in this area and moved to Brisbane. She took another flying lesson in 2001 but because she was married by that time, the cost of flying didn't align well with the couple's financial strategy. They quietly separated.

'He was a lovely man', she says, 'and we're still on good terms. It's just that he wanted to settle down and I realised that I wanted to travel overseas and so at the age of 30 I became the oldest backpacker in the youth hostel, but I didn't mind'.

In early 2006, Kirsten arrived in London and began a nine-month backpacking trip through Europe where she learned about a program in Spain where native English speakers were hosted to tutor Spanish professionals in the language. Some locals, sensing her adventurous spirit, suggested she try 'parapente', but she didn't grasp what that meant. It got lost in translation.

However, a year later, back in London, she looked up 'parapente' and realised it meant paragliding, and found a Scottish couple running courses out of France. The sport was formalised by three French men in 1978 who, building on earlier groundwork around the world, launched the first paraglider. Para (chute) + pente (slope) = running down a slope and flying off it. Designs improved throughout the 1980s with the Swiss holding the first unofficial world paragliding championships in 1987.

In 2007, Kirsten boarded a plane at Gatwick Airport for Marseille and then drove a hire car to the tiny town of La Motte-du-Caire in the French Alps. It is 700 kilometres from Paris, midway between Lyon and Nice. It was so far off the beaten track that the publican wouldn't bother opening his little bar unless he was summonsed to do so.

For the seven-day course, the group started on the baby slope, learning how to handle the wing. They'd run for a bit until their feet lifted just lightly off the ground. They then went incrementally higher and launched for longer until they were flying maybe 20 metres high. Using the run-launch-land technique, they learned the most difficult of the necessary skillsets. It was all done solo and after a couple of days hiking up and down a hill carrying a paraglider, needless to say, everyone was quite worn out.

It certainly wasn't love at first flight, but she was keen to finish the course and so returned to the village later that summer. She was waiting for ideal conditions so she could learn to 'reverse launch' and to be able to launch from a greater height. Le Chabre, the launch site, was about 400 metres from the valley floor and to launch into that requires full confidence and competence. Students needed to learn how to use rising air, working in thermals, and turning in tight circles. Only when the instructor judges you ready, can you go on to the next stage. Students have to hope that the instructor's judgement, about whether they are competent enough yet to launch safely, is spot-on.

It's not the rising air that is dangerous, but the sharp edges of these columns of rising air that can drop the wing over it. And this is where Kirsten's training began to fall down. The weather never held long enough for her to consolidate the last skill: the required three reverse launches necessary to launch safely into stronger conditions. Therefore, she never got the final tick of approval in France, nor back in England where she spent the summer trying to coordinate an instructor with the notoriously bad British weather. The elusive final tick on her licence seemed like a small technicality given she'd done all the work.

Late in the season some course-mates convened a weekend in the middle of England to go paragliding. She spoke to the safety officer at the club and excitedly suited up. What came next shifted her perspective on training, qualifications, rules and safety forever after. It was her next unforgiving lesson.

Because she was only used to forward launching in gentle conditions, Kirsten used the same approach in a stronger updraft, but it quickly caught her wing, which was rising behind her and pulling her upwards and backwards. Caught by surprise, she dropped her brakes but was already being sucked back up the hill by the racing wind, which gained speed as it rose. To the horror of the onlookers, she was dragged across a one-metre-high drystone wall and into a barbed wire fence that snared to her harness. Her wing remained inflated and as she ascended about 10 or 20 metres, the fence, which now tethered her to the ground, reverberated all along its length. Kirsten kited down with a deadening thud and woke on the ground as her friends were calling emergency services.

Her back hurt. A helicopter came. Her elbow was broken, and she had four lonely, reflective days in hospital.

The British Hang Gliding and Paragliding Association politely enquired why she was flying unlicensed and then explained the risks to her personally and to them professionally. She carries this lifetime lesson with her, especially when she sees people not respecting the rules. Sometimes the consequences haven't been spelled out and she understands that there are times when 'You don't know what you don't know'.

By the end of the year her elbow had regained full movement, she was properly licensed and the long and exciting road home beckoned. The ensuing six-week African trip confirmed her love of paragliding.

TAKE FLIGHT

To emphasise the severity of how wrong things can go when a bad decision pairs with bad luck, I feel that it's important here to insert the story of Ewa (Eva) Wisnierska. While Kirsten was flying in Europe, Ewa, a European woman, had been flying in Australia earlier the same year. Though Kirsten has never met her, Ewa's astonishing story is now folklore, and drummed into paragliding students everywhere.

In the Australian summer of early 2007, Ewa was in northern NSW training for the World Paragliding Championships, flying with the German national team. Her group of four were the last to launch, but the weather was deteriorating. With a rush of blood, she succumbed to 'race-brain', where the urge to win the race clouds your better judgement, and she tried to catch the pilots in front of her. Moving towards each other was two towering cumulonimbus cells. These are rain clouds with billowing tops that are responsible for heavy downpours, usually associated with hail and extremely low temperatures. As the two cells moved towards each other, another cloud formed between them, and the white cotton clouds quickly turned into a deadly thunderstorm.

Ewa and a Chinese pilot were both sucked up into the storm clouds. He was struck by lightning soon after and died, but Ewa was spat out the top at 9946 metres (32 632 feet). Most airliners fly around 40 000 feet. The unconscious, frozen pilot circled up there for almost an hour. At minus 45 degrees, her body effectively shut down and she was frozen for that time. Her distraught teammates tried to phone her but got no signal. When she circled to the edge of the storm, she descended and then her wing collapsed, plummeting her at 200 kilometres per hour, before it miraculously reopened.

Ewa regained consciousness and control of her paraglider. She began a slow circling descent until she emerged beneath the cloud and could see the land. Never has a person been so pleased to see the New England Tablelands.

Purely on instinct, experience, and the will to survive, Ewa managed to approach, flare and land safely. The team tried desperately to call her again and were stunned when she answered the phone. From 60 kilometres away out the back of Barraba, she lay freezing in a sodden paddock, covered in bruises from being pelted by hailstones up to 15 centimetres in diameter. After retrieving her instruments, the story was pieced together. She was flying again within the week and the fascinating story is available as a documentary, *Miracle in the Storm*. It's a horror movie.

BY EARLY 2009 KIRSTEN WAS FLYING WITH THE LOCAL PARAgliders of Sydney's northern beaches. There she made new friends with whom she happily launched up and down the coast from hilltops and clifftops, always under an inflated wing and never with the shock of freefalling like the skydivers. She spent every minute either in the air or thinking about it. Inevitably, she began dating another pilot, who had started flying about 12 months earlier than she had. They chased the wind and lived and breathed the sport. She found, however, that she was always comparing herself to her partner as far as her flying went and that she was never 'flying her own day'. It made her feel that she was an average or below average pilot and when she suddenly found herself single after four years, she sought a different angle.

'I had to find some new friends and so I started doing competitions because I could then go away for a weekend, alone, but with a purpose. I spent the next few years doing lots of clinics and in conversation with more experienced pilots. I found I was better than I gave myself credit for and I started to get some strong competition results. My flying really took off once I stopped comparing myself to others. My greatest struggle, though, has always been my size.'

Paragliders classify wings from A to D. An A wing is an entry-level wing that flies more slowly and is easier to recover from collapses. And a D wing is for advanced-rated pilots. It is faster, but trickier to recover from collapses. It appears sleeker, with a wider span and a shorter distance between the leading and the trailing edge. They are generally designed for men, who weigh about a minimum of 80 kilograms on average. Kirsten weighs a mere 52 kilograms and so is not able to fly the bigger, more expert wings. It's like a reverse handicap. A very small pilot on a D can only compete with an average-sized pilot on the next size down so without making some safety-impacting changes, they have no hope against a guy at the top of his game.

There are only a few female paraglider pilots in Australia and so to run a competition with a women's class meant, back in 2014, it was always the same half-dozen women competing. Kari Ellis is an Australian world-class pilot and so when Kirsten was placed second on the podium next to her, she felt that she wasn't necessarily worthy of being there. In a bigger field of entrants, they would never have been in the same class.

There were many discussions between Kari, Kirsten, and an American pilot. Kari at one point didn't want to take part in the women's class as it felt like a participation trophy and Kirsten wrote an article arguing that creating a women's class sets the expectation that female pilots have a need for a handicap. Of Australia's 2500 paraglider pilots of any gender, around 80 turn up for a competition and, at her best, Kirsten has been ranked 24 nationally.

As paragliding became more important in her life, her boss finally said he could no longer fit her work schedule in with her flying schedule, and Kirsten become a contractor so she could manage her work/life balance better. She reckoned that she needed more 'life' in the equation, and so took a trip to Chelan in Washington State. The small tourist town at the edge of a glacial-fed lake is at the junction of the eastern Washington Desert and the 9000-foot Cascade Mountains and National Park. It also has a mighty canyon. The rest of the place is as flat as a concrete floor.

'If you were to dip the landscape upside-down in honey', says Kirsten, 'the first places the honey would drip from is where the trigger points are and the trigger points are the places where you find "lift". Flatlands flying has no such high points so you're looking for things that change the surface temperature, such as water. That's when it will trigger the air to rise. I'm looking for any slight deviation of ground, birds, dust devils or freshly ploughed fields. From the top of the launch, you need to catch enough thermals to give you height to cross the canyon and land in the flat fields. The river has carved out a big gorge and a big lake. It is quite a challenge to get across the canyon; however, the extremely fine dust easily whips up into a dust devil, making the unstable areas easy to see. On a low-pressure day, the landscape is alive with mini tornados'.

On her second trip to Chelan, Kirsten entered the US National Paragliding Championships. When her task was announced, she took one look at the 200-kilometre course and reeled in shock. No way could she fly that far! But a reassuring friend shifted her thinking. The flight tested every paragliding skill that she had. When parts of the course got so choppy that she doubted she could keep her wing open, she'd leave that space and the group of paragliders in it and fly alone. At the 80-kilometre mark she was running seriously low on height but refused to give up. It took an exhausting seven and a half hours with no break, but she made it to the end. It took another four and a half hours to be collected and three more hours before she got to bed, knowing now that she was only limited by her self-belief.

After this huge flight on the last day of the competition, Kirsten returned to launch for fun the following day. With her wing spread on the ground, she considered the cranky reputation of this new launch site and its unstable hot, dry air. She just wasn't feeling good about it and reckoned she'd had her fill of flying after a week of competition. She bunched up her wing and casually walked to a tree a few hundred metres back to repack it in the shade. She passed a local instructor who had spent the last week as part of the group.

'Not liking it?' he asked.

'Nah', she replied. 'Not feeling it today.'

'Good decision', he said.

Focused on folding away her gear, she then heard the distinctive sound of a flutter as the tension went out of a collapsed airborne wing followed by what she knew could only be a wing's leading edge slamming hard onto the ground. With a trembling hand, she nervously radioed a nearby colleague.

'Don't come down here', said the friend. 'Call 911 and tell them he's not breathing. He's not OK.'

Kirsten and the rest of the group visited the pilot's family to talk about his last moments. 'I think his family sought comfort from our visit, because they heard the truth from those of us that were there. To walk into a home where people are seriously grieving is the hardest thing ...' she trails off.

With two weeks to go on the tour, it wasn't a great trip, but having the fragility of life so clearly demonstrated again, she resolved firstly to always trust her gut and secondly to always keep her options open.

The following year her travels took her from Chelan to San Francisco and on to Boulder, Colorado, for a three-month work contract. Determined to make the most of her time, she flew Colorado extensively and quickly settled into a local social group. Boulder sits at the foothills in the lee of the mighty Rocky Mountains. The prevailing wind is from west to east and a look at the differential pressure between the two sides of the Rockies will indicate how much turbulence will occur in the lee. Every paragliding location requires a particular set of skills and Kirsten flew around the foothills of the Rockies and then worked her way back up into the distinctive monolithic snow-capped mountains.

'You're limited on how far you can go into that territory by your landing options. To explore the Rockies, you can fly into the high terrain, but you need plenty of height to glide back out. Part of the risk management is to keep an eye on landing options and to get out if the wind picks up. Anything over 10 knots and I'm concerned but if it gets to 15 knots, I've got a problem because I can't penetrate through. Because my vario synchs into an app on my phone, I can look back on my flight later.'

After three months of gazing from her desk to the huge sheer granite cliffs called the Flat Irons, flying conditions were right. The Flat Irons were difficult to access and required timing and an understanding of the way the air worked. As she flew over the Flat Irons, she whooped with delight in the air, took selfies and cruised on down the range to Colorado Springs.

Looking back on her time in North America, Kirsten marvels at the places and people she met through paragliding. She got to see the landscape from a bird's-eye view, or as a tourist of a different kind. It took her to places that she wouldn't have visited otherwise, like the time she launched from Pine Mountain in Oregon. She had to put down out in the boondocks, walk into a saloon and call her friends for a lift home. The cowboys at the bar were stunned at this woman who appeared in colourful leggings, carrying a parachute. Being so far from anywhere, they could only presume she had just dropped from the sky.

WHILE IN WASHINGTON STATE, KIRSTEN SPENT A WEEKEND IN an Airbnb 'tiny house'. These can be a shipping container, or a house on wheels or on skids. They're different from a granny flat, a garden shed or a caravan. They are catching on in Australia too, and there's now an Australian association. Kirsten was considering living in one; only three small excuses made her hesitate: she hates laundromats, she loves cooking, and she has a tonne of often-used sporting equipment.

TAKE FLIGHT

In Washington, she arrived late on a drizzling Friday night to check out the lay of the land: 'is a tiny house for me?' On first inspection it felt too small, but she soon settled into the space and loved its natural light and wood. In the owner, she found a like-minded soul: a professional woman who had never built before. She was sold. Back in Sydney, Kirsten digitised her music and books, disposed of those that she couldn't and put an ad on Facebook asking for the impossible: vacant land, a knowledgeable landlord, proximity to Bunnings, and tools. Wayne answered the call. He had land at his place in Dural, you could see Bunnings from the front gate, and he had already built two tiny houses. In December 2015, Kirsten arrived with a set of plans, a trailer, and a truckload of enthusiasm. She researched each step of the project and Wayne would appear and ask, 'What do you think you'll do today?' and she would reply and he'd follow up with, 'And how do you intend to do that?' and she'd reply and he'd usually say, 'Well, yes, you could do it like that or ... or this way'. He'd leave and she'd spend the day following his guidance.

For the next two years, construction progressed intermittently as Kirsten built and then travelled overseas to work and replenish her diminished savings. Her blog Lilliput Living has the details of the project.

Because she usually spent her summers in Bright flying, Kirsten was keen to move there, and her breakthrough came when a paragliding couple offered to rent her some land. In Bright, she found all the things she loved so much in Boulder: scenery, paragliding, mountain biking, hiking, and skiing. At Christmas 2017 she and her tiny house moved to Bright permanently. Hopefully, now life could be less about paying high rents and commuting to the city, and more about hobbies, starting with the flying.

The paragliding club at Bright has the perfect playground, with its full surround of mountains to launch from, a steady stream of tourists and adventurers, and beautiful launch and landing sites.

She worked from home on her contract work and flew when the weather was fine. Everything she needed, so it seemed, was at her fingertips. Her conscious decision to reshape her life brought a deep sense of satisfaction, along with fresh challenges in staying motivated to work in the isolation of a tiny house during the long cold winters. The upside is that she was physically and socially immersed in her hobby. But what she noticed one eye-opening weekend was some rampant sexism in this high-risk sport. She felt awkward being around these guys, like an outsider in her own world. Where were the women? 'It wasn't one incident, it was a broader observation based on many smaller incidents. An easy one to reference is the assumption that women on launch were retrieve drivers rather than pilots. The more time I devoted to paragliding, the more I saw some significant barriers to women in the sport.'

Based on her experiences, and her own understanding of how hobbled she was by flying only with men, in her first year at Bright she sourced funding to start Altitude with Attitude, a women's paragliding program. She invited female paragliders to Bright for a weekend of instruction and socialising. It was not a beginner's course, but rather a chance to hone skills and fly together. The results were outstanding.

'Flying without testosterone is a whole different experience. I'm happy to fly with men, but a group of women have a refreshing honesty about their experiences. When we land, we often talk about the quality of the flight; maybe we had a moment with an eagle or a moment when we were in the clouds, or a moment where the view at the top of the climb was amazing. The guys tended to focus on the technicalities like altitudes and speeds, whereas women want to know that too, but will also discuss the feeling of what they've just done, or the view, or the interaction with nature.'

Feedback was strong and positive, with one woman enjoying Kirsten's 'no coddling' style. She liked her calm, determined attitude and expectation that everyone in the group was capable and she felt that coming from a respected pilot like Kirsten, it boosted the group's confidence.

Following this success, more weekends followed at Lennox Head, Dubbo, Rainbow Beach, Corryong and back at Bright. Each weekend provided a different type of flying.

As an example, the flatlands flying at Dubbo requires a tow from either a boat or a car, as there is no hill to launch from. The photos appear to show an old farm ute tied to a paraglider pilot on foot at the end of a rope, but in fact there is a sophisticated winch involved that assists the driver to apply consistent and precise presure. In unskilled hands, this practice can be very dangerous and Kirsten is extremely particular about who she lets drive that ute, given they have her life in their hands. It's actually a tried and tested technique that takes precision and timing, with the ute beginning its roll to bring tension onto the winch rope. It then accelerates, creating a cloud of bright red dust as the pilot begins to run. After a few steps, the wing rises and the ute gathers speed, pulling the airborne pilot faster and forward up through the air, similar to a glider being towed behind a tug plane. It takes a good 1-kilometre straight run to execute, and when she sees the ute come to a stop, usually at a fence, she knows it's time to release from the winch rope, hoping to find some thermals to extend the flight. It is a fun and easy way to get up to 1000 metres without the aid of something to jump from. The women sleep in swags on a watermelon farm and spend a few days camping, flying, camping and flying.

From the French Alps to the Victorian High Country, this progression through paragliding has taken many twists and includes the disciplines of cross-country, coastal, mountain, flatlands, distance and vol biv.

One weekend, Kirsten joined a mixed group to a lake where they practised stall recovery. Towed for height behind a speedboat, the pilot intentionally collapses their wing and learns how to recover. The theory being that a forced landing on water makes less of an impact than it would on land. If the recovery doesn't go well, then a reserve chute can be deployed. The more high-performance the wing, the more challenging the recovery.

In challenging herself to compete with the men, Kirsten entered a competition that required her to use water as ballast to increase the weight, which means she can fly a larger wing that can glide faster and further. On launch, the weight shifted and threw her off balance and she damaged her ankle badly. Shortly after, an Australian friend was seriously injured in Pakistan. It was every paraglider's worst nightmare and required a king's ransom to cover the shortfall in his travel insurance. The details of the accident were chilling and together with another friend Kirsten started a GoFundMe campaign for what became one of the most high-profile accidents in the paragliding world. In 24 hours, they were able to raise more than $100 000 and he was repatriated to Australia but would never fly again. Kirsten vowed that it was time to again check her risk/reward balance.

She recalled the words of her earliest flying instructor, who said that aviation is not dangerous, but it is unforgiving. Every near-miss is a Get Out of Jail pass. It constantly brings you face-to-face with your vulnerability, while affording the most privileged of experiences.

By 2020, Kirsten was president of Australia's largest paragliding club (at Bright) and unsurprisingly, they had double the national average number of female members. She was a committee member of the state association but declined an invitation to join the national board.

The year began with Victoria's worst ever bushfires, which encroached on the surrounding hills. They were 30 kilometres from Bright, and by mid-January 30 000 visitors had fled the little tourist town. Kirsten went to stay with a friend and then had a month in

Sydney to escape the smoke. Bright was starting to suffer upon her return as businesses that had already been affected by the fires were then closed or restricted due to Covid.

Nobody knew how long the pandemic would last or what shape Covid would take. The Paragliding Club was sensitive to public perception and though it could be lumped in with any number of exercise options that were allowed, the committee decided unanimously to cease operations for the lockdown period. It caused a lot of flak and Kirsten struggled with the decision, which threw many people into disarray – particularly paragliding healthcare workers already stretched by events.

By November she stepped down, satisfied that she had led the club through a difficult period and could rest knowing that she had contributed enough. By the second lockdown in 2021, the club opted for a moderated approach that would help members interpret the rules and offered some guidelines. Kirsten got super-fit hiking up Mystic and thinking about how to reframe her flying. Rather than give it up, she stopped worrying about what everybody else was doing and settled on running her own race.

Post-Covid, Kirsten took up cleaning work to make ends meet and enjoyed the team but not the physicality of the work. Her neighbour invited her to consider upgrading her paragliding skills to include commercial tandem flights. His business is often asked for female pilots. It brought more fun than she anticipated. She particularly loves the transition for a new passenger who, on one hand, wants to go paragliding, but on the other hand is crippled at the thought of running off a hill. But when they do, the rewards can be huge. It's one of the few ways you can be intimately connected with another person while paragliding, and for Kirsten, asking permission to bank in a tight turn and be rewarded with squeals of laughter makes her realise how lucky she is to be able to give people this wonderful experience. Flying commercial tandem flights with complete strangers is a greater gift than she'd ever realised. She loves introducing new people to the sport and finds great satisfaction in sharing her love of paragliding with them.

One day she would love to fly Mont Blanc, the mountain range in the French–Italian and Swiss alps. With 11 huge 4000-metre summits to negotiate, it's sure to be the pinnacle of a long association with paragliding that joins Kirsten's ideals of freedom and connection to nature. She'd love to return to where it all began for her in the small French village in 2007.

That connection to nature is one of the biggest advantages of this type of flight, and Kirsten rates one of the best experiences as flying with the native Australian wedge-tailed eagles. It's hard to imagine being so close to these hefty birds, which can stand as high as a metre tall with a wingspan of 2.8 metres. Curious by nature, 'wedgies' will happily join the paragliders in a thermal. While searching for thermals, if Kirsten spots a wedgie, she'll head straight for it as the birds can quickly find the liftiest parts of the sky.

'Wedgies are mostly happy to join us in a thermal, so long as it's not mating season. To thermal with an eagle is to connect with an animal in a way that we humans rarely do. Finding thermals is a game – even the birds don't know exactly where they are – so to join in this game is a treat. I've thermalled wingtip to wingtip with an adult bird for three or four revolutions, eyeing each other to see if the circle needs to be tightened or widened to maximise our height. I've been so close that I can see the unique patterns on the individual wingtip feathers move as they feel for the strongest part of the core. And then, just as it feels like we are aligned, they can fly away and disappear into the horizon.'

Sometimes eagles can get cranky, and this is usually during the June to October mating season. A cranky eagle won't lazily appear looking for a lift. It comes like a stinging bee, starting as a dot in the sky that grows larger as it zeroes in. Sometimes it gives a cautionary territorial squawk. Occasionally Kirsten has missed the cues, only to feel something on her wing and look up to realise there is a problem. There is no competition: eagles are impatient and agile and will dive on and tear the wing with their large talons. It is best practice to return to earth and assess the damage. If you're lucky it will be a few holes the size of a five-cent piece that can be repaired with tape. More often though, you can fit your whole arm into the holes, which cost hundreds of dollars to have professionally repaired in Perth.

On first contact with an eagle in a new area, Kirsten feels a knot in her stomach. Is it friend or foe? It only takes a few seconds to work out and when it works out well, she will crank her wing around to join the bird in the best way she knows how. There is nothing else like it.

Sacha Dench flies her paramotor, specially designed for the Flight of the Swans expedition, over the remote Arctic tundra of northern Russia. *Photo by Dan Burton*

Sacha with her paramotor. She flew a similar machine from Arctic Russia, through western Europe to France and England following the path of the Bewick's swans on their migratory travels. *Photo by Conservation Without Borders*

Above Alida Soemawinata flies the AS350 Squirrel, taking tourists on a sunset scenic flight past Uluṟu, Northern Territory. Her first commercial pilot role was based at the Ayers Rock Airport. *Photo by Natalie Luescher*

Right Having upgraded her qualifications, Alida now flies the BO105 out of Miri in Sarawak, Malaysia, mostly doing aeromedical flights. She is seen here during the 2022 state election, when she transported ballot boxes, armed police and election officials to remote villages. *Photo supplied by Alida Soemawinata*

Wingsuiting is one of the most dangerous extreme sports. It demands perfect body control and balance while flying at speeds of around 200 km/h. It converts vertical freefall to horizontal flight until approaching the ground, when a parachute is deployed for landing. *Photo by Graeme Murray*

Heather Swan (top) and Glenn Singleman, having just launched on their record-breaking BASE jump from Meru Peak in the Indian Himalayas. From an altitude of 21 660 feet, they flew down a 2000-metre cliff face to land on a glacier. No woman has ever repeated the feat. *Photo supplied by Heather Swan*

Catherine Conway and her best friend, Rex, with the rudder from a 60-year-old high wing monoplane, the ES52 Kookaburra glider that she is restoring. The *Kookaburra* is an Australian two-seat trainer that was designed by Edmund Schneider, who emigrated after the Second World War and established a factory in Adelaide. *Photo by Kathy Mexted*

Tim Shirley runs Catherine's wing as the glider gains speed, launching behind the tow plane for a day of competition in the 2018 Australian Grand Prix at Horsham, Victoria. *Photo by Lynton Brown*

Catherine is towed up in the glider during competition in the 2018 Australian Grand Prix at Horsham, Victoria. *Photo by Lynton Brown*

Stefanie Walter climbs out of the open cockpit of a Stearman biplane and onto the top wing. *Photo by Mason Wing Walking Academy*

At the Mason Wing Walking Academy in Seattle, in the US, Stef undertook the one-day course and graduated with an open-air wing walk. Climbing to the top wing, she strapped herself in for a couple of loops, barrel rolls and hammerheads, and then did the same riding a javelin between the biplane's two left-hand wings.
Photo by Mason Wing Walking Academy

Stef's birdwoman costume consisted of 3-metre butterfly wings made of corflute and cellophane, attached to her backpack with wire. Her entry in Melbourne's Moomba Birdman Rally raised money for an animal welfare agency in Bendigo, Victoria. *Photo by* Bendigo Advertiser

Kirsten Seeto prepares for flight from Mystic, the 2200-foot mountain on the edge of Bright, Victoria. *Photo by Kathy Mexted*

Right At Rainbow Beach, Queensland, Kirsten runs across the sand before getting airborne to join the other women in the air at a women's fly-in she organised. *Photo by Molly McEwin*

Below Kirsten flying her paraglider in the Australian Alps over Mount Feathertop, Victoria. *Photo by Mathew Farrell*

At the Air Race Academy in the UK, students were tutored through the art of air racing around these 13-metre-high pylons. Emma McDonald was one of eight pilots worldwide who were accepted to undertake the training. *Photo supplied by Emma McDonald*

Emma with her passenger. In her first role as a commercial pilot, Emma flew the growly three-seat Ag Cat biplane, running joy flights around the Twelve Apostles on Victoria's Great Ocean Road. Emma knew about Ag Cats as the family owned one, which her father flew in his aerial application business. *Photo supplied by Emma McDonald*

At the 2023 Pacific Airshow Gold Coast Emma debuted her solo aerobatics display. Later in the day she performed with Matt Hall. She is seen here flying a mirror-image pass over the beach during a promotional shoot in the lead-up to that event. *Photo by Matt Hall Racing*

Jessica Johnston at her first speed skydiving competition in Moruya, New South Wales, where she earned a gold medal. *Photo by Steve Fitchett*

Jessica flying head down. *Photo by Debbie Murphy*

Krystal De Napoli uses her 8-inch Dobsonian telescope, which is easy to transport and use, yet strong enough to view remote galaxies, nebulae and star clusters. Some of these telescopes have been given to schools by the Scientists Taking Astronomy to Regional Schools (STARS) program. *Photos by Kathy Mexted*

After her mornings flying balloons in Myanmar, Donna Tasker spent the afternoons at the sewing machine stitching together her own balloon. Its pink, green, and light and dark blue patterns make for a striking image in the sky. *Photo by Michael Tasker*

Donna is elated as the balloon she made herself is inflated for the first time. The envelope was sewn together on a company repair sewing machine in Myanmar while she was working there. *Photo by Michael Tasker*

Donna inspects the inside of the envelope before launching for a joy flight with 20 passengers in Northam, Western Australia. *Photo by Kathy Mexted*

7

ON A ROLL

EMMA McDONALD, AEROBATIC PILOT

'She's doing an extraordinary and very dangerous job and there are few people in the world with this type of character.'

Sean D Tucker

TAKE FLIGHT

If 'flying' as a verb describes the action or process of moving through the air, Emma McDonald got some memorable early lessons. When her father strapped his first-born onto the clothesline at the age of three and gave it a heave-ho, the world spun past in a blur of trees and garden implements. It set her little pulse racing, and instilled the notion that being airborne was good fun. More than thirty years later she is still roaring around in circles, climbing and spiralling, spinning, and diving, and clenching every muscle against the *g*-force so she doesn't black out. Emma flies a Red Bull–branded ultra-high-performance aircraft in heart-stopping split-second technical manoeuvres. For the past few years, Australian airshow crowds have craned their necks skywards as her career has taken off.

Under the guidance of and in concert with Matt Hall, the 2019 Red Bull Air Race World Champion and former RAAF fighter pilot, she performs extraordinary aerobatic routines. She is a champion with skill and a down-to-earth nature, but it didn't happen by chance.

Emma was born into aviation on a mild autumn day in Orange, NSW, in 1990. Her father, Richard McDonald, was flying for Hazelton Airlines, before going back to aerial application (also known as crop dusting or simply 'ag'). He has no trouble recalling the day his daughter was born.

'I thought I could handle things, but it was a long day and then it got difficult. She was our first baby, and I was on tenterhooks. It [her birth] was very difficult to watch, and the baby screamed, but I think I screamed harder.' Her mother Cristina says, 'She looked at me as if to say, "I'm here and I'm ready to go". She was born for movement'. It wasn't long before the baby's strength and athleticism revealed themselves. She was fast and agile – a little tot who could get over the neighbour's fence in the time it takes to boil a kettle. She never wanted to be contained. As a three-year-old she introduced herself to the gymnastics teacher by climbing to the top of the ropes, pushing with her legs frog-style right up to the roof of the stadium and back again.

By the time she was five Emma was living in Victoria with her mother, and not far from the McDonald clan at Leongatha. While Richard's parents were farmers, they were also both private pilots. Richard and two of his three brothers, Joe and Mark (and later Emma's brother Peter), took up careers as aerial application pilots – an exacting occupation that requires razor-sharp reflexes and decision-making. For Emma, an outdoorsy kid, it was normal to be riding around on a motorbike with her uncles flying off small strips nearby in the verdant hillsides. She was as revved up as they were.

'She was a monkey!' says Richard. 'As soon as she had the strength to lift herself up, she'd ride around on my neck. One time she slipped straight off my shoulders, and I turned back to find her hanging from a branch she'd grabbed hold of. She loved me tipping her upside-down and swinging her around. She was incredible. For some reason she is hard-wired not to get motion sickness. She hung on to the clothesline and thought it was great fun.'

That athleticism saw her through to state and national level in athletics, swimming, and gymnastics. She worked at a riding school as a strapper in her early teens and enjoyed competing on horses as well. However, she couldn't wait for school holidays to spend time up north around the aeroplanes.

'Dad would come down and collect us in various aircraft. I could barely see over the dash in the early days, so I'd fly by looking at the instruments. Up in Warren, New South Wales, we'd go out to do paddock marking when Dad was night-spraying. It was always a great highlight. He always wanted to fly a jet so when a Russian MiG fighter training aircraft came up for sale, he bought it to do joy flights and perform at airshows. It was cool flying around in that when I was only ten. I worked as ground crew for him organising flight suits for passengers, sitting in on briefings, and doing ground signals as part of his pre-taxi routine, checking external flaps and air brakes. The MiG had a distinctive smell – I've only smelt it again in the World War Two Mustang at Matt Hall Racing (MHR) and it certainly brings back that early memory. It's a rigid metal smell, kind of like oil, kerosene, guns, ignition, and green war paint. There's no way to pretty it up.'

For her 16th birthday, Richard took her for a joy flight in the MiG. 'She was big enough to be strapped in safely to do aerobatics and old enough to understand the emergency procedures.' He let her take the controls and she flew around and got to do an aileron roll. This is when you push the control column to the side, so the aircraft rolls 360 degrees around its axis as it continues to fly forward. The fact that she never got sick or got headaches from the high-stress manoeuvres has stood her in good stead. Maybe it was being conditioned from such a young age that helped her care less about how she felt physically, and more about what she was doing.

'It was the most gorgeous-feeling aeroplane to roll. Even though I now fly one of the most high-performance aircraft in the world, the MiG's roll was smooth and light. You drove her where you wanted to go and she was there, but it was also a smooth graceful application with so much power in the same action. I thought I'd love to fly it for real one day, doing joy flights. It's decommissioned now and lives up at Raglan, Queensland, on static display. Dad starts it up for the Raglan Airshow and does a ground run show. I always wanted to do what Dad was doing – airline, ag, aerobatics. I didn't know what sort of job I would end up in, but I looked on it as an adventure of a massive undertaking.'

With a desire to go where Richard and the flying was, the pull north won out during Year 10. Her school science teacher in Victoria was sad to be losing his best student when Emma decided to finish her education up at Rockhampton. She left a room full of trophies and prize ribbons and said goodbye to her mother. '[Children are] not ours to keep, and it was the best thing for her, but it was the hardest thing to do. I knew her father was able to help if she decided to follow her dreams, and I would always be there cheering any of her endeavours. But it was hard to let her go.'

Aviation was right in front of her there and she was especially interested in a low-level career spraying and sowing crops. She readily admits, though, that she got distracted, took a different turn, and lost direction. Though she was a bit rebellious, Richard was pleased that at least she'd veered away from the difficult life flying ag. Instead, she went out into the 'big bad world' to try her hand at many other things. She worked in succession and sometimes simultaneously as a veterinary nurse, air conditioner installer, bar waitress, school run driver, and a racehorse strapper and trainer. Predictably, she quickly burned out, but on the way, she found and loved pole fitness. The sheer athleticism appealed to Emma and before long she was teaching the sport and was offered a franchise for a Rockhampton studio. Despite his concern for where this might lead, Richard found himself forking out for a pole so she could practise. It was a strange Christmas present to be handing over, he felt. Under her guidance, though, while she was still working for the vet and the stables, the studio flourished and in the years that she owned it, won three business awards.

Her other career break came in the junk mail. She loved knowing how things worked and had explored a career as a Licensed Aircraft Maintenance Engineer (LAME) but the opportunities were all based too far from Rockhampton. Among the unsolicited mail, she found an advertisement for diesel fitters and applied for an apprenticeship. It was a satisfactory alternative to being a LAME, and in a class of twelve people, Emma was the only woman. She laughs now at her boss, who singled her out on the floor and told her she didn't belong there and he doubted she could pull her weight. He later admitted his mistake, because she thrived on learning to work on anything from little bobcats through to large mining machinery. Everything about the place was exciting – the sound of engines starting up, learning how they produced power and how they worked mechanically, including the hydraulic and electric systems. And on a roll, she opened a second pole fitness studio.

There is no end of explaining this sport to a sceptical public, but the tide of opinion shifted in 2010 after Emma and two friends – Michelle Hefner, a boilermaker from Mackay, and Kim McGowan, a graphic designer from Brisbane – made it to the finals of *Australia's Got Talent*. This reality TV show takes all comers, from singers to musicians and magicians, but by the judges' reactions this was the first time they'd hosted pole fitness performers.

Pure Pole Angels blew it out of the water. In midriff tops and exercise briefs, Emma and the girls wrapped their calf-length boots around a pole for a jaw-dropping display of agility, strength, and fitness. Judge Dannii Minogue talked about the difficulty of the sport after trying it herself. 'So hard, you have no idea', she claimed, and enthused that she would book these girls as a warm-up act for any major concert. 'I've got so much admiration for you, and yay for the sport of pole dancing.' They'd helped turn it into a widely recognised sport.

Used to her hi-vis yellow work shirts and safety glasses, Emma's colleagues saw her in a surprising new light and commented on Monday, 'Nice abs!' as they commended her sheer strength and skill. Her studio business took off, with people of all shapes and sizes wanting to improve their fitness and strength. Her parents were proud of her work ethic, and the studio ran well, rejecting any 'creepy observers'.

At the engineering works, she finished her apprenticeship a year early and won local Apprentice of the Year. Her boss conceded that he had judged her wrong and congratulated her. 'Good job', he said. They remain firm friends.

Eventually, while competing nationally and working from one corner of Queensland to the other as a mobile mechanic, injuries slowed her up on both fronts. As she nursed a sore shoulder from the office, the flying dream reignited. It was an expensive proposition, and the shift would require large sacrifices. After a couple of false starts, she realised it would take all her time, energy, and cash if that was to be her next move. Sadly, her partner of seven years felt she was wasting her hard-fought career on the tools to pursue an aviation pipedream. It can be hard to see the benefits of flying at that early standpoint. She got serious about her ambition and started her journey having sold the studios, and as a single woman in her mid-twenties. The future was beckoning. She hoped for a career that was bigger than simply flying from A to B. 'I didn't know what it would look like. I had always wanted to do aerobatics as a job and I applied to the RAAF to fly fighter jets, but they'd offer me anything but. I had to wait another six months to re-sit the entry exam but by then I'd have been too old to be accepted.'

With all these swirling thoughts, Emma stood with her dad in May 2016 at the Raglan Airshow. She had just achieved her private licence and flown in some friends. They watched Matt Hall throw his Extra 300L around the sky in a precursor to his second place in the Red Bull Air Race Championships that year. She turned to Richard and said, 'I want to do what he does for a job. That's what I want to do with my career as a pilot. How can I get to do that?'

Well, thankfully it wasn't ag flying, but was it any safer or easier? Richard thought carefully, knowing it was not impossible, but only a meagre few get to do it. 'It's a lot of hard work, time, effort, and money – but not impossible.'

At the end of the day, Emma and some of her students performed a pole expo. Feeling relaxed after a day of flying, Matt commented to Richard about this unique performance, but was surprised to learn that it was his daughter. 'There was serious strength there, and I knew I wouldn't have a tenth of the strength that they had', says Matt. 'Richard asked me to talk to her about joining the RAAF and I still remember that she turned up at the plane and was staring me down with a disturbing intensity. I couldn't work out if she was angry or intent or absolutely focused. I gave her about 20 minutes of my time and she asked some very pointed questions [about both the RAAF and air racing]. I gave her a big long list, because I get asked this question a lot.'

Emma made careful notes. She'd need a commercial licence and then as many endorsements (extra training qualifications) as she could get: tailwheel, aerobatic, retractable, constant speed unit, pressurisation, turbine, instruments and more. He stressed that she also had to invest in her physical and mental health. Physical fitness was paramount and should be maintained and developed to ensure she could handle all the stress, fatigue and professional growth that would come with the plan. Mentally, she'd need a positive outlook, a supportive group of people around her, and a set plan with stepping stones towards her ultimate dream job. She clung to that list and, though she doubted she'd ever get to experience half the life Matt had, she started working through it. After completing her tailwheel endorsement a few months later, word came through that some Victorians needed a driver for their growly three-seat Ag Cat biplane. They ran joy flights off the state's southern coast. Emma knew about Ag Cats as the family owned one, which her father flew in his aerial application business. But Emma had not flown it. And she knew the Victorians, because they were close family friends. With a brand-new commercial licence and tailwheel and turbine endorsements, she sent off her thin résumé and was lucky enough to get the job.

As spring 2017 crept in, she installed herself in a granny flat at the Peterborough Airfield and got to work, flying tourists around the Twelve Apostles at 500 feet with the wind in her hair, the salt on her face, and a thumping radial engine making it possible. It was her first paid job, and she was extremely grateful for it. Her boss, Paul (Woof) Steinberg, says, 'I know the McDonalds, and I know Emma. I knew she was capable of doing the job and she didn't disappoint us. The aeroplane always came back in one piece – we get some hairy crosswinds on the home strip – and she was handy mechanically in the hangar. Sometimes the passengers would be surprised to see a young woman flying the plane, but nothing untoward.'

By season's end she was already planning for the following summer, when she would bring back a 1950s Chinese training aircraft, a Nanchang, and run the two operations in parallel, using the Nanchang for aerobatic joy flights. Still working through Matt's list, over the winter downtime she went to Cowra to flight instructor Lyn Gray's flying school, Fly Oz, and completed her two-week instrument rating (learning how to fly on the aircraft's instruments for use in inclement weather). Lyn was featured in *Australian Women Pilots*. When one of her fellow students said his mate needed a pilot/ground crew, Emma replied that she was committed to her next season at the Twelve Apostles. He pressed the point and revealed that his mate was Matt Hall, and Emma's eyes popped. 'Oh no!' she said, stunned. 'He wouldn't want me because I've got so few hours and have no military training. I'm probably not ready or in a position to apply for that job', she blurted. 'No, I think you'd be perfectly suited', he replied. If she didn't get the job, then she'd lost nothing. If she did get the job ... wow! It took confidence to submit the application and it was probably the first time she doubted her ability. At the online interview Matt recognised her. 'I reminded him of the Raglan Airshow and pulled out the list with the (so far) ticked-off items. He was blown away because he gets so many people asking him how to do it, but nobody had ever come back to show that they'd done it. I asked if there would ever be an opportunity to possibly fly the Extra, because I knew he only employed military guys to fly it on the joy flights. He replied that it was generally his turf, but that nothing was impossible. "That's not a no", I thought, so I knew there was the slightest chance of doing that and that is where my dream was. I was searching for that opportunity. I rang Woof and told him about the interview, and he said, "just don't forget about us little people". He knew these chances don't come along often and he said, "you've got to take these opportunities when they arise and you know you can always start your own business somewhere if you want to", and so with that blessing I packed my whole life again and moved to Lake Macquarie, New South Wales.' The little people, Emma jokes, are anything but. They are the important people who gave her a start in the industry. She was extremely thankful for the opportunity they had given her; that difficult first job.

Her XR8 ute pulled up at Lake Macquarie with a dirt bike in the back and her worldly possessions around it. She started work the next day. It was a jam-packed week and in the first couple of days she went for a fly in the Extra. 'Kenny Love from the Instrument Rating course in Cowra was there in his little two-seat Piper Cub. We took off [with Emma as a passenger] in the Extra and flew in formation with Kenny, and then we went off and did some aerobatics. The Extra is super-responsive. The whole point was to go for a fly so I could sell the product with confidence. It was an amazing moment. I finally got to meet Matt in person, who spelled out his expectations. He was impressed that I'd stuck to my guns and made my own way. It was cool to come full circle from seeing him two years beforehand at Raglan, to then working with him. It's not a normal pathway – actually, there is no pathway designed for pilots to become airshow pilots.'

Emma threw herself into the job and spent a couple of years proving her enthusiasm to fly anything. She began flying the six-seat Piper PA-39 Twin Comanche, as MHR contracted to 'Wings4Kidz', a not-for-profit group that fly sick children from rural and regional areas to major centres for medical treatment. She fell in love with this aspect of her job, which was no surprise to her parents. They both understand her affinity for kindness, especially towards kids, and for saving lost animals. 'She never shied away from rescuing things', says Richard. She naturally got to know many patients and families well.

It was a fulfilling and grounding counterbalance to the 'selfish fun' she was having in the other part of the job.

'Wings4Kidz has always been extraordinary to me, and a privilege to use my flying skills to help somebody. I didn't know it was something I could do for a job. We work with critically ill children, one of whom was a little jaundiced baby, Ayla Allan. While she was waiting for a liver transplant, we flew her to Sydney for specialist treatment. There is no way her mum could disappear for a few days and leave the other three children at home, so this way we have them back home the same night. Ayla has had some close calls, but miraculously has made such great progress that she is living like a normal kid. It's so fantastic to see. She's a full-on six-year-old little disco diva now and flies up the back with her sparkle handbag and massive diva glasses. She sits on the seat looking out the window like a rock star. She calls me Emma Wiggle. I've known them for the entire length of her treatment.'

Ayla's mother Dannielle reinforces the sentiment. 'Emma Wiggle is her name here in our house and Ayla really loves it when we have "her Emma Wiggle" as our pilot. My husband Brett is a miner and I became a "stay-at-home-mum" in Cobar looking after our sick baby, who spent most of her time in hospital. She is almost seven and still enjoying Year 1 at school, but still is a very sick little girl. This is a forever thing for her. She had two liver transplants when she was two-and-a-half; the first one failed in surgery and the second one shortly after had lots of complications, but she takes it all in her stride and smiles though it all. Without pilots like Emma flying us to and from Sydney, we would spend days in the car, but instead we were there and back in hours. It made a huge difference. Ayla would say, "Yes! It's my Emma Wiggle", when she flew with her. They have a very strong connection.'

While flying Wings4Kidz as a solo pilot at least weekly, Emma quickly found it too hard to keep up with both the office work and the joy flight operations and so another staff member was employed, and Emma quickly became a full-time pilot. She moved on to the King Air, a ten-seater turbine aircraft that flies at almost half the speed again of the Twin Comanche. Flying corporate charter clients around the country, she also took on the role of MHR Operations Manager – a coveted job. She was finally earning a great wage and edging towards her dream – to fly the MXS as an airshow performer, and as an air racer.

The hard work didn't go unnoticed and when she was asked if she'd like to do aerobatic training in the Extra, and finally in the MXS, one of the Red Bull race planes, which is what Matt now uses for his high-intensity displays, Emma was all in.

'I had previously done formation displays in 2018 with another pilot', says Matt. 'I've done flying displays with Air Force mates; however, as we now have the planes that we've got, we can do a very unique display. Leading a formation with a wide-open throttle is unique. I've always known it could be special, but it is hard to work up a display that is reliable. As we developed Emma as an aerobatic pilot, she wanted to fly formation. We built a display to fit her style and level, and then I jumped on the wing, and we started training.'

The MXS single-seat race plane is a high-performance and very sensitive aircraft. Emma knows that it's a huge privilege to be trusted with it. She started training for aerobatic competitions and performing with Matt at airshows across the country. She also travelled as part of the team that year when Matt won the 2019 Red Bull Air Race championship. She was well positioned to follow distantly in his footsteps, hoping to enter the air race circuit within a few years.

Then Covid hit, and in the same breath corporate interest waned in the expensive event and the air races were cancelled for the foreseeable future with a question mark over their viability.

'Covid was a complete show stopper. Every part of MHR (except for charter flights) ceased. There were no keynote talks, no events, and no air racing. These were all the main income. It was a formidable time to try and run a business. Matt kept us all employed and eventually used his own savings, not knowing when it would end. There were seven of us and that kind of outlay will sink you as a small aviation company. Initially we were considered essential services on the charter front and that work picked up, but then Queensland locked down the borders, then Victoria, and then we were grounded. All the bookings disappeared, and charter ceased to exist. It was sudden death. As the charter flying bled off, we wondered if this would ever end and what business would look like in six months' time. The constant opening and closing were like a yo-yo and the mental strain on everybody was huge. Matt was incredibly positive for most of it, but sometimes you'd see little holes. He eventually banned television as the constant news loops were so depressing. We decided to keep things positive, and the team met weekly to formulate income-producing ideas. At one point I remember he was just looking out the window and said, "I don't know how to navigate this much longer. I'm going to do my best as long as I can, but the money will run out at some stage". Us employees were happy to go on leave, or partial leave to help.'

Matt churned through all the money he earned from racing, in 18 months of lockdown. 'It all went back out the window paying bills and wages to keep the business open. I reckoned that if people were loyal enough to stick with me, then I'd be loyal enough to pay their wages. I couldn't have them not pay their mortgage.' It was down to the wire, though, by the time business was allowed to reopen. A fortnight later it would have been a different story.

While Covid continued to close almost everything down, a new Air Race Academy at Sywell in England started up. Emma didn't think she had quite enough training to race yet; however, the old voice of reason kicked in – believe in yourself and apply. The in-depth application included a video submission. Having MHR backing helped. Both Emma and her colleague Kris Sieczkowski, a RAAF fighter and aerobatics pilot, did a month of training with Matt, learning about air racing. It was an intense period, but they were accepted, along with another six applicants from a world-wide pool of submissions.

At Sywell, they stayed on the aerodrome in the Airport Hotel, an art deco building that was formerly a clubhouse and officer's mess from the 1930s. It was totally decked out with wartime aviation paraphernalia, and the staff dressed in themed outfits. A glass wall in the bar overlooked the aerodrome. Emma's mind was spinning, not only from the place, but the buzz of what she was about to do. She joined another couple of women on the course, Alice Junker from France, who is placed in the international aerobatic championships, and Melissa Burnes, who is on the American team. When training began, Emma was with Klaus Schrodt, who is a celebrated aerobatic coach and air race pilot. She also trained with Steve Jones and Ben Murphy, who are the main judges and part of the Blades, a British civil aerobatic team.

The course went through the process of who flies when, and then a walk around the pylons as the races are flown in a circular pattern around 25-metre-high inflated pylons. There is a process of learning how to inflate and deflate them, and importantly, how to get one off your wing if you hit it, because the material sticks to the aircraft. (It's pretty much a tail slide – which involves pulling the aeroplane straight up so that it flies vertically until it runs out of momentum, and then slides back down tail-first.) As the track was laid out on an airfield, they had to learn how to manage an engine failure and conduct a landing. That involves zooming as high as possible and then gliding back to the ground, rolling out and treating the aeroplane as though it has a dead engine. This is never really practised in Australia as we usually push the throttle in and do a go-around at the last moment. (Abort the landing by applying power before the aeroplane touches the runway and go around for another circuit.) There was also a component on professionalism and how to talk to the media. Emma's presentation was on hydration and the effects of *g*-force. She was judged on how she spoke and how much information she could understand and convey. There was a practice media interview that tested how she could respond to on-the-spot questioning. She has a special interest in health and fitness because they have always been so important for her high-energy activities. 'When I'm training for racing, the hardest thing is not to get too fit, because then your *g* tolerances reduce due to a lower heart rate and blood pressure. I do a specially formulated routine of 45-second reps with 15-second intervals. I try to have a smoothie in the morning – berries, spinach, and banana – and omelettes, fruit and veg and a variety of meats. I love red meat.'

With her head still spinning after the course, Emma found work in a local hangar with Richard Grace. His Australian mother Carolyn flew the Grace Spitfire, a restoration project begun by her husband. After his early death, Carolyn took on the monumental task of learning to master the Spitfire, which she did, and flew more than 900 hours doing joy flights, aerobatics, and formation exhibitions. When her then four-year-old son Richard grew up, he took over the family restoration business and employed Emma for six weeks until the Australian borders reopened. She finished the most incredible experiences of her life so far, and with a full heart flew home to Australia, where the shine went right out of things.

The country was in chaos due to Covid and Emma had to spend two weeks isolated in quarantine. It was a long fortnight for the former kid who couldn't stand containment. When she was finally allowed out, she returned to Lake Macquarie and prepared for the next round of air races, due to be held there the following year. When they were cancelled due to a lack of sponsorship, she turned her attention to aerial displays. She had just finished her formation rating and Matt reckoned they could do something with it. They came up with a routine, which they debuted at the 2022 Raglan Airshow. Emma was flying the aircraft she'd watched Matt fly six years previously. She was proud. She had come full circle, from saying to her father that she'd love to do this, to then be flying off Matt's wingtip. On the ground, her family and friends watched with excitement, especially remembering those who doubted and discouraged her at the beginning. 'You're wasting your time', they said. But here she was, and she worked hard to improve and create new, unique, and 'quite cool' routines. Some of these routines are an extension of precision military manoeuvres Matt performed in the RAAF. It's impressive stuff.

'One of our latest routines has us rolling inverted together. Matt doesn't change positions. He'll roll with me at the same time. I'll pop the nose (a tiny quick lift of the aircraft nose) and we're both inverted in the same position. That transition is rare and only performed by the US Navy's Blue Angels and the US Air Force's Thunderbirds. We also do an opposite rolling pass, where I fly straight in a corkscrew roll, while Matt flies around me rolling in the opposite direction. Normally when this is performed, the leader is inverted; however, I'm actually rolling at the same time and setting the height. Matt is slightly behind me looking forward. I'm amazed at how he manages to maintain separation and spacing.'

Even the uninitiated can't ignore the thrilling spectacle of a dual tumble, where the two planes fly side by side vertically. Straight up! When the aeroplane runs out of ability to climb any higher, Emma kicks on her left rudder for a stall turn and points the Extra earthwards, trailing smoke so the crowd can see how dangerously close, but carefully spaced the pair are as they roar towards the ground and then at the crowd. The aim is to create something new and different and their Derry Roll Cross Turn, which comes next, both delights and shocks the viewers. It looks as though they're side by side; however, Matt is slowing down so they are staggered. Then they create an optical illusion by rolling to the outside, so it looks as though they're going to roll away from each other, but 75 per cent of the way through the roll, they reverse direction and cross paths with a synchronised tumble away in opposite directions. It is over before the crowd can register and think, 'Oh! Did something bad just happen?' In that turn they are pulling about 7 or 8*g*; that is, 7 or 8 times the gravitation force on their bodies. To the uninitiated, not expecting to be in this situation, most will black out between 4 and 6*g*. Somebody at the peak of their performance fitness level with the right aids can possibly sustain 12–14*g*. Emma is flying full throttle at about 180–200 knots. Matt keeps pace in the race plane as it can fly faster. It's enough to give the average person a headache; however, Emma has never suffered from doing aerobatics as she was conditioned early, flying around in the agricultural aeroplanes with her family, where the extreme manoeuvres could pull around 3 or 4*g*. When Richard pulled the MiG into a roll, it pulled 6*g* sustained. All part of the experience!

To maintain consciousness at these speeds a person must take a big breath and squeeze their calf, thigh, and core muscles, together with their jaw and teeth, to hold the blood in place. Matt pulls some funny faces which force his face to go red, but it stops the blood being pulled from his head. Emma is less dramatic in her moves but she did pack a punch big enough to impress one of the military bigwigs with her debut solo on a trade day at the 2023 Avalon International Airshow, just outside of Melbourne. He and his colleagues were impressed with the type of flying and recognised the military moves worked into the routine. Angela Stevenson is an airshow commentator, and she watched the performance also. 'It was simply a joy – her clean lines and immaculately timed manoeuvres demonstrated a connection to the aircraft in flight that's difficult to explain, but you know it when you see it – the plane and pilot are just working it together. She has such a calm, decisive demeanour, both in the plane, pulling it through all those *g*'s, and on the ground.'

Down on the ground Cristina, who never tires of watching her daughter fly, listened as the crowd went 'Woah!' and then erupted when the pair of pilots got out of their aeroplanes to sign autographs. A little girl nearby said, 'Mummy, Daddy, I want to be like her'.

Six months later, Emma made her grand entrance with a solo aerobatic routine at the Pacific Airshow Gold Coast in Queensland. The 'stage' was a one-square-kilometre performance box in the sky, and the audience on the beach below was 100 000 strong. As the announcer, Matt Jolley, urged the crowd, 'Please welcome EMMA McDONALD', loudspeakers blasted the thumping rock beat of AC/DC's 'Jailbreak'. The royal blue Extra 300L ripped in from the south and Emma pulled it up and rolled vertically skyward before it ran out of airspeed. Hanging on its propeller, the aeroplane momentarily slid back, as though on a thread, before rolling forward and with a blast of smoke spun nose-first towards the ground and repositioned into a backwards loop. She did a neat half-turn towards the sun and pulled over backwards for another pass before the crowd. For six minutes, the only thing showing beneath her oversized black reflective visor was the occasional smile on a concentrated face and blonde hair falling in the direction of the earth, no matter the orientation of the aeroplane. On the beach a young fan watched eagerly. She'd waited in vain for an hour the day before to get her poster signed and lined up at the autograph stand again for another almost three hours the following day. When Emma finished her shut-down routine at the airstrip, she returned to the beach, went straight to the stand, and found her young fan. The treasured 'Emma McDonald' signed poster is now on 15-year-old Millie's bedroom wall and she is considering joining the Sunshine Coast Airforce Cadets. Such is the power of a role model. One of Emma's own role models is Sean Tucker, who is America's favourite aerobatic pilot and an Aviation Hall of Fame inductee. He enthusiastically complimented Emma on her solo performance and acknowledged her potential. Stick with it, he told her.

They met again soon after in California for the Pacific Airshow at Huntington Beach. 'I had to do a US commercial licence conversion test and a low-level endorsement that would allow me to fly down to 250 feet, which I asked Sean to approve. He was impressed enough to do that, and he expected that next year he'd be clearing me to fly down to ground level. It was an amazing opportunity to stay with him and get to know him. It was a wonderful welcome to the US.'

To put that in context, Sean has been flying aerobatics and airshows for more than 40 years. He has been named a living legend, and his specially built competition aeroplane is now next to Wilbur and Orville Wright's historic flying machine in the Smithsonian Institute in Washington, DC. For anybody else it would be like meeting Elvis.

Buoyed by all this American enthusiasm, Emma hooked into the flying, but it started with a bang when she hit a bird and broke her borrowed aeroplane. Chuck Coleman had lent her his aeroplane for the performances. She and Matt were practising about 300 feet off the ground in typical fashion – fast and inverted and in formation. Without warning, Emma collided with a 'massive seagull thing'. Oh shite! 'It's lucky I didn't have an engine failure and drive Matt and myself into the ground.' In the following critical 30 seconds, she drew on her training and got upright and as high as possible. The bird had smashed in half of the front engine cowl. She had to check whether it had taken out an oil line, or a fuel line, or if she was about to catch on fire because the bird was burning. Even though she could smell it caught under the cowl, it didn't cause any of the above problems and thankfully Emma was able to land safely. It was a massive disappointment after all the effort that had gone into flying halfway across the country to collect the two aeroplanes.

TAKE FLIGHT

'I saw a very large explosion of stuff', says Matt. 'I started to ease away, but Emma pushed up and rolled away from me, so I went with her. She did a climbing left-hand turn. I told her to leave everything set, keep climbing and get as much height as possible while we figure out what's going to happen from here. We got her steered back towards the airfield. I moved closer and had a look. I couldn't see any obvious damage, but that's because I couldn't see the front of the cowl through the prop arc. I've had many close calls in flying: dodged a missile in the F-15 in Iraq, taken a bird down the side of an F-15 and ripped a hole in the fuel tank; I've hit birds in the canopy of the FA-18, and I hit the water in one of the Red Bull races. If you do extreme flying for long enough, operating on the edge, you accept the risks. For me it was another event, but for Emma it was a bigger event because she doesn't have my level of experience, yet she showed incredible maturity. It could easily have been a mid-air collision if she'd panicked or lost awareness.'

'I was completely convinced I'd be grounded, and that Matt would have to perform solo. Sean walked over and said, "Oh man, that sucks. We'd better get my aeroplane out of the shed. It's having its annual inspection".'

Sean knew that Emma had spent thousands of dollars on licences and expenses to be there and he didn't want to see her have to pull out because 'a dumb-arse bird got in the way'. The engineers were set to double-time, then Sean tested it and handed over the keys.

'It would have been selfish of me to withhold my aircraft because I was worried about another bird strike – I'd be doing a disservice to the industry', says Sean. 'We could have patched the other one together, but you must do the right thing. I've been in the airshow industry for my whole career. I believe that we need women like Emma who are fierce and strong of conviction. She's in it for the right reasons – not for the accolades. Her family fly crop dusters. They get up every day betting on their skills. It's dangerous work (both crop dusting and airshows) and her most important strength is her reverence for what she is doing, her unbridled joy, willingness to face her fear and push herself, while knowing who to trust. She's doing an extraordinary and very dangerous job and there are few people in the world with this type of character. You have to be intuitively connected to the machine, and 100 per cent laser-focused on the moment. She was under a lot of pressure at the Gold Coast show, but it helped make her, and set her provenance. She was about to top off her year by headlining at the biggest and best show in America.'

Millions of people watched the performances.

The three-day Pacific Airshow at Huntington Beach was an unfathomable experience, joining the line-up of US military Thunderbirds, Navy parachute team, F-22 Raptor, Navy's Growler and Super Hornet, Mustang, B-52s, helicopters, fire bombers and other legendary performers over a one-mile stretch of Californian beach. It was packed with party-goers who enjoyed live musical festivals in front of them, a boat race around them, skydivers above them, and rip-roaring aerobatics that 'make you turn your head and scratch it at the same time'. Hopefully at least a few of the punters having a piña colada on the beach will take inspiration from her pursuit of excellence. As their reputation grows, the MHR team plan to immerse themselves in the biggest airshows where they can reach the highest number of people. And hopefully soon the air races will return, either to Reno in the US, or to Australia, so Emma can get her go at the ultimate dream.

At the airshow at Raglan (population 146), an event held in a paddock at the Old Station, Emma found the spark that lit the fire, set years before by her father. She had headed off on a General Aviation track, but changed tack when she got that important list – a concrete set of challenges to throw herself into as surely as she had to everything else. Matt places her determination and proactive approach to self-development as among the best in the field. 'I know and have worked with a lot of talented people, from chiefs of various air forces to world champions, and she has the same type of drive.'

It's hard to imagine her anywhere else now but drawing 300 horsepower circles in the air at more than 400 kilometres per hour. Such is his faith in her career, Sean concludes with, 'I will loan her my aeroplane again next year. Let her read that in the draft of this story'.

'I'll take that!' Emma says excitedly.

In a prelude to the return of any big air race meets, with the onerous cost of transporting crews and gear around the world, a group of Red Bull pilots have created Air Race X. Pilots with the world's best flying skills compete remotely around a physical race course that is set up at their home base, and mirrored globally using Virtual Reality technology. Each pilot effectively flies the same race around virtual pylons with sensors mounted on their aircraft that collect precise flight data. In the first round in May 2024, Emma was placed fifth out of a field of eight. There was a mere three seconds between first and eighth place.

8

HEAD DOWN, FAST AS YOU CAN

JESSICA JOHNSTON, SPEED SKYDIVER

'Skydiving has brought me self-awareness.
I'm trying to be the best version of myself.'

Jessica Johnston

TAKE FLIGHT

The navy and white Aermacchi AL-60 Atlas Angel aircraft climbs through a smattering of puffy clouds into an azure African sky. Up around 12 000 feet, its self-loading cargo makes an orderly departure out the skydiving door. Jessica Johnston, sick with nerves and dressed in a jungle character onesie, joins the group in doing Horny Gorillas with a few mates. She is a cheetah, and her friends are a tiger and a lion. The language of the skydivers is as unique as their pastime and the outfits on this day are for a bit of fun. Horny Gorillas is an entry-level move into the serious business of formation skydiving, where teams perform complicated manoeuvres in larger groups. Their circular patterns in the sky are kaleidoscopic. For Horny Gorillas, the routine is to exit the aircraft together with linked legs and/or feet. In this configuration, the aerodynamics cause the group to fall semi-upright, so they're effectively sitting in a circle. Once they're established, they then lean back and beat their chests ... like gorillas. If it doesn't work out, Jess's group will abandon the idea and simply come together and hold hands, before peeling away to pull their parachutes at 5000 feet above the ground. This leaves ample time to slow down from 200 kilometres per hour to a more manageable speed for landing safely. It takes about 500 feet for the chute to deploy and the deceleration to begin. From there, the muted green plains around Rustenburg (near Pretoria, the capital of South Africa) splay out below. This is Jess's mother country. The land of her birth is foreign to her now, on her first trip back after growing up in Australia. Down below, the roads and tracks around the town of Rustenburg are laid out in an orderly grid at odds with the chaos of earthly life. It is March 2016, and the 32-year-old has been in the sport for just over a year. She is joyous beyond words and totally focused on the moment.

Back inside the Angel later that day Hendri Liebenberg, dressed in a wingsuit, gives the 'clenched fist with thumb and little finger up' shaka sign adopted by popular culture to mean 'hang loose' or 'good vibes'. His broad smile is at odds with how many people would feel about jumping from a plane in a wingsuit. The aircraft's passenger seats have been removed for a skydive configuration and Jess is kneeling on the floor between Hendri and Barend Pretorius, who has a helmet mounted camera; the bouncy footage adds an extra urgency to the frantic wind-slapping of the wingsuit's synthetic fabric. Jess gives a broad laugh and makes the same gesture with both her hands, turning her helmeted head to include the cameraman in the fun. Her mouth, dry from nerves, is appeased with chewing gum.

The Angel maintains a steady airspeed and direction, and before anybody jumps out, the pilot locks the brake on the wheels. Hendri steps carefully onto the stabilised left tyre. Appropriately, a large outline of an angel's wing is painted on the underside of the aircraft's high wing, but Hendri is not looking up. He steadies his left foot on the wheel, clutches the strut, which connects the wing to the aeroplane, with both hands and brings his right leg alongside. Behind his slapping wingsuit, Jess quickly grips his shoulder straps and, with her right foot on the aeroplane's tiny external step, draws her left leg out to parallel his. In a heartbeat, she pivots from her right foot and the coupled pair effortlessly disappear. While the Angel flies on to dispense the rest of its jumpers, Hendri falls from 12 000 feet like a starfish as his wingsuit inflates and then flies. With Jess piggybacking, they power along like a badass Jeannie on her magic carpet. It's called a wingsuit rodeo.

With only about a minute of playtime, Jess raises herself onto her elbows. She reaches across to her left boob and from within her ebony crop top and snowy white bra, retrieves a small plastic ziplock bag. Her bug-eyed smile reaches her eyes in genuine delight and she rubs the bag with one hand, softening and loosening its contents and breaking its seal. It takes about half a second for every year of her brother Daniyel's life to release a portion of his ashes into the sky. She raises both thumbs and forefingers to the camera in an L-shaped gesture and gives them a shake. Job done.

TAKE FLIGHT

In the rush of the descent her face contorts, with her skin stretching and flapping around her jaw. She checks her altitude on the yellow altimeter wrapped around her left wrist and thumb, and with another skydiver's wave, pokes her tongue out at the rear-facing camera strapped to Hendri's helmet. Her mum, Leacette, will laugh at that later. And that's it! She raps on Hendri's rigid shoulder to signal her departure and, releasing her grip, draws back from her friend, rolls to her left and falls away. She pulls her parachute at somewhere around 6000 feet; 1000 feet before she needs to, but she doesn't want to push the friendship.

This could have been one of the saddest days of her life, but back on solid ground Jess ecstatically throws her arms around the necks of Hendri and the cameraman. It's a 'look what we just did!' hug. With high adrenaline roaring around her body, she dances on the spot like an excited kid – or like a young woman bringing some balance into her once-messy life. It is her fiftieth jump.

Jess remains grateful for the direction that her new sport has brought, and she has spent almost a decade travelling around Australia working and competing. Work packing parachutes fits beside her own skydiving and after well over 1300 solo jumps, she says that it's the people she has met, as much as the sport itself, that she loves. It's hard to rival the endorphin release that goes with freefalling at around 200 kilometres per hour from up at 14 000 feet, then floating under the canopy for the last 4000 feet. It takes around 20 minutes for each jump and sometimes Jess can jump a few times a day, depending on whether she is in training. Much of the time she works, packing parachutes.

Now you need to meet the sub-culture of speed skydiving – the art of 'going as fast as you possibly can over a set distance'. Speed skydiving is said to be the fastest non-motorised sport on earth. These skydivers flog along at least 50 kilometres per hour faster than a Formula One car. Even though they are only doing it for 30 seconds, it still requires steely concentration and the discipline to calm your mind at that speed. 'If you get the speed wobbles, you must speed up during those moments or you cork out and lose control a little bit', Jess says. Keep calm. Go fast. Don't cork out. Got it? I've enquired for you. When a skydiver 'corks out' it means they lose stability, which then slows their descent rate. If performing in a group, the group continue descending while the corked-out person appears to shoot up like a popping champagne cork. In fact, they are not ascending, but rather descending, albeit more slowly. Don't cork out, people. But if you do, modern equipment is so accurate that you can look back on your jump and learn from your mistakes. There's no time for evaluation on the job, though, because, with all flaps, straps and pilot chute secure, your streamlined self is pin-dropping head-first at 427 kilometres per hour for the fastest half-minute of your day.

Jess stumbled upon this competition when she was packing parachutes at the 2018 National Championships at Moruya, on the south coast of New South Wales. They had some new technology that switched from a barometric measuring device to a GPS tracking device. Old records were archived and new ones up for grabs, starting that weekend. Jess asked what she would have to do, and the reply was simple: fly head down as fast as you can. Simple.

She nutted out the finer points, starting with how to fly head-down and how to do it alone, because she usually jumps with friends. She gathered the gear, starting with an audible altimeter in her helmet that will scream an alarm when she gets down to 5500 feet. She also wears an altimeter on her wrist that records the heights, and back on the ground she can check the GPS tracker to learn the speed she has reached. The GPS tracker provides real-time audible indications of glide ratio, horizontal or vertical speed.

She knows that once the audible altimeter alarm sounds, she will have to angle out to a more belly-to-earth position to slow her speed and open her chute. If she opened the chute at those high speeds, it would probably disintegrate, but with her disciplined mind she would calmly reach for her reserve.

Once she'd left the aircraft, Jess did what she was told and as she bulleted towards the ground, she reached 375 kilometres per hour. For most of us reading this, that seems like a lofty effort for a first-timer. She won first place and in her understated manner says, 'I was pretty happy with that'. There was more to come.

In 2017 she was part of the four-way formation team in the Western Australia state championships. Ronnie Perry, the national coach who managed the Australian team, says he's never seen her so excited as when she was selected for the 2018 Australian team. In March 2019 she won Fastest Female Speed Skydive at 370 kilometres per hour in the Australian/New Zealand championships. In October that year she earned a Bronze in the Speed Skydiving World Cup in the UK. Her speed of 400.36 kilometres per hour meant she cracked the Australian and Oceanic female speed record also. The record was certified by the Federation Aeronautique International (FAI). The FAI is an independent non-profit organisation that oversees and encourages the conduct of sporting aviation worldwide and certifies aviation records.

Jess's record was later smashed by her good friend, Queenslander Natisha Dingle who maxed out at 491.99 kilometres per hour. The fastest male skydiver is Marco Hepp from Germany at 529.77 kilometres per hour. Natisha has been jumping since she was a 16-year-old, a decade longer than Jess. These experiences are consistently critiqued and analysed. The 2019 records were described by the Australian Parachute Federation (APF) as the most successful chapter in competition history with 'three national and three international records broken by some of the country's (now world's) fastest athletes'.

They are fast all right, and it's easy to assume that the skydivers are 'adrenaline junkies', but Jess refutes that. There is nothing cavalier about what she does. The distractions of everyday life are left on the ground, and she takes only the task at hand with her into the air. 'When I'm skydiving, my mind is not going 100 miles per hour – it's the only time in my life that I have really found peace.' Her personal best was set in 2021 at a 'peaceful' 423.18 kilometres per hour. To prepare for that, she used visualisation, meditation and exercise to perfect the art of controlling her mind and body. Beyond what you can do in the quiet of your lounge room, the rest needs to happen in the sky. It is harder to critique the speed skydives than the normal ones, though, because they are only recorded on the FlySight GPS tracker, not visually.

SPREADING SOME OF HER BROTHER'S ASHES IN SOUTH AFRICA was a watershed moment and a welcome salve. The siblings had been incredibly close and weathered many storms together, including sexual abuse by a distant relative. The nightmares still haunt her, sleep is a torturous affair and trust is a broken memory. It affected the rest of their lives, which for Daniyel ended when he was 21 years old. Jess had only turned 18 a week before and his suicide shattered her entire world. So much had happened since the high energy of an early life racing each other on motorbikes around the bush at Rockingham in Western Australia, where their parents owned a motorbike shop. 'I definitely had a lot more courage then', says Jess. 'Now I'm timid on a bike as I have to worry about injuring myself and not being able to work and create income (and pay to fix the bike).'

For most of her teens Jess lived with her mum, and guardian Dave, at Dwellingup, a tiny country town a bit over an hour's drive south of Perth. It's an area filled with mountain bike tracks, bushwalking trails through towering jarrah forests, a river for canoes and a big sky for camping under. It was also perfect horse country and as Jess has always had an affinity with animals, she was desperate for a horse. They have empathy, they can feel your energy and they were perfect for Jess, who enjoyed the uncompromising companionship of an animal.

Mostly (except for a spirited two-year-old horse that was difficult to handle), the horse world was a great confidence booster, and when she saw her first rodeo at Pinjarra, she delighted in the atmosphere and the excitement of the event. She loved the culture and the costumes, and so aligned herself with the rodeo community. Under a broad-brimmed Akubra hat, she learnt to rope cattle, and give it her all in barrel racing, a time test of the fastest horse and rider combination around a clover leaf pattern of three 44-gallon drums. She was rewarded with some trophy belt buckles. The rodeo world gave her something to sink her energy into and it was more engaging than school. 'How was your day at the river?' Leacette would ask. She was a school bus driver, and she knew stuff, including when Jess didn't get on her bus!

It was obvious that she needed another option, and an agricultural boarding school was deemed a better fit. The skills she learned there are still useful in the evolution of her career. She spent half the week in the classroom and the other half outdoors doing practical subjects like farming skills, metalwork, woodwork, automotive, building and construction, and animal husbandry. She began a school-based traineeship in Year 11. After leaving school, when Daniyel passed away, Jess went searching for her place in the world. Who was she, where did she fit? The answers, she thought, were best sought in a campervan on a long and meandering, self-medicated drive around Australia. She headed for the coast to check out some surfing, and then south around Albany, the town described by Australian author Tim Winton like this: 'For a young person who felt claustrophobic surrounded by strangers, it was reassuring to know that within minutes I could be … on a beach with no other footprints in the sand'. A perfect place for a teenager to contemplate a confused life, having just learned how easily it can be ripped away. From South Australia,

Jess worked for a while in Tasmania. It took a year and a half, but she finally made her way home via the east coast, Queensland, the Northern Territory, and the Pilbara. These were small steps towards maturity; her choices were still evolving, and by her mid-twenties she was in a relationship with an older guy, settled in a house with a great job. Sadly, it was a house of cards. 'When he broke up with me, I felt like I'd lost too many people and things that I valued. People that I thought I knew turned out to be strangers, some of whom intentionally tried to hurt me. Everything was side-tracked.'

She rang her permanently worried mother and asked for help.

Three weeks before Christmas 2010, Jess was on the other side of the country. She was keen to try a non-medicated approach to her recovery from addiction. The facility presented as reputable but expensive. Leacette was out of her mind with worry and, clutching at straws, prayed that her daughter could pull through. Jess would give it her best and was prepared to embrace this opportunity.

'I didn't consider the details, I just wanted to do it. I wanted to get off drugs without antidepressants. Mum didn't know what to do. She'd already lost one child. I quickly realised at the place, however, that things didn't seem quite right.'

In February 2015, the media raised serious concerns about the facility's professionalism, practices and legitimacy. Those concerns continue to be aired. She stuck at it for nine months, but when she was asked to yell at an ashtray to stand or sit, and other bizarre things, she wanted to get out. These objectives were meant to bring about life-changing cognitions, which they didn't; however, Jess is firm that it was the connections that she made with her 'twin', the person she was partnered with, and with the other program participants that helped her. 'I did get a lot of stuff out of the rehab, even though I didn't finish the program. I had done the best that I could and, having learnt a lot by being in there, I came out much stronger than when I went in. Some of the people around me had been doing heroin. If they could recover from that, then I knew it should be easier for me, because I wasn't that bad.'

The hardest part was telling her mum, who got no refund on the up-front fees – tens of thousands of dollars. Jess felt that she had not delivered. Leacette glumly shrugged at the latest false start, but respected the decision when she learned the details.

Jess re-entered the world and soon went looking for work again. As a FIFO worker at BHP's Mulla Mulla iron ore mine, she had to be drug-tested simply to get the job as an underwater porcelain technician. 'It was tough. I didn't really want to tell anyone in the interview what I'd been through, because some people kinda think less of you.' Nevertheless, she got the job and began a two weeks on/one week off roster, flying 1300 kilometres in and out of Perth. The money was brilliant and it went on travel: Cambodia, Bali and New Zealand with her best friend Leshana, and to Fiji with her mum and Dave. Nothing compares to her own country, though. 'I've been all around Australia, done the Nullarbor four or five times now and the Outback Way straight across the middle – I love Australia so much.'

She also worked on Barrow Island, a barren, protected little island about 40 kilometres off the Pilbara coast. Surrounded by cobalt and turquoise waters, it has a beautiful and unique habitat and is fringed by sandy beaches. Workers were to stay within camp boundaries unless working out onsite and so the pristine beaches remained untouched by Jess's boots. 'You make some really good connections there, for sure. However, there's also some challenging people in the workplace, which challenged my resolve.'

Twelve-hour working days formed the bulk of her work-eat-sleep-repeat work pattern. There was no arguing about the pay benefits, though, and she thought back to her days working in the snowfields where she was charged board for a shared room. At the mine she was paid almost the same amount as compensation for having to share a room. The flow of funds allowed her to explore as she'd never been able to before. She joined the new crowd of 'flashpackers' (cashed-up backpackers). But the rewards matched the sacrifices and as she began to draw up the threads of her life, she took one of her breaks over in Cairns. 'The thing to do in Cairns is to go skydiving', a friend said.

I lived in Cairns for three years and found plenty of other things to do; however, life takes you where it has plans for you and before she knew it, she was sitting down with Ronnie, a tandem instructor from Skydive Cairns. Now a lifelong friend, mentor and life coach, Ronnie came across as a really cool skydiving instructor. He saw Jess as pleasant and happy. They had a level conversation about his enduring love and respect for the sport. In a pivotal moment, he said to the 28-year-old, 'You know, you could do this!' They were weighty words. Not issued as a challenge but spoken with practicality. He could see that she was an excited student and he trusted that she would make the most of the experience.

Could, or should, she jump out of a perfectly serviceable aeroplane? It's an old question. Other people have done it. She wondered why she was putting limits on herself. On the bus ride to the airport, Jess ran through a raft of disaster scenarios, wrote the headlines, and imagined the social media profile the media would use for the news that night. By the time they arrived at the airport, she'd decided that she just had to trust in the people she was with.

She jumped out of the plane in a tandem with Ronnie. Exiting onto their bellies, it was a fast and wild freefalling minute. With so much information to take in, it felt like sensory overload, and it probably was. She blacked out and then rallied. Under the inflated canopy, when the world slowed down, she was able to take in the city and the beaches, the ranges that ringed them and the rivers flowing through the landscape. They floated 5000 feet down across rainforests and cane fields to a beautifully manicured drop zone in Page Road, Edmonton, on the south side of town.

Jess's smile was unmatched. Her life was changed. The future had begun, and she followed up the next day with another tandem. She excitedly told Ronnie that she was going to pursue the sport, which he hears all the time. It's the excitement.

Life ticked along back at the mine for another couple of months, until there was first one suicide, then a second on the island. Both times it was her friends who found the deceased. The whole thing was too close to her heart and too much to bear in the long and mind-numbing weeks at the camp. She shook her head. 'Nup. I'm done.' It was scary to give up a regular income, but the cost had become too great.

She rang her mum on the Sunshine Coast in Queensland. Leacette agreed with Jess who reckoned that if something wasn't working, then it was up to her to change it, so she packed her belongings and drove 3700 kilometres across the country with Leshana to learn skydiving. 'She is one of the very few who backed up what she said she was going to do', says Ronnie.

At Toogoolawah, north-west of Brisbane, Skydive Ramblers have been training skydivers since 1972 and Jess was their next customer. A very nervous one. Ironically, given she now skydives competitively, her nerves almost put a stop to her before she got going. The most obvious hurdle was her fear of heights, for even helping friends with roofing she clutched the house frame for dear life while her surprised friends wondered what to do with her.

'I'd drive three hours out to the drop zone, throw my guts up and chicken out. Then I'd drive home to the Gold Coast again – that's how nervous I was', she says. 'Mum would laugh that she'd come all this way from her home on the Sunshine Coast to watch me be sick. Once I mastered it, though, there was a great feeling of accomplishment at how far I'd come. I'd thought, *holy cow, I felt like that and then I did this!*' She has since found many kindred souls who, similarly, had to overcome their fear of heights to pursue the sport. The introduction to the course includes learning about the equipment, *jumping*, emergency procedures and landing. It was on the second day she had to actually jump. It was action stations with an instructor either side holding the handles on her suit during the freefall. Then they moved on to 'under canopy', where she was jumping by herself and deploying her own parachute, but with a system of radios to communicate with instructors, and flags on the ground for guidance. Aside from the main parachute, there is an emergency parachute, and a little device called an Automatic Activation Device. If for some reason you are rendered unconscious, it will register that you are falling at a certain speed below a certain altitude and automatically deploy your emergency parachute. 'Sara aka Bear was the best female instructor I could ask for. She has been teaching people to skydive for many years and is one of the most humble experienced skydivers I know in the community.'

All these safety precautions were reassuring and slowly she was released into the wild blue yonder. She started doing flips, learning how to control her body in the sky. On lesson nine she jumped from 5000 feet and deployed the parachute immediately. This last stage demonstrates that you can jump out of the aeroplane, get yourself stable and land safely. 'There's so much to fit into one minute. On my first solo I jumped out and felt like I had plenty of time to do a lot of things. A minute is actually a long time. I could breathe and enjoy the ride.'

She enjoyed it so much that she urged Leacette, who was a regular supporter out at the drop zone, to give it a go. On her second tandem, Leacette looked out to her right, where she saw Jess fly up and extend her arm. They held hands in what Leacette describes as a moment of pure connecting joy. If finances ever allowed, she'd consider one day following her daughter into the sport, which sees about half a million skydives around the country annually.

TAKE FLIGHT

EVENTUALLY, SKYDIVING SUITED JESS WELL AND SHE JOINED the more than 3000 licensed skydivers registered with the Australian Parachute Federation. Surprisingly, about 13 per cent are women, which is double that for female powered pilots.

Jess is philosophical. 'We all put limits on ourselves, but I recommend you try skydiving at least once, because it's life-changing. I feel so present when I'm in the air because there is nothing going through my mind except what I'm doing, usually executing the planned dive, focusing on the leader, and once the parachute opens, looking around for the others, looking down at where I'm going to land or looking off into the distance, checking out the horizon. When I do take in the beauty of the jump, we see some cool stuff, such as full-circle rainbows, which are absolutely beautiful. We can be floating down past a cloud mass and see the whole circle in front of us. Occasionally, if the sun is setting, we see it setting on the ground and then again from altitude when we go up and do a freefall and it's a real "Oh wow – that's magnificent!" moment. Once I release the 'chute, everything slows down and, after I locate everyone else and run through my safety checks, then I have time to take in the beauty of it all. You have the view to yourself. One of the most gorgeous places to jump is at Tully in Queensland. There is a stunning variety of blues in the Great Barrier Reef off the coast and the sunsets there are something else!'

It's one part of what keeps her coming back, and so is the continual challenge to create interesting and fun jumps. Jess will generally jump with friends. Occasionally, if they're doing a belly jump, they will brief the flight beforehand using creepers (metre-long y-shaped skateboards on rotating casters that allow you to lie flat on top of them and move in any direction). Skydivers can lie on a creeper with their legs bent back at the knees and their arms spread-eagled. They can then simulate their in-flight routines by rolling around on a flat concrete pad, coming together and moving away in fluid movements that they will replicate in the sky. Belly jumps are the first configuration you learn, the same as a tandem flight. The next position is head-up in a sitting position and then head-down orientation, at the same time learning angle and movement jumps across the sky. This is learning how to fly your body, even during your training, when you do backflips to prove that you can stabilise again. If you follow instructions, you can usually land wherever you want to. Another of the beautiful jumps Jess does is down onto Taylor Cay, which is a sandbar in the Great Barrier Reef. In a sea of cobalt and turquoise, the reef has a partly submerged sandbar that is large enough for a cricket club picnic and small enough to challenge approaching parachutists. Land wide and it's a soggy affair.

Landing is crucial to the whole exercise and a stand-up landing is a show of true skill that all and sundry can admire. The little handles on the steering lines are pulled at the same time in even motions to slow down and eventually arrest the descent while maintaining a straight heading. 'Sometimes we are travelling a bit too fast and so we have to sit down. If you flare wrong, at the wrong time, it can put you down with a thud.' Not ideal. But a stand-up landing will result in whoops and hollers between the group. They call it 'frothing'. So, after a graceful stand-up landing, be assured the group will be 'frothin'' with their friends and feeling empowered, because, uninjured, they can jump again. Most injuries do happen on landing and Jess has been lucky that the only time she's hurt herself was when she landed on the grass and rolled her ankle in a hidden pothole.

The skydivers jump in a well-planned sequence that starts with the order in which they're loaded into the aeroplane. Still prone to nerves, Jess will calm herself with some breath work. She has learnt to process her emotions much better than in her early nauseous days. The atmosphere in the plane on the climb out is one of high energy. In a Cessna Caravan there can be up to 16 people on the nine-minute flight to altitude. In the smaller Cessnas, it will take about 25 minutes to carry the five passengers up to their jumping height. When she's doing it with her mates, they are busy visualising the jump and how they will execute it; trying to calm themselves amid the noise. Just before they jump, they will get information on wind speed and direction from the ground crew.

The smiles are 'awesome' when they are under canopy. The team will always be looking for their own clear airspace to ensure vertical and horizontal separation to land in. They load onto the plane in order of first in, last out. The first groups to exit the aircraft are angle groups (people flying through the sky at a certain angle), big and then small belly groups (people flying on their belly), large then small free fly groups (people who may freefall for longer than the others), tandems and then wingsuits.

'I've jumped out of hot air balloons and helicopters. They are stationary and you really get the sensation of falling as you exit – usually around 4000 feet.' Freefalling from an aircraft at 14 000 feet is a noisy whooshing affair for about a minute at 220 kilometres per hour before opening the canopy. In a speed jump, which is from around 14 000 feet at double that speed, the roaring sound of the freefall is like putting your head out of a speeding car, until 30 seconds later when you open the parachute and peace is upon you. It all requires a fit and healthy body, which will ensure a longer skydiving life.

Jess sees it as a lifelong journey, working towards being the best she can be and doing it for as long as she can. 'When you find something that makes you this happy, you do what you can to be able to keep doing it.' And while 1300+ jumps sounds like more than enough for most of us, she admires her old boss, the owner of the Innisfail drop zone, who at 70+ years old has recently passed his 37 000th skydive; still jumping and doing tandems.

Ronnie has seen Jess from first jump through to coaching her to the world championships and he admires her gusto. 'She doesn't give up. She digs her heels in and gets on with it. She's not a flim-flammy person who doesn't follow through. I'm really enjoying her successes and, continually working on mindset, we learn how to enjoy and understand any perceived failures. We spent a lot of time working on that. She's super coachable as she'll shut up and listen. She has good focus and is really keen to share her knowledge.' One of her strongest points is her role as a rigger (someone who re-packs the parachutes). Now running courses herself, she is sought after for this important skill. Ronnie recognises her growth mindset and her ability to overcome the obstacles that get thrown in her way. 'Sometimes she'll call me if she is upset, but quitters are never winners and she knows that. I actually think her greatest achievement has been conquering herself!'

So, what is next? Jess has taken her closest companion Rusta, a loyal blue heeler cross, and moved to various outback jobs to save for a BASE jumping course. She's got her eyes set on training with Australian Chris 'Douggs' McDougall, one of the world's most experienced BASE jumpers, who is running courses out of Croatia. It's riskier than skydiving and the appeal for Jess is in doing this extreme sport safely and seeing whether she likes it.

'Everyone I knew before skydiving that died, did so in shit circumstances. The skydivers and BASE jumpers I know that have died, died doing what they loved; they were pushing their limits and … I don't know … they were living! Skydiving has brought me self-awareness and I'm so glad I found this journey. I can't imagine what other sport would have done that for me. I realised that I was often a victim and I no longer want to be a victim of my circumstances.' Jess is only in her mid-30s; Ronnie agrees that she still has plenty to give to the sport and the world around her.

Having dealt with Daniyel's death, and her own depression, addiction and recovery, Jess is still trying to create the best version of herself. I know that if opportunity doesn't knock, you have to build your own door. 'I've got a long way to go and still struggle with self-worth, but reflection helps. I remind myself that if I was looking at myself as another person, I'd admire their courage and ambition. You've got to be sure to remember to do that with yourself.'

9
IT STARTED WITH THE STARS

KRYSTAL DE NAPOLI, GOMEROI ASTROPHYSICIST

'My engagement with Indigenous knowledge perspectives has entirely changed the way I view not just the skies, but the land around me. Everything is connected.'

Krystal De Napoli

TAKE FLIGHT

A summer breeze in Benalla, Victoria, gently lifts the leaves on the trees in a backyard. A second-hand trampoline bows under the weight of two children and their mother, lying in the dark, slightly removed from a family gathering. Eight-year-old Krystal, the younger of the two kids, strains her little eyes. She is scanning the dark sky to see what her mother is describing to them.

'Can you see the Seven Sisters? They are faint, but they are my favourite. They are a group of girls huddled together in strength and safety. There's something that draws me to them – the power of feminine love and protection. They are always pursued by Orion as he chases them across the skies, but they always have each other.'

The story is one that belongs to many cultures around the world, arising with a similar narrative despite the oceans that separate those communities. To Aboriginal people, the story of the Seven Sisters is one of the most well known, belonging to many nations in the form of a Songline that describes an epic tale of desire, pursuit, and familial strength.

It tells of the seven sisters that represent the Pleiades star cluster in the constellation 'Taurus' in Western astronomy. In Australia we see the stars come up just after sunset and travel low across the horizon. They are followed closely every night by the constellation representing a man who desires the women, whom he is forbidden by lore to marry. Some aspects of the story, and its timing, relate closely to sacred men's ceremonies and cultural lore of Australia's central desert regions.

If you have the patience and the skills to search a clear night sky, you may be able to find the Seven Sisters. They are faint, but they are there. Its theme of sisters was important to Krystal's mother, who was the youngest sister in her family, and Krystal is the second sister in hers. On this night the sky is bursting with celestial light, putting on a shimmering, showy performance against the deep black background that you can only get out in the country. They pop, the way a photograph will pop out from a black frame and border. Her mother's soothing voice is hypnotic to the child as she loses herself in the spectacle, which reveals itself more fully as her eyes adjust. First the brightest stars grab her attention, and then she notices the twinkling soft blues, reds and oranges as the smaller ones emerge. She is drawn upwards into the darkness.

While her mother tries to share a sliver of ancestral knowledge, as fine and fragile as a thread on a spider web and mostly lost to the effects of the Stolen Generations, the elder sister marvels at all the shooting stars. Krystal couldn't see them and to this day believes her sister was taunting her. Despite her frustration, this moment stays imprinted on her mind. Her childhood was fractured and messy, but in the depths of her troubles she would always return to the comfort of the stars and eventually pursue the mysteries they hold.

'I grew up in difficult circumstances, Mum grew up in way worse and Mum's father [Pop] had it bad too. I've grown up in a matriarchal family with my mum, nan and aunties.' Krystal's Pop was adopted too young to have any memories of his mother; however, he became aware of his adoptive status at the age of nine, when his surname was changed from Kennedy to that of his adoptive family.

'I may have been adopted, but I've always known me own crowd. Y'know what I mean?' he says to his granddaughter. As an adult, he was finally able to contact his younger paternal siblings. A joyous occasion that came with the sad revelation that his birth father, a German man, had passed away just six months prior. 'His siblings welcomed him into the family and shared stories of their life with their father, with assurances that he would have been loved', says Krystal. 'They gave glimpses of a childhood that in another time would have been his own. Pop continued this journey of reconnection with his mum's family, who quickly embraced him into an extensive network of loving Aboriginal cousins, aunts, and uncles – a family that provided the cultural and community grounding that he had lost many years ago.'

Krystal's own paternal genes run straight back to Italy about 40 years before she was born, hence the De Napoli name. Despite her Pop's removal from his Gomeroi mother, Krystal's maternal lineage can be traced back to the 1800s.

She is the second eldest of seven children who all share their matrilineal Kamilaroi heritage, but only three have the patrilineal Italian line. The family lived on Pangerang Country at Wangaratta in northern Victoria, which is a regional city of around 20 000 people right by the Hume Highway, where the snowy waters of the Ovens and the King rivers meet on the eastern side of the town. Its nearby tourist trail, designed for people of greater means, winds around the King Valley. The hilly landscape, wineries and festivals would have reminded her Italian forebears of home. The Italians came here as tobacco growers, until tobacco was replaced by wine. The Kelly Gang bushrangers made nearby Oxley, Greta, and Glenrowan famous in Australian folklore around the mid- to late 1880s. Before them, Chinese prospectors had come for the gold. And until then, the Taungurung and Pangerang people lived a traditional life, which was interrupted and almost eradicated by colonial invaders seeking the fertile lands of this lush, mountainous country.

Krystal and her siblings grew up knowing they were Aboriginal, and her mother was particularly interested in that part of her life. She'd try to discuss it with her kids and only recently Krystal has learned things from her siblings that they remember. They are originally from around Tamworth on Kamilaroi Country, one of the largest Aboriginal nations in Australia. The Kamilaroi area begins in the Hunter Valley and extends west to the Warrumbungle Mountains and north into south-west Queensland. Her mother learned from her father (Pop) what little information he had about their Aboriginal ancestry. With only a small photo to reflect on and a legacy of trauma, there is so much that he is unable or reticent to recall. However, he is encouraged by the younger generation seeking answers and pleased to connect them with their Tamworth community.

Krystal's biggest insecurity was always because of her family being displaced from their own community. 'There was a group of about twenty other Indigenous kids brought together through a school-based social and wellbeing group. It served its purpose but did not provide us with any real connection to our own culture or families. Only when I got to Melbourne did I gain a real sense of community through the science world.'

Many of these children lived and played together in the Yarrunga housing commission area between Wangaratta's main street and the King River. The houses were built after the Second World War for the city's factory workers. By the time Krystal was born in the late 1990s, most manufacturing had closed and the town's population growth steadied. While she always had a roof over her head, she says there were times when there was no peace beneath it and Krystal spent time in emergency housing, often with the family of her best friend.

Just getting through high school was a monumental effort, and Krystal says that it was in Year 10 that she realised how abnormal her circumstances were. Other kids in her classes didn't have to contend with the same constant interruptions and distress and feelings of inadequacy and desperation. Her saving grace was her maths teacher, Mr Barron, who asked why she was crying in class. 'I know it's not about the maths', he said, and she unloaded to him about the difficulties of her life and her fear that she'd never graduate from Year 12. He calmly replied that they'd just have to work around it and find a way forward for her.

In seeking her own identity, she dyed her hair a statement blue. At least the colour of her hair was something she could control. With this as her point of difference, she felt confronted when a new kid,

Michael, arrived. He had all the things that made Krystal unique: bright blue hair, a beautiful singing voice, and the same birthday. At first, she baulked and then they became best friends.

By the time she got to Year 12, she had moved from a C grade through to an A grade in Legal Studies. Being able to speak to people about her problems shifted their weight and Krystal credits her success to her teachers, extremely hard work, the ear of some close friends, and the Indigenous Support Unit. Her one aim was to finish high school. When asked if she could ever have seen herself being where she is now, Krystal sighs and replies, 'Oh my god. No … It's weird to accept the life I have now and I'm almost starting to disconnect from the kid that I was. Man, I was so hopeless. I thought I had no future at all'.

There were threads of kindness around her, including from a family who cared for her during tough times. When they moved away, they arranged a musical scholarship for Krystal that lasted until she finished school. It brought opportunity and comfort. With support from her Nonna, she was able to tour with the music school locally, state-wide and even nationally. It was a compensation for not being able to go on school camps and in everyday life the singing also brought a semblance of calm. She sings like a bird! But she wasn't singing when she got her final school results. She thought they would reflect her hard work and the other great results she'd got during the year, but she was crushed and still won't reveal her score; it doesn't matter now, anyway.

An offer came from Monash, which began with acknowledging that they didn't like her results but suggested that she contact their Indigenous Support Unit. The unit was 'phenomenal' and could see the depth of her desire and ability yet to be tapped. They offered her a way forward with a six-month bridging course. She had to forego her planned gap year studying at her music school and get herself to Melbourne within four weeks.

A good friend's mother took up the reins and supported Krystal for the initial six months until government assistance could be sorted. As the $300 per week campus fees were unattainable, she took the cheaper option and moved into a small flat, a 90-minute bus ride away. The six-month program was intense, with a few hours' extra weekly tutoring for each class. There were three exams to complete for acceptance into a science degree. Everything hinged on those results and failing to complete or pass any of them would result in loss of government funding and the chance to stay at uni. Basically, her future hinged on passing the bridging course.

Exhausted while preparing for her third exam, Krystal emerged from a deep sleep one morning to answer a slew of phone calls informing her that her mum, aged in her late 30s, had passed away unexpectedly. The delivery could perhaps have been better than, 'Krystal, your mum is dead'. The shocking news knocked her off her feet and could easily have been her breaking point. She had only been in Melbourne a short time, and everything was already difficult: housing, driving, uni, money, separation from her community. 'I was in immediate shock and wanted to go home to my family. I had to start the degree and complete the third exam at the same time, knowing that if I failed it, I would get kicked out of the degree and the government funding agency would put me into $7000 debt and cut off my payments because I hadn't completed the unit.' Somehow, she rallied herself enough to complete the final exam and passed the course with high distinctions and honours. She started a Bachelor of Science (BSc) in the mid-year intake.

When selecting subjects for the BSc, Krystal chose astronomy, to learn more about what her mum had been trying to teach her. Because she was starting mid-year, she began astronomy in the second semester and loved it: life, the universe, and astrobiology. With great determination, she latched onto the subject; she was missing her mother and felt nostalgic about the stars. Krystal loved the stars, she loved maths and felt she could engage with astronomy. She was determined to make the most of her opportunity. Her lecturer, Jasmina Lazendic-Galloway, made that possible with her enthusiasm and knowledge. She gave out clear printed notes, which Krystal pored over, highlighting text, and excitedly reading forward to the following semester's topics. She unfortunately missed many classes in the semester following her mother's death as she could barely bring herself to leave the house. 'I still have nightmares and hallucinations. That belongs to PTSD. One thing I really struggled with in uni was having small things completely unsettle me. When my car broke down before an exam, instead of being able to call a parent to come and get me and help sort the problem, I had nobody to collect me, no money to sort the problem, everything then became triggered, and I found myself in completely difficult circumstances where things are so much harder than they ought to be for a young woman.'

Our conversation stops a few times when memories invade, and her trembling body warns of the surfacing trauma. Its repercussions are ongoing, but were tempered when her initial spark of interest in astronomy became an unstoppable bonfire as the class worked cohesively to complete quizzes and activities, which were a welcome respite from the ongoing grief and panic attacks that come with complex PTSD. Jasmina's classes brought her levity, fun, learning and inspiration.

In that first year, Jasmina organised stargazing nights. As Krystal stepped up for her first look through a telescope she saw Saturn, Jupiter and other 'cool, bigger stars'. The bonfire blazed as Saturn's perfect rings, texture and colour came into sharp relief. While it looked fake, Krystal knew that there was no reason for anybody to be lying about it. Then she saw Jupiter. Her general knowledge about the planet was that it has four main moons, and she was aware that Galileo, the Italian astronomer, physicist, and engineer, had built some impressive telescopes in the 1600s and named Jupiter's four moons. The four little 'stars' around Jupiter in the telescope were clearly Galileo's moons.

'The first telescope I looked through was a visual/mirror telescope. I could see the colour and [the famous] spot on Jupiter. I always thought the colours of space were phenomenal, but now I've learnt that the colour is an illusion, and we don't actually detect it very often. Another thing that blew my mind was that we were using the Hutton-Westfold Observatory telescope at uni and we imaged a galaxy. It immediately looked like those crazy beautiful images that you normally see of space, but these were in black and white. Even without the colour, I was wowed by the depth, features, and details in the images.'

Krystal met her partner David in Jasmina's class and formed a strong relationship with Jasmina, who in later years became a mentor and a supervisor for further studies. It took almost six years to complete the science degree due to more family disruptions, but despite the gaps, she always felt connected to the university and her studies. She graduated with a major in astronomy and a minor in physics and mathematics. There was so much to know and so much she would have loved to share with her mum.

A SOURCE OF STEADINESS IN HER LIFE WAS HER CLOSE AND loving relationship with her Italian Nonna, who still lived in Wangaratta. Krystal is calm as she sits on my couch, apologising for crocheting, which she is finishing off as a gift for her brother. As a knitter, I find it comforting to be around somebody using their hands to create, and as memories of my own yarn-bearing days bubble up, we slip into an easy conversation about the positive role models in our lives. Again, balancing the demands of a disintegrating family and a career in the making, in 2021, having already lost four close relatives in as many years, Krystal deferred her honours degree so she could go home to Wangaratta, live with her best friend, and spend time with her ailing Nonna.

'For the first time I had a warning that somebody was going to leave me. I could prepare for it and say everything we wanted to say. I spent an intense month visiting Nonna every day. It was very helpful when she gave me a bag of unfinished crochet projects to continue with. I could happy-cry and process what was happening. I'm the only one she taught to crochet and my siblings love to see me using up her supplies and finishing her projects. Nonna made a huge blanket that won a prize in the Wangaratta Show. She finally got some acknowledgment for her skills. The blanket goes almost all the way to the floor, and it has a grid of 17 x 20 crocheted roses attached separately. There is a bag of yarn and roses left over and they're beautiful and so it's up to me now to design the end of the project, which is the pillow shams. I like the yellows, oranges and pinks.' With each stitch, measured and gauged against the oddments, her grief eases in a healthy, calm manner.

WHILE ENJOYING THE JOURNEY, KRYSTAL WAS STILL UNCLEAR about her future pathway until in 2017 she saw an advertisement for a talk by American-born cultural astronomer Dr Duane Hamacher from her home university, Monash. His research explores how astronomy is thoroughly embedded in the practices of Indigenous communities, focusing on the intricate layers of scientific information embedded within these ancient knowledge systems and passed down through oral tradition over thousands of years.

For Aboriginal and Torres Strait Islander communities, the skies are a reservoir of knowledge. Each star behaves as a book of information; twinkling gently in the sky to help inform communities of seasonal change, impending weather events, changes in animal behaviours, while also serving as memory devices in the form of star maps which help map out routes across Country. In this way, the sky becomes a library that needs to be able to be seen, to be read. Today, Krystal and her colleagues work to develop dark sky parks to protect our collective view of the stars.

A dark sky park will allow you to see the stars in more detail, without the light pollution brought on by artificial light (projected by cities, for example). Designated dark sky parks in Australia and Aotearoa/New Zealand are Aoraki Mackenzie, Aotea Great Barrier and Stewart Island/Rakiura in Aotearoa/New Zealand, and Jump-Up, Queensland; River Murray Dark Sky Reserve, South Australia; and Warrumbungle Dark Sky Park, New South Wales, in Australia.

Duane moved to Australia to undertake a Master's degree at the University of New South Wales, which was shortly followed by a PhD at Macquarie University. Now an Associate Professor of Cultural Astronomy at the University of Melbourne, he readily acknowledges that as an American he is an anomaly when it comes to Australian Indigenous astronomy, but on visits to many parts of the country he was astonished by the depth of knowledge still held by traditional owners. He has since devoted his time to cultivating this knowledge and become an expert in the field. Unsurprisingly, Krystal was keen to hear Duane's presentation and managed to fit it in. By chance, he was talking about Kamilaroi Country that day: Krystal's Country and her mob – a land and people she had never met. She'd known that he specialised in Indigenous astronomy, but this was an altogether unexpected coincidence. She approached Duane at the airport. 'I was with Alan Duffy, and I'm used to people approaching him. When Krystal came up, walked past him, and asked if I was "Duane Hamacher, the astronomer", I was a bit taken aback.' The pair spoke after the lecture and that meeting changed Krystal's life. 'I'm sure I would have found work and ended up in some nice place after my studies, but now a lot of the work I do and a lot of the opportunities I get all trace back to that meeting.'

Duane was told for years that there were no PhD-qualified Aboriginal astrophysicists. After he finished his PhD, he learned about Dr Stacy Mader, a Gidja man from Western Australia who earned his PhD in astrophysics at the University of Wollongong over ten years before! Stacy now works for the CSIRO as an astronomer and experimental scientist at the Parkes Observatory. Stacy was the catalyst for the renaming of Murriyang (formerly known as Parkes), which is a 64-metre-wide radio telescope renown for being a prime receiving station for the 1969 Apollo 11 mission to land on the moon. Stacy connected with local Wiradjuri Elders who in kind proposed the name Murriyang for the telescope in honour of Wiradjuri Dreaming traditions. Stacy has also won two NASA awards for Group Achievement; Curiosity Rover Support and X-BAND Upgrade Path. Stacy, Krystal and Duane now work together to promote Indigenous astronomy.

Krystal continues to break new ground and Duane acknowledges that she is making incredible progress despite all the trauma she has suffered. The Stolen Generations is not that long ago; the policy, along with colonisation, had a huge impact on her Pop, who raised her mum, who raised Krystal. The trauma was real and passed on directly. If not for that trauma, she wonders if the close relatives who died during her university years would all still be alive today. Krystal has encountered some people who are confused when she tries to talk about intergenerational trauma, but for her and her siblings, it is not in the past. She still lives with its impact, but she is trying to override it through education and understanding.

'Until very recently, the education system treated Indigenous culture as lesser-than. The narrative of "there was nothing but bush here before invasion" is changing. There would be so much more respect and love for each other if we had a better understanding as to why Indigenous people have this strong connection to the land. It's a continual thing that didn't stop 200 years ago because of colonisation. It was interrupted but not obliterated. We have the world's oldest continuous thriving culture and it's still here; we were the first bread bakers and the first astronomers. We're trying to make sure that it doesn't get erased. Indigenous science, and astronomy in particular, is spectacular and specific to these lands. It's something that every Australian can be proud of, and I think a lot of good can come from it. In Aboriginal cultural traditions there are infinite layers of knowledge embedded into stories and Songlines that help inform us of the land around us. Our science is intrinsically interconnected with threads of knowledge that tie star positions and their paths across the year with plant harvest and animal breeding cycles, seasonal change and forecasting weather patterns, helping us track the flow of time and navigate across this marvellous continent. This is a different way of conceptualising and communicating knowledge than we use in Western forms of education, and it's a way that suits my way of thinking much better. In Western classrooms we tend to compartmentalise knowledge into separate baskets or silos, containing our arts away from our sciences, and then eventually, our sciences away from other sciences like the divide between physicists and biologists. I used to struggle to understand the impact and context of things I would learn at school in isolated boxes. For me, Aboriginal science shows that the entire universe is really just a cosmic web that connects us all.'

Krystal is committed to sharing her knowledge with schoolchildren, to inspire them and spread awareness. She is humbled by the opportunities she's been given and the help she's received to navigate seemingly impossible hurdles and meet her full potential. Her beautiful brown eyes light up when she talks about a short research project she undertook on exoplanets (planets that orbit around stars, rather than around our sun). Did they find a crystal planet? Krystal says there is a planet made of diamonds, which she believes might be a nice crystal planet. 'My name is interesting. I do remember that Mum had an interest in astrology so I'm pretty sure maybe her observational knowledge came from her interest in star signs. I dunno. It's funny that somebody with such an interest in astrology raised an astronomer. Some astronomers get so offended when you call them an astrologer. It's just a similar word – people make a mistake.'

Astrologically, Krystal is a fiery one – Sagittarius. Her star is rising, driven by her own determination and commitment, but fuelled by those around her. She admits that it's hard to deal with the bad and the sad things that have happened to her. But as those days dim and she gains more control over her life, she says brightly, 'I have a radio show called *Indigenuity*. It's a weekly program where I get to interview all these cool Indigenous knowledge holders and showcase many forms of Indigenous ingenuity. There's no way I'd get to have those conversations normally!'

She has helped create an Indigenous science course at Monash and is taking that information out into schools to educate kids about Indigenous astronomy. She enjoys that this gives the participants the chance to gain a new perspective. One of the best and most unexpected opportunities, though, was a once-in-a-lifetime trip from Melbourne to the South Pole to see the aurora australis – the southern lights. The surprising thing she learned is that the auroras are normally portrayed in photographs as stunningly beautiful energetic coloured objects, but actually, it's only the camera that sees the colour. Our eyes aren't sensitive enough to see the colour and so we see mostly black and white. That was compensated for, though, by the energy and the movement. Her absolute highlight was the rapid movement of the lights that danced across the sky in a stunning show.

'That is the part of the aurora that you see coming over the horizon. The red is associated with things relating to red vibes, with a negative connotation, often like a warning or taboo. The colour is very important in that regard. The aurora was seen as a warning. Gunai have a creation story about the Creator putting his son in charge of ceremony (men's business) and people in the community leaked sacred knowledge to women and he was so upset he caused almost like the apocalypse with massive flood and fires in his rage and response. It did a lot of harm to people. In the end he said, "Look, I'll let you continue to practise ceremony, but you cannot break this taboo again". It is said that the aurora is like a constant reminder that ceremony is sacred business and not to share it. There are many things in Indigenous astronomy that are tricky to see, such as an eleven-year solar cycle with peaks in aurora activity. Indigenous Australian Elders have long been experts and masters of astronomy knowledge. Many creation stories feature flight, and the moons and planets often have some connection to the earth first and then get cast up into the sky. They teach that everything on the land is reflected in the sky, and everything in the sky is reflected on the land.'

She was invited to speak on cruise ships going from Perth up to Ningaloo Reef to view the solar eclipse on 20 April 2023. Nothing can really capture what the naked eye will see of the eclipse in real life. The colours are gentle pale blues and whites. There was beautiful detail and fine crisp wisps of light (prominences) appearing like thin white strings.

Ever since she has been able to, Krystal has dyed part of her waist-length dark hair blue. She finds the colour calming. 'I have always had a strong connection to the colour blue that even to this day, when I see people for the first time in years, they will bring up how much they associate me with it. What was really incredible to me was that on my first ever trip on Kamilaroi Country in 2017, I was taken for a walk on Country with a wonderful Kamilaroi woman, Tania Marshall. She independently started to describe to me that blue is an important colour on Kamilaroi Country. This throwaway comment obviously caught my interest and I asked her what she meant. She described how for us, Gawarragay (the Emu in the Sky in Gomeroi language) tells us of the Dhinawan (emu of the ground in Gamilaraay) and describes the emu egg collection cycle (gigantic blue eggs, speckled with white, like stars in the night sky). The kookaburra has the blue in his wing and that the blue-bellied black snake, the variety lesser known than the red-bellied black snake, is almost exclusively found on Kamilaroi Country. This is probably a bit silly but to me it was an incredible coincidence.'

Hundreds of miles south of Tamworth, on an ink-black night on an isolated coastline in southern Victoria, the young university student takes her partner's hand and steps onto a beach. The air is heavy with salt and through the silence she approaches the moody water. Waves pound the shoreline with hypnotic irregularity. Beyond them the sea stretches 500 kilometres to Tasmania. It is impossible to tell where the sea finishes and the sky begins. It is one big body of darkness, from her feet in front of her, to the horizon behind her.

Lying on the cool sand, Krystal takes in the 180-degree view and scans the twinkling sky for the constellations, configurations, and familiar patterns. Once again, she feels completely lost in the stars and she challenges herself to find them: the saucepan is high above, and low in the south is the Southern Cross. Scanning to the left she finds the Coalsack Nebula, a dark oval shape. This is the head of the Emu in the Sky with its beak pointing downward. Its long neck stretched out to the east between the Southern Cross's two pointer stars. Orion the Hunter is now a familiar friend who visits in the warmer months. She follows Orion to the Seven Sisters, whose resilience and camaraderie mirror her determination to fiercely protect her own darling sisters. In her mind, she withdraws to the trampoline in Benalla, searching for her mother's voice one last time.

To the young astrophysicist, the stories of the sky make perfect sense and on that quiet stretch of Gippsland sand, she lies back, feeling in harmony with the world and her place in it. 'Now I understand', she thinks. 'I see it, feel it and know it.' To her great delight 'heaps' of shooting stars crisscross before her. She's never seen a shooting star before, but they present themselves, cutting the sky like rockets.

Immersed in that place on the beach Krystal is enveloped by the universe. This is how her Kamilaroi ancestors had viewed their world, where earth and sky exist as one. She now knows that so many Aboriginal Dreaming stories start on the earth and end in the sky. That Creation stories, especially, tend to engage the night and tend to feature flight, reflecting the action of the land and sky which are then separated; sun, moon, stars and planets have names and stories. Quite often they have a connection to the earth first. 'This happened and this happened' and then they've broken some sort of taboo and the two are separated.

Lying on that dark beach, where the water and the sky had no delineation, Krystal began to understand the teachings that she had learnt at university on a deeper level, rooted in a curiosity that began on the trampoline in the back yard at Benalla 20 years ago.

10

THE EARLIEST AVIATORS

DONNA TASKER, BALLOON PILOT

'I love that no two flights are the same. The passengers, seasons, colours all change. I love sharing it and watching people's faces as we inflate the envelope. It's big and unexpected.'

Donna Tasker

Donna Tasker, balloon pilot

A dragon's breath leaps forth, biting at the cool dawn. Pha-whhhhooooar. From a couple of gas cylinders in a huge wicker basket, the bright orange tongue rages forth, reaching into our enormous yellow hot air balloon. This is the hot air. At the base of the flame, Donna Tasker controls the fury. The balloon – or envelope – has already been hit with cold air to inflate it from a flaccid pile of fabric on the ground to a fully rounded, marvellous thing lying on its side in the frosty grass. Now the pilot, dwarfed by the size of the envelope, walks inside to inspect its integrity. The balloon's initial predecessor, 250 years ago, was made of layered cotton and paper, but today's version is a highly strengthened urethane nylon fabric, large and strong enough to carry 20 people. As the hot air is now directed to its interior, the envelope rises with the warmth, lifts from the ground and angles the tethered basket up on to its base. Not enough flame and it will be left teetering. Too much and it will try to fly.

Donna throws the flame and flings the ropes. When the first gas allocation runs dry, she spins the faucet, disconnects the hose, and hoicks the metal bottle into the hands of her ground crew. Spread around her, joy-riding passengers eagerly or nervously wait for lift-off.

Beside us are a few more balloons from the same company with their fare-paying passengers equally gog-eyed. The glorious envelopes inflate and the wind ambles in from the north. We can only go with it.

There's a pre-flight briefing: don't touch anything, don't go inside the ropes while we inflate, don't hang out too far, don't drop anything, brace when I say – and enjoy the ride. We're an orderly crew inside the basket, all with cameras at the ready.

To our left, 30 two-person balloons create a popping kaleidoscope. They are all piloted by women, who have come to the West Australian wheat belt from many corners of the world to compete in the 2023 World Women's Ballooning Championship. It is being held in Australia for the first time. Competitors and spectators are excited, and the organising team are slightly exhausted. With the week drawing to a close, there is a palpable buzz about the field as the placegetters are still up for grabs.

With a couple more squirts from the gas, the earth sighs and the balloon breathes. As softly as a mother settles her sleeping infant, we are released like its dreams into the gentle dawn, lifted by the envelope's warm air and carried on the whispering wind. We can't even determine the point that we launched because it's as though the earth has just naturally stepped out for a moment. Like Elisabeth Thible, the first woman to fly in a hot air balloon, it would have been fitting to break into an opera and sing ourselves into the sky. In the French summer of 1784 Thible did so, dressed as a Roman goddess, but we have neither the costume, nor the voice. It's surprisingly warm and welcoming, though, here beneath the dragon's breath.

Donna calmly leans over the basket's edge to chat with people as they slide by, ever so slowly, about fifty feet below. 'This is a very interactive form of aviation', I tell her as the support crews and onlookers eventually reduce to waving miniatures on the ground. With her right arm raised to fire the burner, Donna smiles in agreement.

We turn to the morning's long shadows cast across the valley ahead. The competitors, in balloons of every colour and geometric combination, are the aviation version of the Melbourne Cup spectacle. They are shimmeringly gorgeous in the soft morning and rise in their own time, like bubbles in the breeze. The sun kisses their bulbous sides and highlights the Australian aviation registration numbers. VH-NKS, with variegated patterns against a pleasing aqua base, slowly drifts between us and the half-moon. The farmers here around Northam are used to the occasional balloon visitor, but so many of the conical shapes, sharply imposed on the clear morning sky all together, look like a superimposed, computer-generated image. They are strangely calming to watch.

We fly up to about 1500 feet high, turning occasionally to share the view with everybody on board, while still being carried by the breeze. Within a short half hour we are looking for a suitable landing spot. When the airport appears over the horizon we gently put down into a cow paddock beside it. The surprised crew can't open the locked gate, so Donna injects more hot air for a fence-hop and crosses to a wide grassy verge on the other side of the runway. It's then like the end of a camping trip, with passengers and crew helping to deflate and roll the surprisingly heavy envelope back into its carryall. We're back on the ground, but for weeks I remain aloft on the feeling of that stunning flight. In a sharp contrast, a couple of days later, I'm blasted back home on a Boeing 737, which seems so aggressive. I hesitate to leave the ballooning behind. My pilot will be back tomorrow morning like she's done a thousand times before. She loves this job. And she hopes to do it a thousand more in her role as one of Australia's few commercial balloon pilots, of whom even fewer are women.

DONNA CAN TRACE HER FASCINATION WITH AVIATION BACK TO the 1980s at Hawkesbury High School, a few kilometres north-east of the RAAF base at Richmond, NSW. Life back then was a bit of a messy affair, with family disruptions, for the academic but strong-willed teenager. She laments that perhaps the RAAF sensed her lack of direction when she approached them about a flying career. It was a confronting 'No' when they told her that women couldn't fly (yet – the RAAF's first intake of women pilots was in 1988). It didn't end her fascination with flight, but neither did it help!

It was a relief to leave her childhood behind and move to Perth with her mum and stepfather. She was studying hospitality over there when a classmate invited her for a trial flight in a little Cessna 152. It sparked her interest in aviation again and she considered becoming a RAAF flight attendant, but they sent her away again. There was nothing for it but to sign up and learn to fly herself. Her parents were supportive, and she lived at home while she worked and studied. Donna really loved the flying, but encountered a frustration familiar to many: an unreliable instructor. She was deflated when he didn't turn up again for a booked lesson one weekend, but that was tempered when she was offered a flight with 'Jingles', an older instructor who only worked on weekends. It was a fortuitous shift in the program, because he sent her solo on the next flight. Donna loved fixed-wing flying and Jingles got her through to her first milestone, a Restricted Licence, in 1992.

There was another instructor at Jandakot who she didn't fly with at that time. She did, however, marry him! When Michael Tasker's career took him to Singapore, Donna looked into doing her commercial licence, but funds wouldn't stretch that far and so she shelved that ambition, instead working in everything from retail to hospitality to the casino as a croupier and, finally, in Canberra with Michael, as a scuba diving instructor and a veterinary nurse. It was a vibrant, varied career path, which faded to grey when ballooning came into her life.

In the nomadic mix of a commercial pilot's life, the couple were packing to leave Canberra when Donna pulled a ballooning voucher from an entertainment booklet. It was to be a last hoorah. 'I'd seen balloons flying around, so we put it on the list of things to do. [After that flight] I fell in love with it and knew this was to be my job. Jackie Jantz was a balloon pilot and instructor and maybe that made a difference [seeing a woman in the role] to the way I saw my place in aviation. I bailed her up at breakfast and peppered her with questions. When we settled in Bunbury in Western Australia, a friend gifted us a balloon flight a few hours away at Northam. The day of the flight was raining, foggy and horrible. I thought it was ridiculous, but when we popped up above the low cloud it was a sea of white below, with a bright blue sky above. It was another world. I then bailed up that pilot at breakfast. He was dismissive, but I was determined to get into ballooning, so I started turning up as ground crew. I just kept turning up until I wore them down.'

Learning to fly balloons in Australia is completely grassroots. You have to find somebody with one of the country's 200 balloons, then convince them to teach you to fly it, and that's never an easy task. Each flight requires a ground crew of at least three people, who need to be there before dawn, help load the basket and the gear, drive to the launch site, help set up, then drive to the landing site and help pack up. It ends up being a coalition of the willing, and owners cultivate close bonds with their teams. Donna's break finally came when she found Liz Marrick. With Liz, she went out to Canowindra to get her ab initio balloon training started, spent three years getting her private licence, and another three years qualifying as a commercial pilot. It was arduous but worth it and eventually she was flying balloons for a living.

'Lots of the women who fly competitively have it as a serious hobby. The dedication and focus they put into it is brilliant, but that is not for me. I need to be paid for it', says Donna. 'I've only ever wanted to fly balloons commercially.'

Michael watched on as his fixed-wing wife swapped her avgas for a gas burner. 'It was a dogged determination that got her through. I joke that when I go to work, I strap it on and go flying. When Donna goes to work, she must build the thing and then pack it all away at the end. The reason there is such a shortage of balloon pilots is partly because it's so difficult to get into.'

The 2023 championships at Northam were won at the end of the week by Nicola Scaife, Australia's poster girl for women's ballooning. Like Donna, Nicola went for a commercial flight and immediately asked the company if they had any jobs. She is now a beaming three-time women's world champion who, together with her husband, runs a commercial operation in the Hunter Valley. Nicola came from a background of competition sport as a teenager. In contrast, Donna shuns competition of any kind, not just ballooning. 'I really admire the women who compete, but it's not for me. There was pressure on me to nominate for these championships because I'm local, but my father was a really competitive man – I hate it.' Both women are united in their love for the sport and are happy to promote it where they can. For Donna, the joy is in sharing the ballooning experience with her passengers.

'I love that no two flights are the same. The passengers, seasons, colours all change. I love sharing it and watching people's faces as we inflate the envelope. It's big and unexpected. Everybody loves ballooning. They don't know what to expect, and many are scared of heights, but their experience is usually calm. You're not shot out of a cannon! The departure is gentle, and we move along at treetop height. The landings can be fast sometimes.'

When a professional career was still some way down the track, Donna was 'working as a biscuit chucker from Bunbury to Perth' on the railways. When they wanted her down in Perth, she ended up doing passenger announcements, before becoming a train driver. She gave that up to do train control.

During this time she got invited to Malaysia, where she brushed shoulders with international balloonists. It opened her eyes to different countries' experiences, because in Malaysia they couldn't fly any higher than 500 feet, whereas in Australia you're not allowed to fly that low! They 'just bobbed around over the lake'. The flying was fun, but the connections she made were life-changing. A balloon company consultant invited her to Bristol, UK, to train and convert her 200-hour Australian licence to a UK licence. This would allow employment with the British company at their Myanmar bases.

Cameron Balloons, widely regarded as the world's favourite brand of balloons, are based in Bristol. It is the home of ballooning royalty, and a short hop from France, where ballooning had begun around 200 years earlier when two brothers, Joseph-Michel and Jacques-Etienne Montgolfier, experimented after noticing that hot air from a fire would cause paper to lift. Hot air rises.

Louis XVI thought it would be a good idea to send up a couple of criminals, as ballast on the test flight; however, the brothers opted for a more agricultural approach and sent a sheep, a duck and a rooster. The craft landed safely, and the animals received a more civilised welcome than the un-piloted prototype earlier that year. It had launched from the site of the future Eiffel Tower and landed some miles away in the village of Gonesse. Terrified locals attacked the strange object from the sky with pitchforks and knives. In contrast, the Montgolfier sheep was given prime position in Marie Antoinette's menagerie. There doesn't seem to be any reports on the fate of the fowl.

In early 1785, the first balloon crossed from France into England. In the 1970s Bristol started running a successful Balloon Fiesta. It began with only a few flying over the city, and has grown to be Europe's largest free annual hot air balloon festival. Half a million visitors come for four days to watch a hundred craft in an event that defines the city's skyline. The balloon festival is one of Bristol's main tourist attractions. For Donna, it was an introduction to the area and her host, Phil.

This UK licence training would have a dignified start, not from an isolated airport or just any old paddock. In this new world, it would begin among jolly picnickers and curious deer in the rolling grasslands of Ashton Court, just south of Bristol. Ashton Court is an 11th-century Grade 1 listed manor house set on 850 acres, and includes a couple of ancient deer parks, historic gardens, minigolf course, and an enormous house to rival any in Europe. The historically significant building is loved by visitors, but a burden for the local council, as the cost of upkeep and restoration is almost beyond reckoning. Only a fraction of the building is used and that is for tourism or public hire.

It's a stunning estate that butts up to the cavernous Avon Gorge, and sets the backdrop to the balloons that launch nearby.

In this exotic environment Donna undertook two training flights, which went well, but it was the final check flight with Phil that caused some excitement. They departed in a gentle wind and tracked straight for the city. Donna looked around in wonder. *Oh my gosh, I'm flying over Bristol and these beautiful buildings and parks.* The flight on a balmy summer's evening was a dream, until Donna looked up into the yawning envelope and ... holy hell! Uncontrolled flame was dancing out of the burner. The dragon was about to escape!

Phil put the fire out and, keeping her cool, Donna took control because this was her flight test. She was lead pilot! She ordered an immediate descent to the deer park below, still close to where they'd launched. Phil, with a lifetime of experience, was more circumspect and reasoned that they really had to get the flight done. Donna thought he was joking, or that it was some kind of trial to see how she would react. Against her protestations they continued their flight over the city. Despite being busy, Air Traffic Control granted clearance for them to climb, to access a faster wind. Donna's pulse was running flat out as she re-calculated their flight path, endurance, and emergency procedures. They tracked towards the chocolate factory – a large old brick factory that is now a housing development – and Donna made a determined run for the park beside it. No way was she missing that field. They avoided the historic Greenbank cemetery nearby and, though just clipping the top of a fence railing, made it in safely. Britain's newest balloon pilot got out of the basket and lay on the ground. It had been a big build-up, too much excitement, and she now had to regain her equilibrium. Phil leaned over and smiled, 'You've passed'.

There are shades of history about this story that refer back to Sophie Blanchard, the first female professional balloonist. When her husband died in a ballooning accident, she continued the family business of showmanship in the air, and was made an official aeronaut, performing for Bonaparte and Louis XVIII. After about 60 successful flights, while wearing a dramatic white dress and hat topped with ostrich plumes, she performed an airborne fireworks display, but inadvertently set the balloon alight. The poor brave woman survived the crash, on to a double-storey house roof, then fell down to the street and joined her husband on the list of pioneers who 'died doing what they loved'. It's probably for the best that Donna didn't know this story before setting off.

Recomposed after her test flight, Donna prepared to take her British licence to Myanmar and the Bristol Boys Club. They were a cohesive group of balloonists from Bristol who ran the Oriental Ballooning (OB) operation in Myanmar. Donna was the outsider when she arrived in 2013 to start with them. 'The Chief Pilot asked if I'd be his alternate chief pilot because most balloon pilots just want to fly, they don't want to perform any of the administrative tasks. I was quite happy to do that.'

Her arrival in Yangon, the capital of Myanmar, was confronting. The walls of the hustling, bustling airport were stained red from discarded betel quid (nut or tobacco leaf). The dank concrete smell was compounded by monsoonal rains. 'I collected my bags, then had to go to the old domestic airport next door, which was quite rustic. They weigh your bags by picking them up! I was given a sticker for my lapel so the airport staff knew which airline to put me on. The PA announcements were unintelligible to me and there were no boards advertising flight times or destinations. There were masses of people everywhere, but they had a distinct calm within them. It was an energy like nothing I'd ever known. Despite being shy, they were quick to smile. I finally caught my flight, which I think was the milk run from Yangon to Heho and on to Mandalay. It dragged on all afternoon, and I kept wondering if I should be getting off.'

TAKE FLIGHT

Eventually, the little plane touched down in Bagan, and Donna says it was a 'late afternoon charmed arrival'. She was shown to her concrete bungalow-style hotel. Each room had a small verandah and access to the central pool. It was probably a two-star place, but it had hot and cold water, power and a basic bathroom. Her single bed stood on a timber floor and the room opened to the back, so she could come and go quietly if it suited her. It was close living but the balloon pilots were a small and supportive group.

On her first morning she was taken out for an observation flight, and then a quick check flight. Then it was down to business and the thrill of her first balloon job. The early mornings were magical and she was now flying a slightly bigger balloon than she was used to. It was an exciting time. She was part of a start-up company, joining its competitor, who had held the market for 14 years.

With the necessary early starts and midday naps, the days could be a bit fractured and the one thing she missed was good coffee, so when Michael arrived to visit a month later, he brought a coffee machine with him. A touch of home. However, she embraced a deep respect for the local people and their customs, including the clothes. Her shoulders were covered and her legs covered to below the knees. She admired the local women in their collared fitted blouses worn over long wraparound skirts. 'They always look good in them. The guys wear the traditional *longyi* (skirt) also. I am always respectful of dress standards when I am there.'

There was no shortage of work, as Western tourism increased after Hillary Clinton visited the tiny town, a UNESCO world heritage site. The tourists came for the spectacle of the temples that were strewn across the countryside, their spired peaks rising like scattered anthills. As the kingdom's ancient capital, Bagan once boasted approximately 1000 stupas, 10 000 small temples and 3000 monasteries. The patchwork 104-square-kilometre plains around Bagan hold 2200 remaining temples, which the balloonists weave around in lazy morning flights. The largest of the temples is the 12th-century Dhammayangyi. Strangely, although its massive square 78-metre-wide base recedes up through six stepped, terraced layers, its interior is sealed off, leaving just the outer features accessible; four porches and verandahs. Beautiful artwork adorns the lower walls, but you'd have to come back in a taxi to see that. The most highly revered of the Bagan temples is the perfectly dimensioned Ananda, which is carefully maintained. Its golden peak reaches 51 metres, or 150 feet in flying terms, and shines like a lamp when the rising sun creeps up on it. Donna's most recent photo from 2023 is looking down onto the top, which is covered in bamboo scaffolding so thin that it looks like spaghetti. The top is being redone with new gold leaf.

Usually, the balloons take off and fly over a golf course and the temples. They can fly down to 500 feet and the hour-long flight begins with a golden dawn departure, then passes over the rich countryside, where kids in traditional dress ride bikes on dusty roads, past rows of thatched housing and into the city, where concrete grids lay out the throng of daily life.

The other OB base is at Inle Lake, further east, and presents a few more challenges – mainly flying over water. Inle Lake is a 22-kilometre-long and 11-kilometre-wide farmed lake system, and the balloons depart from the middle. Even though a balloon will travel with the wind, the wind is reliably south to north for six months of the year and vice versa. Boarding a boat in the dark, the group travelled to the middle of the lake for departure. 'When you take off, you fly over an ordination hall, surrounded by floating gardens. The surrounding mountains are at five and six thousand feet. The Burmese allow us to go up to ten thousand feet in this location, and somewhere there we'll usually find a wind. Some days, though, we could be completely becalmed, and we'd have to land back on the lake. This involved the unenviable task of manoeuvring the balloon down onto a square platform that is strung across the top of two long tail boats. Helpfully, the platform is painted black with large OB in white lettering. I've had flights there that were surreal.'

As Donna departed for her second season in Myanmar, Michael helpfully suggested she could use her spare time to do something productive. 'We have a lot of time off, because we are up at 4 am but we're home again by 10. I have the rest of the day to myself, and Michael suggested I build a balloon. I had done a week-long maintenance course on how to sew and repair balloons at Kavanagh's.' Kavanagh Balloons are Australia's only hot air balloon manufacturers, and one of only a handful worldwide.

Using her established sewing skills, in Myanmar Donna acquainted herself with the company sewing machine, normally used for balloon repairs. They kindly let her use the machine for her own project. 'I talked to a few people about building a balloon and decided that if I could get a kit, then I'd do it. It costs about the same price to make your own as it does to buy a Chinese one. One of our guys, Jonny Smith, had been a balloon cutter, so once we got the pattern, he knew how to cut and make it. He got the software to spit out the numbers, and I ordered the fabric. The main thing I needed was a big table, so the crew made one out of scrap and I put it in the back of the hotel. Somehow the fabric from China found me addressed to 'Pilot Donna, Bagan'.

The fabric is rip-stop nylon – it feels like an unusual cross between canvas and silk – and 800 metres of it turned up on Pilot Donna's doorstep. To aid with the pattern making, the chief pilot, Piers Glydon, went to a newspaper factory and came back with a massive roll of unprinted paper. Someone else sourced a welded frame to hold the three different coloured rolls of fabric – green, pink, and blue – and by 2 pm each day Donna and anybody else who was interested would emerge from a sleep and go to their tables.

The balloon was made in 20 pieces and required precision cutting of the heavy fabric. In the back lanes of Yangon there were people who specialised in fabric, needles and haberdashery. In a dusty corner of a market stall, an old fabric-cutting tool lay waiting. Jonny the balloon cutter messaged enthusiastically, 'Grab it!'

To the tunes of Taylor Swift, Donna immersed herself in her project at the workshop. With Jonny and his methodical approach, they bagged and labelled the pieces quickly, and then Donna set to work sewing. She expected to ask one of the crew to help, but she became surprisingly protective of the project. The longest panel of the twenty large segments is thirteen metres long by one and a half metres wide. Each panel is a tetrahedron shape; narrow at the top, bulbous in the middle and narrow at the bottom. It has a camber on the top and the bottom. 'I made each join with a French seam using the industrial twin needle machine. It has a metal seam folder, which automatically folds the fabric as it is fed through and sets it at the correct width. I then sewed load tape over the top of the seam. I had great advice from the experts.'

Back in Australia, Steve Griffin, who had built his own balloons in Queensland and in his capacity as a Civil Aviation Safety Authority (CASA) official, weighed and inspected Donna's creation for Certificate of Airworthiness. As the balloon is classed EXPERIMENTAL due to being homemade, she had to do her own five hours of required test flying. The most nerve-racking part was standing it up! She was supported by Michael, who met her at the landing site with flowers, as it was their wedding anniversary, and another friend who brought champagne. It was a momentous occasion for Donna. After the test flying was completed, she loaned her balloon to friends, one of whom was flying it in the competition at the start of this story. Another friend, Ben, flew it in the national championship. It has now done around 50 hours and Donna loves to see it out and about. Because she is always flying commercially, she can't use the little balloon in her everyday work as it is too small, and also not certified for commercial flight. She estimates it has another 10 or

15 years' flying left in it. 'There are quite a few home-built balloons in Australia and that's why I had the support of other people around to do it. Mine is a basic French design.' The envelope was task enough; she bought a ready-made basket.

The greatest compliment came from Phil Kavanagh, whose company has been manufacturing hot air balloons since 1972. He's seen some good, and some shocking, home-built efforts and he congratulates Donna. 'She did a great job on the colour scheme, and the balloon itself is well made. Like many of these things, it's the design that is important and hers hangs together well without any sags or bulges. She's a clever lady – ask her about her beekeeping.'

Back in the commercial world, Donna was invited to fly alongside Allie Dunnington in Mongolia to help establish a ballooning operation there in 2018. During her month in the country, she flew over the Terelj National Park, which, after unseasonal rain, was lush and vibrant. Her accommodation was no longer a concrete hotel room; she was now staying in a traditional *gher* (a round tent covered with skins or felt), with windows and a bathroom. 'There were horses running around outside and the famous Mongolian Plains were not far away. Our passengers were the locals.'

On the home front, Michael's career required another shift and Darwin became their new home. From the extremities of Asia and England, Donna now also worked seasonally in Alice Springs. Down in Alice, home was a small accommodation unit on the side of the shed where the balloons are kept. The flights out there are stunning, with sublime sunrises, amazing outback night skies, and a workday that takes her above the MacDonnell Ranges and the Central Desert. Another favourite place to fly is Kununurra in Western Australia. They still love to return to the outback, though they are now living back in WA, where Donna is chief pilot of one balloon company, while flying as a line pilot for another.

ABOUT ONCE A YEAR A SKYDIVER OR TWO WILL MAKE CONTACT, wanting to jump out of a balloon. It's not for the faint-hearted and initially Donna sought plenty of advice from other balloonists who had done it. She also spoke to some balloonists who were skydivers, and then she laid down the law. Each skydiver needed at least 200 jumps' experience, and they had to jump individually. They need to fall separately, and the balloon needs to be slightly in descent at the time of the exit, because the biggest challenge for the pilot is when the passengers exit. It lightens the load in the basket, making the balloon rise sharply. The record for a parachute exit is 72 000 feet, or 13 miles, up into the stratosphere. Most jumps are done at a few hundred feet. These particular passengers jumped from 6500 feet.

'At the beginning they were really pumped up. They had never seen a balloon before and were surprised at how small it was. As they watched it inflate and realised the size of the basket, and that they had to get in, they were a little less excited. It was a quiet ascent and I climbed straight away. As the first skydiver sat on the edge of the basket, I anxiously raised my camera. On the count of three, he fell forward and slowly disappeared into the eerily quiet sunrise. Watching someone fall out of your balloon basket is horrendous. It was a horrible feeling, and a relief when I saw his parachute open and then when I knew he was on the ground and OK. Once I got them out, I had to fly back down myself at an average of 500 feet per minute.'

Her photo of the parachutist looking back up at the balloon is a great shot. But, to a balloonist who is in it purely for the joy of hot-air travel, it is completely unnatural to watch a person charge at the air, rather than sail through it as nature and the apparatus intend. They would rather work with the wind, than try to overcome it.

Ballooning consistently brings Donna some of life's most beautiful moments; the sunrises, the excited passengers, the landscape and the serenity. But which way do you look when somebody proposes mid-flight? Usually, it's joyous. Where else would you rather be than totally relaxed, adrift in a dream so high in the sky? If a proposal is what you are seeking, then it would be perfect. If not, then 2000 feet in the air with a misguided beau and a stranger at the helm is, well, hell – including for Donna, who didn't know which way to look when her passenger proposed and got a rejection. How fast can you get that thing on the ground? Not fast enough, and the painfully slow descent was endured by the proposee, curled in a ball in the bottom of the basket. There's a pointed lesson there for anybody who needs to hear it!

Donna is a bit nostalgic as she recalls that story, sitting on the deep verandah of their new home between Perth and Northam. The historic weatherboard house has a lush, extensive garden – the birds are singing as loudly as Donna is speaking into my voice recorder. There is a picture-perfect white picket fence, and it's a breathe-deep kind of place, a little *Out of Africa*, a little 1930s Australia. Beyond the garden, a couple of horses, her new love, graze on the rest of the five-acre property. An equine's warm beating heart brings balance to the years of gas-fired cold mornings.

Slowly, but surely, our conversation starts to fade as the day gets old. In a world where sleep is meted out in small doses, the 4 am schedule catches up with her. I seek out Michael, who tells me his wife is teaching him her craft. 'After a briefing we set up the balloon, inflate it, and she shows me how the burners work. I have to do a minimum of 17 hours, which is about 25 separate flights. Her reading of the really fine weather details of the specific areas they will be flying in is incredible. It is at odds with my usual flying, in a jet, which requires me to point the nose, put the power on and the rest is brute force over ignorance. I usually have a large airstrip to land on, but balloonists know where the wind is taking them, and how to counteract their direction by going up or down to where the wind is blowing a different direction. It uses fine controls, anticipation, and a mastery of reading the wind. I have been waiting for the day when I'm flying into Alice Springs with a couple of hundred people on board, and I have to give way to Donna and her few passengers in her basket, because speed always gives way to sail. There are times when she will half-jokingly call it a stupid sport – most often when the alarm goes off at 4 am. It's always cold at 4 am.'

Any thoughts about the stupidity of a 4 am get-up are quickly dispelled once the flame is lit and the envelope is rising. In the Avon Valley earlier that morning, the dew had burned off the fields and we drifted into the soft light of the rising sun. It was the most incredible place to be. The world was at peace, and Donna was every bit at one with it.

GLOSSARY

This is a general guide to some of the terms you will find used throughout the book, which can be useful to put the story into context. Aviation covers a broad area of activity, and various aspects of aviation in Australia fall under differing associations. I've also included some useful websites as resources.

Ab initio In Latin, *ab initio* means 'from the beginning'. It is a widely used term in flight training and refers to the foundations, such as aircraft handling, flight rules and navigation.

Aerial application (previously known as aerial agriculture, and crop dusting) includes: spraying of crops; applying granular products; fertilising crops and pasture (top dressing); sowing seed; and firebombing.
<aaaa.org.au>

Aileron roll A manoeuvre whereby the aircraft rolls 360 degrees about its longitudinal axis. It is most commonly performed by turning the control column to one side, while the aeroplane maintains the same altitude and flies straight.

Altitude Altitudes are generally given in feet, which is standard aviation practice.

BASE jump BASE jumping is the sport of jumping from a Building, Antenna (radio mast), Span (bridge) or Earth (cliff). The thrill is in the freefall, which can be anything from a few seconds, depending on the height of the jump. A parachute is deployed in time to land safely. It is banned in Australia, but celebrated in other parts of the world.

Cessna 172 The Cessna 172 is a four-seat, general-purpose aircraft made by the Cessna Aircraft Company in the US. It has one

Glossary

engine, wings fixed above the fuselage, and a fixed undercarriage. Larger variations have a retractable undercarriage. It is versatile as a trainer and a touring aircraft. It first flew in 1955 and has since sold more than any other aircraft in history.
<cessna.txtav.com>

Comanche The Piper PA-24 Comanche aircraft is made by the Piper Aircraft Company in the US. It has one engine, wings beneath the fuselage, and retractable wheels. It generally has four or six seats. It is made of all metal.

Endorsement *Ratings* have a number of endorsements that define the extra knowledge and skills you need to conduct these flights safely. Examples of endorsements are: aerobatic (performing airborne manoeuvres such as loop or barrel roll); formation (where pilots qualify to fly within a few metres of each other in formation, such as the RAAF Roulettes); low level (qualify to fly below the standard minimum altitude allowable. Useful for aerobatic and airshow pilots, mustering and station pilots, aerial application, and search and rescue pilots); retractable undercarriage; tail wheel; and twin engine.
<https://www.casa.gov.au/licences-and-certificates/pilots/ratings-reviews-and-endorsements/ratings-and-endorsements/operational-ratings-and-endorsements#Gettinganoperationalrating>

Extra 300L The Extra was designed by one of the world's most successful aerobatic pilots, Walter Extra. From a one-man experimental design, the range has now grown to include the aerobatic EA-200, EA-300L, EA-300LP, EA-330LT, EA330LC, EA330LX and EA-330SC aircraft.
<www.extraaircraft.com>

Fixed wing A fixed-wing aircraft generally refers to a powered aeroplane that has wings fixed to the fuselage.

***g*-force** A measurement of acceleration.

Glider An aeroplane without an engine. Gliders have *fixed wings*. The fuselage and wings are long and slender. Gliders are launched by a winch, or towed by a powered aeroplane up into the air and then released. They sail or soar on the winds, increasing height by thermal lift (rising air), which can be caused by rising warm air, or by ridge lift (air coming up the side of a mountain).
<glidingaustralia.org>

Huey Bell UH-1 Iroquois military helicopter. It was made by Bell Helicopter in the US and was used extensively in the Vietnam War.

IFR Instrument Flight Rules means a pilot is flying the aircraft relying on instruments for navigation. This is usually due to bad weather, when it is impossible to see outside and gain visual reference, which is important for navigating and orienting the aircraft.

Knots The measurement used for airspeed. It equals one nautical mile per hour, which is the same as 1.852 km/h. One nautical mile equals 1.1508 land-measured (statute) miles.

Out-landing In gliding, this refers to when a glider can't make it back to the airstrip and has to land in a paddock or some other location that is not the airstrip, therefore landing 'out'.

Paraglider A lightweight fabric wing (parachute-like aerofoil) with no rigid structure. The wing maintains its shape by the suspension lines, and the pressure of air entering vents at the front of the wing. Aerodynamics does the rest. The pilot is suspended beneath the wing on the bottom of the lines and uses either a hard plastic seat, or a pod to sit in for comfort and warmth (depending on location, weather and duration). Using a similar principle as *gliders*, paragliders can thermal in warm air or updrafts to gain altitude, before gliding down.
<www.safa.asn.au>

Paramotor A foot-launched paramotor, such as in Sacha Dench's story, is a 'wing' connected by ropes to a frame and harness (like a

backpack). It has a fuel tank, engine and propeller. The propeller is protected by a large hoop that is covered by protective netting to restrict movement of loose objects through the propeller.
<www.safa.asn.au>

Rating A rating is a course of study to enable a pilot to operate in certain conditions on certain general types of aircraft and includes: aerial application rating; instructor rating; instrument rating (*IFR*); and night rating (allows pilot to fly at night).

Skydive Skydiving is the same as parachuting. Whereas parachuting involves deploying a parachute to slow a descent to earth, skydiving developed by delaying the parachute's release so as to enjoy a longer freefall. Skydivers perform many aerobatic manoeuvres during freefall, including group patterns and dances.
<www.apf.com.au>

Sling A cable or rope that is strong and flexible enough to attach a helicopter at one end, and secure a load at the other. Commonly used to carry a fire bucket or lumber, or for retrieving larger objects like a small aircraft or vehicle.

Trike A trike uses a rigid structure to support a fabric wing, as used on a hang glider. This is fixed to a small, powered tricycle fuselage that has a seat (or two), and is steered using weight shift by the pilot.
<www.safa.asn.au>

Twin Comanche A variant on the *Comanche*, it has two engines and four or six seats.
<www.piper.com>

Vario A variometer can be an instrument worn on the wrist that can read wind speed, direction, rate of height increase, variations of wind and height, glide ratio, and barometric pressure. It can synch to an app on a phone that can be stored for review. It is also the most important instrument for gliding.

TAKE FLIGHT

Wingsuit Wingsuiting is a step further than *skydiving*. A wingsuit is a fabric jumpsuit with three 'bat wings': one between the legs and one each joining the arms to the torso. The suit has dual surface cells that inflate during freefall to create flight. Wingsuits fly at angles around 200 km/h forward and 50 km/h down. They are typically launched from an aeroplane, or as part of a BASE jump. The wingsuiter deploys a parachute for landing.
<www.apf.com.au>

Useful websites

Air Force Cadets <www.airforcecadets.gov.au>
Aircraft Owners and Pilots Association (Australia) <aopa.com.au>
Airservices Australia <www.airservicesaustralia.com>
Antique Aeroplane Association of Australia <antique-aeroplane.com.au>
Astronomical Society of Australia <asa.astronomy.org.au>
Australian Ballooning Federation <www.abf.net.au>
Australian Helicopter Industry Association <www.austhia.com>
Australian Indigenous Astronomy <www.aboriginalastronomy.com.au>
Australian Parachute Federation <www.apf.com.au>
Australian Space Agency <www.space.gov.au>
Australian Transport Safety Bureau <www.atsb.gov.au>
Australian Women Pilots' Association <awpa.org.au>
Aviatrix International <www.aviatrix.com.au>
Civil Aviation Safety Authority <www.casa.gov.au>
Conservation Without Borders (Sacha Dench) <www.conservation-without-borders.org>
Dark Horse Farm (Heather Swan) <www.darkhorsefarm.com.au>
Gliding Australia <glidingaustralia.org>
Honourable Company of Air Pilots <airpilots.org.au>
Lady Aviators <www.ladyaviators.co>
Mason Wing Walking Academy <masonwingwalking.com>

Matt Hall Racing <matthallracing.com>
Moomba <moomba.melbourne.vic.gov.au>
The Ninety-Nines <www.ninety-nines.org/Chapter-Australia_2.htm>
Recreational Aviation Australia <raaus.com.au>
Royal Aeronautical Society <www.raes.org.au>
Space Australia <spaceaustralia.com/index.php/>
Sport Aircraft Association of Australia <saaa.asn.au>
Sports Aviation Federation of Australia <www.safa.asn.au>
Whirlygirls International <whirlygirls.org>
Women in Aviation Aerospace Australia <www.aviationaerospace.org.au/>
Women in Aviation International (Australia) <waiaustralia.org>

SOURCES

1   Sacha Dench

5 News, 'Woman flies with swans for 4500 miles from Russia to UK', YouTube, 2017, <www.youtube.com/watch?v=etG8W9AaAvE>.

ABC News (Australia), 'Three bushfires merge in the Bega Valley to create monster firefront', 2000, <www.youtube.com/watch?v=yldtWoGxPms>.

British Women Pilots' Association, Award Winners 2017, <bwpa.co.uk/scholarships/award-winners-2017/>.

Conservation without Borders, 'Sacha Dench showreel 2023', YouTube, 2023, <www.youtube.com/watch?v=aHWA58CC5Wc>.

Conservation Without Borders website, <conservation-without-borders.org>.

Everything Electric Show, 'Adventures with Sacha Dench – "the Human Swan"', YouTube, 2022, <tinyurl.com/ms7cdj3r>.

Ewing, Ed, *XCmag.com*, 'Sacha Dench: Profile of "The Human Swan"', Issue 171, July 2016, <xcmag.com/news/sacha-dench-profile-of-the-swan-lady/>.

Guinness World Records, '"Human Swan" Sacha Dench sets record crossing the English Channel', 10 October 2020, <tinyurl.com/j2cf5tau>.

Hogan, Clover, 'Let your courage take flight', YouTube, May 2021, <www.youtube.com/watch?v=kAmYiJ9S86E>.

McKnight, Albert, 'Two years after Black Summer bushfires, the Bega Valley continues to rebuild', *About Regional*, 31 December 2021, <tinyurl.com/4vj2kx8m>.

Odell, Michael, 'Sacha Dench: the woman who flies with swans', *Times UK*, 2019, <tinyurl.com/yc4psrhn>.

On Demand News, '"Human Swan" to fly 4500 miles from Russia to Britain by paramotor', 2017, <www.youtube.com/watch?v=jnAcMcH_eiw>.

Russell-Stevenson, Alyson, *The Think Podcast*, 'Sacha Dench – The Human Swan', 2021, <open.spotify.com/episode/6UbwNxYM2O4LeufxrUVAUc>.

Sacha Dench website, <www.sachadench.com>.

Science Direct, 'Economic assessment of wild bird mortality induced by the use of lead gunshot in European wetlands', 1 January 2018, <www.sciencedirect.com/science/article/abs/pii/S0048969717314900>.

Wildfowl Wetlands Trust, <wwt.org.uk>.

Wright, Helen, 'Flying Like a swan: Sacha Dench is Estonia', *Estonian World*, 13 December 2016, <estonianworld.com/life/sacha-dench-estonia-flying-like-swan/>.

WWT, 'Introducing Flight of the Swans', YouTube, 2016, <www.youtube.com/watch?v=v54tA71dZAs>.

WWT, '"Human Swan" is first woman to receive prestigious aviation award in 50 years ...', 22 May 2018, <tinyurl.com/ymrj2da2>.

Sources

Sacha Dench, interview with author, 2024.
Kathleen Retourne, interview with author, 2024.

2   Alida Soemawinata

Chauhan, Shreya, 'These animals are getting to meet other animals and they just can't contain their excitement!', *Times of India*, 4 April 2020, <tinyurl.com/27wddmdj>.
Green, Louis, Ernest Giles entry, Australian Dictionary of Biography website, <adb.anu.edu.au/biography/giles-ernest-3611>.
Gosse, Fayette, Sir Thomas Elder entry, Australian Dictionary of Biography website, <adb.anu.edu.au/biography/elder-sir-thomas-347>.
Giles, Ernest, *Australia Twice Traversed*, Gutenberg Project website, <gutenberg.net.au/ebooks/e00052.html#ch2.3>.
Stoneham Graham, 'Melbourne Stage 4: Come and meet me in the middle of the air', YouTube, 2020, <www.youtube.com/watch?v=pwfXxrcVJjU>.
Austin McNally, interview with author, 2023.
Tia McVeigh, interview with author, 2023.
Rob Mengler, interview with author, 2023.
Darren Neal, interview with author, 2023.
Lachie Onslow, interview with author, 2023.
Alida Soemawinata, interview with author, 2023.
Margaret Soemawinata, interview with author, 2023.
Jessica Van Der Meer, interview with author, 2023.

3   Heather Swan

60 Minutes Australia, 'Wingsuit flight over Antarctica Part 2', YouTube, 2019, <www.youtube.com/watch?v=0IuvdVYZfqE>.
Baseclimb website, <Baseclimb.com>.
Bullei, 'BASE Jump Trango Tower 1993', YouTube, 2014, <www.youtube.com/watch?v=LfCFhKMoKVk>
Great Expectation Speakers and Trainers, 'Heather Swan and Glenn Singleman', YouTube, 2016, <www.youtube.com/watch?v=52-PJjEVzFY>.
MrZaratustra32, 'Meru Peak Jump', YouTube, 2010, <www.youtube.com/watch?v=MKInS2p-6sE>.
New York Times, 'Mount Meru: Climbing the Shark's Fin', YouTube, 2016, <www.youtube.com/watch?v=seCiupa4I6U>.
Swan, Heather, *No Ceiling,* The Five Mile Press, Scoresby, 2005.
Swan, Heather, *Love Flying*, Icarus Films, New York, 2016.

4   Catherine Conway

Australian Aviation Hall of Fame website, <www.aahof.com.au/inductees/Harry-Schneider>; <www.aahof.com.au/inductees/Ingo-Renner>.
Fincke, Michelle, *New Daily*, 'Catapulted to fame: Queen's Birthday award for Catherine's unique passion', 6 November 2018, <thenewdaily.com.au/news/national/2018/06/11/catherine-conway-queens-birthday-honours/>.
Oberhardt, Amelia, *Secrets We Keep: Shame Lies & Family* podcast, 2024, <www.listnr.com/podcasts/secrets-we-keep>.

Catherine Conway, interview with author, 2023.
Peter Conway, interview with author, 2023.
Simon Hackett, interview with author, 2023.
Mark Newton, interview with author, 2023.

5   Stef Walter

Bendigo Animal Welfare and Community Services, 'Moomba Birdman Rally 2017 BAWCS represented', YouTube, 2017, <www.youtube.com/watch?v=tzPZKpEpLs4>.
dangerouslytalented, 'Moomba Birdman Rally 2017', 2017, <www.youtube.com/watch?v=5axhq5F0J1Q>.
Discovery UK, 'Are you brave enough to do this?', 2018, <www.youtube.com/watch?v=iiKRgdfL4K8>.
Mason Wing Walking Academy, 'First time wing walker shows no fear', YouTube, 2021, <www.youtube.com/watch?v=lNZjX0EdPZg&t=50s>.
Mason Wing Walking website, <Masonwingwalking.com.au>.
Linda Beilharz, interview with author, 2022.
Michael Mason, interview with author, 2022.
Stefanie Walter, interview with author, 2022–24.
Michael Walter, interview with author, 2022.

6   Kirsten Seeto

ABC1 and France 5 film, *Miracle in the Storm*, 2010, <vimeo.com/20320893>.
Adams, Michael, *Wind Beneath His Wings, Lawrence Hargraves at Stanwell Park*, Michael Adams, 2004.
Altitude With Attitude website, <www.facebook.com/altitudesass/>.
Australian Transport Safety Bureau Report No. 199002035.
British Hang Gliding and Paragliding Association website, <www.bhpa.co.uk>.
Jay Shafer Tiny Houses website, <jayshafertinyhouses.wordpress.com>.
Lilliput Living Tiny Living Consulting website, <www.lilliputliving.com>.
McClurg, Gavin, Cloudbase Mayhem website, Episode 137, Kirsten Seeto and Making the Jump, 2021, <www.cloudbasemayhem.com/episode-137-kirsten-seeto-and-making-the-jump>.
North East Victorian Paragliding Club website, <www.nevhgc.net>.
Pelletier, Antoine, 'Skydiving over the Namib Desert – Swakopmund, Namibia', 2018, <www.youtube.com/watch?v=4WYW8Fe_zcc>.
Tiny House Australia website, <www.tinyhouse.org.au>.
Scott, Tony, *Top Gun*, Paramount Pictures, 12 May 1986.
Seeto, Kirsten, 'What Holds Women Back', *Cross Country Magazine*, 8 January 2016, <xcmag.com/news/comps-and-events/what-holds-women-back-kirsten-seeto-takes-aim/>.
Waller, Kevin, *Suddenly Dead*, Sydney, Pan MacMillan, Sydney, 1994.
Wedge-tailed eagle, Wildlife Fact Sheet, <www.wildlife.vic.gov.au/__data/assets/pdf_file/0017/115343/Wedge-tailed-Eagle.pdf>.
Sue Derrett, interview with author, 2021.
Kari Ellis, interview with author, 2021.

Sources

Lucy Legget, interview with author, 2021.
Kirsten Seeto, interview with author, 2021.

7   Emma McDonald

Alerts SoCal, '2023 Pacific Airshow Huntington Beach CA', YouTube, October 2023, <www.youtube.com/watch?v=42_4IYbv5aU>.
Avalon Airport Spotter, 'Making Her Mark; Emma McDonald', YouTube, August 2023, <www.youtube.com/watch?v=Y8RU6Fgt0zQ>.
Avalon Airport Spotter, 'Emma McDonald Extra 300 Display Pacific Airshow 2023', YouTube, August 2023, <www.youtube.com/watch?v=w1xj7eVFquo&t=7s>.
Folksalert, 'Emma McDonald – Flying High', YouTube, 9 May 2023, <www.youtube.com/watch?v=kEBTTd2VQyU>.
Geraets, Neil, '"It's probably the freest I feel": A day in the life of a stunt pilot', *The Age*, 5 March 2023, <tinyurl.com/65sydky5>.
Matt Hall Racing website, <www.matthallracing.com>.
Moore, Anne Wason, 'Stunt pilot Emma McDonald breaking barriers at Pacific Air Show', *Gold Coast Bulletin*, 22 July 2023, <tinyurl.com/33j845js>.
Reaching for the Skies, Lake Mac., Lake Macquarie, 2024, <www.lakemac.com.au/Lets-Lake-Mac/Emma-McDonald>.
Dannielle Allan, interview with author, 2024.
Kristina Brown, interview with author, 2024.
Matt Hall, interview with author, 2024.
Emma McDonald, interview with author, 2024.
Richard McDonald, interview with author, 2024.
Angela Stephenson, interview with author, 2024.
Sean D. Tucker, interview with author, 2024.

8   Jessica Johnston

7NEWS Coast, 'Part 1: Coffs Harbour speed skydiver Jessica Johnston has brought home the bronze from the UK World Cup', YouTube, 24 September 2019, <tinyurl.com/26xref4r>.
Australian Parachute Federation website, 'Speed Skydiving (SS)', <www.apf.com.au/Sports-Jumping/Australian-Parachute-Team/Athletes/Speed-Skydiving-Jessica-Johnston/speed-skydiving-ss>.
Beagleweekly.com.au, 'World Records at Moruya skydiving championships', 18 March 2019, <tinyurl.com/5br9r4b6>.
Kanowski, S, 'The fastest woman in the sky', *Conversations* podcast, Australian Broadcasting Corporation, Brisbane, 3 March 2023, <shorturl.at/eoW14>.
Ramsey, Britt, 'Coffs Harbour speed skydiver chasing world record', *nbnnews*, 30 July 2019, <www.nbnnews.com.au/2019/07/30/coffs-harbour-speed-skydiver-chasing-world-record/>.
Jessica Johnston, interview with author, 2023.
Ronnie Perry, interview with author, 2023.
Leacette Read, interview with author, 2023.

9 Krystal De Napoli

Allan, Jeff, 'How to spot the emu in the night sky', *Australian Financial Review*, 19 August 2022, <tinyurl.com/mr4bzbyw>.
Noon, Karlie and De Napoli, Krystal, *Sky Country*, Thames & Hudson, Sydney, 2022.
Krystal De Napoli, interview with author, 2023.
Duane Hamacher, interview with author, 2023.

10 Donna Tasker

Australian Ballooning Federation website, <www.abf.net.au>.
Bristol Balloon Fiesta website, <BristolBalloonFiesta.com>.
Oriental Ballooning website, <Orientalballooning.com>.
Rogers, Helene, *Lighter Than Air*, Affirm Press, Melbourne, 2021.
Phil Kavanagh, interview with author, 2024.
Donna Tasker, interview with author, 2024.
Michael Tasker, interview with author, 2024.

ACKNOWLEDGMENTS

My first thanks must go to the women in this collection of stories. Alida, Catherine, Donna, Emma, Heather, Jessica, Kirsten, Krystal, Sacha and Stefanie, you are all incredible. Most of you were a bit surprised to be asked, but happy to share the love of your chosen field of aviation. You have all been obliging, and patient, with my persistent questions and general interruptions to your daily lives.

I also thank your friends, colleagues and associates for sharing their time, anecdotes and expertise. Particular thanks to Jessica Van Der Meer, the Neal family, Dr Julia Newth, Marta Empinotti, Michael Dillon, Vonna Keller, Mike Barker, Mark and Leslie Walmsley, Leacette Read, Ronnie Perry, Matt Hall, Sean D Tucker, Lachie Onslow, Katherine Retourne, Simon Hackett, Duane Hamacher, and the many other people I spoke to – for your inclusions and for generously sharing your time and input.

In the engine room was my publisher, NewSouth Publishing, who were quick to take up the offer of a second book and have been very supportive throughout, even when I had to delay it by a year because I got a job. These include Joumana Awad, Harriet McInerney, Elspeth Menzies, Jocelyn Hungerford who politely and patiently edited, Camha Pham who did a thorough proofread, and Luke Causby who designed the cover – we all love it!

Thanks also to the photographers and videographers who have shared their work but perhaps have not been acknowledged in the photography section but appeared in the promo videos; Cameron Reynolds (aviation videographer), Ryan Imeson (Ryan Imeson Photography on Facebook), Mason Wing Walking Academy in Washington, USA, Erin Menhennit, Amelia Mexted and Peter

Brunton for the glider footage, my sister Fran Whitty for jumping off the shearing shed into my 13-year-old waiting arms and presumably filmed by our brother Brendan, Bendigo Animal Welfare and Community Services for the Birdman footage, Matt Hall Racing for the aerobatic footage, Heather Swan and Glenn Singleman for the Baseclimb footage, Debbie Murphy, Hendri Liebenberg and Barend Pretorius for the skydiving footage and Natalie Luescher for footage of Alida at Uluṟu (also used on the cover). Apologies if I've forgotten anybody.

Another special thanks for the library staff at Finley, Ros Rowe, and Tocumwal, Jennifer Congdon (author of *Woodstock*), who generously accommodated me as I made the big push to get the second half of the book written over a couple of months of coming and going.

And the book wouldn't be complete without a few promotional videos for which I thank my youngest brother, Damian 'Whitt' Whitty for all his creative support and for creating the soundtrack, and to Janet English for harmonising on it, and to Conor Whitty (sound engineer) for doing a much better job than I can on the shorter clips.

I encourage you to seek further information on some of the women you've just read about. Sacha Dench sadly experienced a terrible accident shortly before I commenced her story and she has been largely unavailable, due to a lengthy hospitalisation and an exhausting recovery, while still managing to execute another expedition. As we go into editing there is a fundraiser for prosthetics to enable Sacha to walk freely again after almost becoming a double amputee. I encourage you to follow her charity Conservation Without Borders and keep an eye out for the film, Flight of the Swans, which is winning international film awards.

Emma McDonald is making her mark in the world and is available for corporate events, keynote talks and flying experiences. Sponsorship is always welcome too! Heather Swan is a fabulous motivational speaker and has her own book *No Ceiling*, which is a fascinating in-

Acknowledgments

depth account of her story. Kirsten Seeto is a tandem pilot and can take you on a paragliding joy flight and do corporate talks on tiny houses and paragliding. Donna Tasker is a ballooning instructor and can be contacted for one-on-one training, or can give a unique talk on sewing, ballooning, or sewing a balloon! Catherine Conway is a gliding and flying instructor, who is also available for talks, and can do fabric, wood and composite repairs. Krystal De Napoli presents on astrophysics and Indigenous astronomy, while Jessica Johnston does parachute packing. If you got something out of their stories, please feel free to reach out.

Thanks to Windward Balloon Adventures who allowed me to fly with Donna during the Women's World Hot Air Ballooning Championships 2024 at Northam. What a beautiful morning! And to Kirsten who took me paragliding off Mystic in Bright.

Lastly, I must thank my husband Denis for his endless support, and congratulate our kids on their recent achievements and ambitions. Thanks also to the Whitty and the Mexted crew for all their support.

Apologies if I've forgotten anybody. I hope you have enjoyed the stories.

Oh, and guess what? I've finished another book and this time I'll make special mention of the women I worked with who watched me as I performed the tug-of-war between the office and pursuing this project. Amanda Western, Sue-Ellen Cook and Narelle Conroy who were all very supportive in and out of work. Also to Maria Abate, Lisa Shiner and Michelle Dove. Lastly, because I know she's read right to the end to find it, thanks to you, another Finley girl, for your constant encouragement Judy McNamara.

Contact: flystory10@gmail.com
http://www.youtube.com/@TakeFlightBook

www.ingramcontent.com/pod-product-compliance
Lightning Source LLC
Chambersburg PA
CBHW041311240426
43661CB00065B/2899